TALKING FOOTBALL
(HALL OF FAMERS' REMEMBRA
VOLUME 2

AUTHORS:
DAVID SPADA & ELLIOTT HAI

EDITOR:
MELINDA SPADA

Table of Contents

ABOUT THE AUTHORS

David Spada is a successful attorney whose dream was to become a sports talk show host. Elliott Harris is the former Chicago Sun-Times Quick Hits columnist who has covered the worlds of sports for decades.

David and Elliott teamed up in 2011 to host the sports podcast "Sports & Torts" on talkzone.com. "Sports & Torts" was a finalist for Sports Podcast of the Year in 2013 by the website podcastawards.com. David and Elliott have interviewed over 200 Hall of Famers from the world of football, baseball, and basketball since 2011. They are pleased by share their interviews with 46 Pro Football Hall Of Famers who talk about their careers in this book.

Chapter 1

Jim Otto

College:
Miami

Career History:
Oakland Raiders (1960–1974)

1980 Inductee Pro Football Hall of Fame

<u>College Choice</u>
When I was a senior in high school I had 48 university scholarships. Miami was one of them, but I hadn't really thought that much about Miami until I had visited Minnesota, Wisconsin, Northwestern, and some other schools. I think it was 30 below zero when I left Wausau, Wisconsin. I visited Miami in February. When I got to Miami, it had to be about 75 degrees.

I couldn't believe it could be so cold in one spot and so nice and warm in another. Everything smelled fresh because everything was so green. For a country boy from Wisconsin, it was really just a dream that I never thought would come true.

When it came time to go away for two days in August, I went to Minnesota. We got there in our old car, and the next morning we turned around and drove right back to Wausau. I think we had about 20 dollars from my parents. I was able to make it with gas money all the way down to Miami.

Northwestern recruited me just before Ara Parseghian was hired as head coach. I was recruited the spring of 1956, during my senior year in high school. Wisconsin and Minnesota had two great teams as well. I would have played in Rose Bowls if I had gone to either one of those two schools.

Miami is hot and humid, and the college was on probation. I really had to think hard before going there. That held me back from going there to begin with, but then I looked at their schedule for the four years that I would be there. The University of Miami would be playing schools in the Atlantic Coast Conference, Southeast Conference, Southwest Conference, and the Big Ten. I'd be exposed to a lot of different types of football, and I'd play against almost every conference in America.

Weight Training

Jim Ringo was probably the premier center when I got out of college. He was with Green Bay and weighed about 245. They might have thought he was a little small. When I got out of college, I weighed 217. I went to training camp and lifted weights, and weighed 240 my rookie year.

I gradually worked my way up through weight training. There weren't too many athletes doing weight training in those days, but I believed in it. I studied kinesiology in college and understood how I could build muscle, strength, and quickness. I did a lot of weight training and working out to the point where I worked my way up to 276. That was the biggest I was.

Nobody believed I would get that big. A lot of the teams tried to acquire me from the Raiders. When Mr. Davis came in 1963, he wouldn't let me go for anything.

Early Years With Raiders

I didn't know what I was getting into because it was a step up in the pros. In 1960, the American Football League wasn't that good. We didn't have that good of football players to begin with. It took a couple of years for guys like Al Davis, Sid Gillman, and Hank Stram to really start recruiting and signing some better players into the league.

Even though I had hopes that I would be a part of that all along, I just wanted to play. The National Football League didn't draft me. They said they were going to draft me, but when draft day came, the NFL didn't draft me. I just wanted to play football and get the chance to play with Oakland. Playing in Oakland was the best thing for me because I grew up there. I grew up there, got big, and I learned how to really play football.

Let's just say that in 1960, '61, and '62, we were kind of the doormats of that league. My first year with the Raiders we only won a couple games.

It was tough, it was really tough, but I new that there was a light at the end of the tunnel. If I played hard and got my teammates to play hard, and we had a coach that we had faith in, then we would be good. Al Davis did that for us, so I was happy while I was there.

I used to think that maybe they would trade me, but it never happened. There were teams trying to trade for me, but the Oakland people wouldn't let me go. When Miami got their franchise, since I was from the University of Miami, the Miami Dolphins would have liked to have me there as a player. They would have liked to have a University of Miami player on their team, but Al Davis wouldn't let me go. I didn't mind it. I loved the entire time I was in Oakland; I'm still an Oakland boy.

Al Davis
As a coach, Al Davis was far superior to anyone. I think Sid Gillman was an excellent coach for the San Diego Chargers. He was a very fine coach, and so was Hank Stram. But, Al Davis put so many innovations into football while he was coaching and he did so many different things while coaching players. He was excellent at working with wide receivers, like Lance Alworth, who is in the Pro Football Hall of Fame. He worked with him in San Diego. He also worked with Fred Biletnikoff and a lot of our wide receivers and offensive linemen, like me.

He would come up to me during the practice and say, "Jim, just move your right foot a little bit more to the outside and then drive off of that foot." He had different little things he'd help everybody with, actually.

We played in some games where it was very similar to what Baltimore did recently when they got a direct snap from the center and ran around the end zone to run the clock out.

The very first time we did that, people thought we were nuts. I predicted Baltimore would do it when I saw the situation they were in. I said, "They better take the ball on a direct snap and run the clock out." I was kind of excited about that. Al Davis did a lot of things that were innovative.

I know that Al Davis also had the help of Ron Wolf, who was an outstanding football person as well. He was a big help to Coach Davis.

Tom Flores
I didn't envision Tom Flores ever coaching the Raiders when he was playing. I knew Tom was a football person. He knew what he was doing out there on the field. His first three years in the league he didn't do that well because he was sick. After his illness he came on and showed what he could do. He had a football mind and he had a mind for coaching and it was no surprise to me that he became the Raiders Head Coach and then later on with Seattle.

Look at both Tom Flores and Jim Plunkett. They're both Hispanic, and you don't like to think that's what holding them back from being named to the Hall of Fame. The selection committee for the Hall of Fame, I wouldn't want to say they are racist or anything like that, but I think a lot of them thought that Tom Flores and guys like Tom were tutored so heavily by Mr. Davis that it wasn't really their ability to do what they're doing. They were getting it from Mr. Davis.

I think that's unfair because even back a few years ago when John Madden went into the Pro Football Hall of Fame, the selection committee wanted to put him into the Pro Football Hall of Fame as a football related person, not as a coach. I was very, very upset about it. I went to the Hall of Fame for one of the selection committee meetings and I sat before all those people and really called them out and told them what I thought about the situation. John Madden was a football coach and the greatness of the Raiders at that time was because of John Madden.

Raiders Going From Doormat To Successful
It was fantastic. A football player loves good coaching and he will respect the coaches, because it's important for a coach to take you all the way. You saw the two Harbaugh brothers coaching in the Super Bowl and prior to that, everything they did throughout the season. These are the kind of coaches that a real football player loves to play for. Players would give their shirt off their back to play for a guy like that.

Back in the day when Jon Gruden was a Raiders coach, every young guy in the National Football League would have liked to have been with the Raiders at that time. When you get a coach who has the ability, the desire, and the drive like the Harbaughs, Gruden, and Davis, it's like a dream come true to play for him.

First Raiders Super Bowl
They said it was going to be a lot of hoopla, and there was, but I didn't let that stuff bother me. I didn't get into that at all. All I knew was I'm a kid from Wausau, Wisconsin, going against Lombardi's Packers; Ray Nitschke, those guys in the inside, that's what I was after. That's what I prepared for and I'm very proud of the way that I played against them. Vince Lombardi complimented me on my play, but we lost. But I was after a win, not a compliment.

Toughest Defensive Player Went Up Against
If you go to the Pro Football Hall of Fame and look at my era, the middle linebackers and the defensive tackles that are in there, were pretty darn good. You got Bob Lilly, Joe Greene, Ray Nitschke, Dick Butkus and all these different inside guys; linebackers. There were some great ones in there and those were the guys that I had to prepare to battle for.

To get the notoriety of the Hall of Fame or All Pro, you've got to be able to handle guys like that and I'm proud to say that I did a pretty good job at that.

Success Of Raiders Offensive Line

It was the weightlifting we did, but there was just an awful lot of pride and poise in those guys and we worked hard together at practice. We wanted to be the best. Gene Upshaw and Art Shell had tremendous pride in themselves, and naturally I was very proud of my team. I tried to exude that pride out there on the field every day in practice and every Sunday in the game.

It was something that I think Mr. Davis instilled in us; the pride, the poise, the dedication, the commitment to excellence, all those things that you've heard about over the years, that was the Raiders. That was our Raiders team.

Favorite Quarterback

I didn't have a personal favorite quarterback. When George Blanda took a snap from me, I knew we were going to do something special. I knew that he had a plan to complete some passes; get in position to get a field goal or get in position to get a touchdown. When Ken Stabler was in there we knew that it was going to be bam-bam; you're going at it, let's go. There was a lot of commitment and pride out there.

It was the same with Daryle Lamonica. Lamonica was a super athlete. We practiced hard. Teams today don't practice like we did back then. To be successful, a team has to work on it. Look at the 49ers and the Ravens in the Super Bowl. Those guys worked hard for the last couple years. Jim had two playoffs and John had five playoffs in a row.

You don't get there if you don't work hard. Every team out there has to work hard if they want to get to the big time.

Injuries & Physical Problems

I had my leg amputated a couple years ago due to football injuries and nobody really said, "Jim, I'm sorry. What can we do for you?" There was no insurance for dismemberment or anything like that. As far as concussions are concerned, I think it's being overplayed a little bit. I've had probably about 25 concussions, more than that when I played, and I'm not complaining. My wife thinks I'm a little goofy at times, but every wife thinks that about her husband.

I don't have Alzheimer's. Doctors have examined me and they said I'm not going to have Alzheimer's. I do have some cognitive problems, though. A doctor I saw in Southern California is concerned about some of the cognitive tests that I didn't do well on, but I feel very good about it. I'm going to go along. I punished my body playing football like we all do, but some of these guys, I think, are just looking for a handout after they get through playing. They're looking to get a paycheck from some insurance, or someone who is going to pay off the guys that do have some memory problems.

I played 308 straight games and hurt my knee; well, that's an understatement. I hurt my knees and I kept going. In 1974, I thought, wow, it's getting kind of tough out here, and yet I made Second Team All Pro after all those years. In my 16th year of football I had a feeling in my knee that I didn't like. It didn't seem as though I would be able to play up to the standards that I had played to all this time, and I just didn't want to be the guy who's hanging on out there.

I didn't make much money at all. I think the most money I made was $70,000 a year, in my 16th year of pro football. You've got Flacco talking about $20-$27 million now. I wouldn't mind hanging around with him and being his water boy or something. I think they're just making a lot out of this thing. Sure, we all have memory loss to a certain extent. You can't think of a professor's name, where you went to college, or sometimes your wife might ask you to pick up a loaf of bread and you bring home a pound of cheese instead. That's no big deal as far as I'm concerned.

We've been playing football for many, many years and there have been a lot of headaches and a lot of concussions out there. I've had amnesia for three days. I didn't know who I was or where I was, but I can still remember when it happened. As long as I can remember when that happened, and that's been a lot of years ago, I think I'm in pretty good shape. I wish guys would quit crying so damn much. If they would have had some strength and been a decent football player to begin with, they wouldn't be crying right now.

I hit with my head all the time. I would lead with my head. That's the first thing I would hit the opponent with, then my forearms, then my shoulders. I blocked the way I was taught to block and that's the way I was taught. I tried to be a perfectionist at my trade and that's what I did every time. You get headaches doing that.

I had a concussion three weeks ago. I was in a wheelchair because when I take my leg off at night to sleep, I have to have a wheelchair to get me to the restroom. I was in a hotel and I backed up with the wheelchair in my room and it tipped over backwards. I hit my head right on the tile floor. It sounded like a coconut broke open and I had a headache for about four days; so I had a concussion. What the hell, I've had a lot of concussions.

There I was, I didn't feel too good for about four or five days. My wife and I are in this hotel; we're off having a holiday and visiting and I got a headache. Big deal. I probably got hit in the head that time harder than most guys ever get hit in the NFL. I was a little dizzy for a while, but you've got to suck it up and get off your backside.

Bill Bergey
John Madden is chewing me out from the sideline. Bill Bergey was a rookie and Bill was setting up his defensive line to free him from me. I couldn't get a free shot at Bill Bergey, and Bill was making some tackles. Madden was kind of hollering at me, "Otto, can't you get that rookie?" Then there's Bergey, he's saying, "Yeah, Otto, can't you get that rookie?" I said to myself, you're damn right I can get that rookie. I went after him and put him out of the game.

John Madden
John Madden was only about a year and a half older than me. I had tremendous respect for Coach Madden, as did the rest of my teammates. He wanted the game played a certain way and we played that way for him. He was demanding. He would demand that we play the game that way and that's what we would do. He was like

one of the guys, but he was also a taskmaster and he wanted the game to be played that way. We all loved John Madden. He was a great guy to play for.

Al Davis
I normally called Al Davis, Coach. When I would come up to him, I would usually address him as Coach, whether we were in the office or on the field. Then there were times when I would refer to him as Mr. Davis. On the field and in football, I'd call him Coach Davis.

Greatest Football Player
I think that person has yet to be seen. As far as I'm concerned, you've seen a lot of great football this past football season and in past years. We see great football players, great plays—fine young men doing well for football. Football is a way that we can communicate with people to be good leaders, good Americans, and be great football players. I think the greatest football player is yet to be seen.

Reflection On Life
You look back and you say, gee, Johnny Unitas died young. Gee, so and so left us too soon. Ray Nitschke was a tough son of a gun. How come he had to die so young? I had my 75th birthday and I sat with my grandchildren and I just said, "Children, can you believe Grandpops is 75 years old? I don't feel it, but I am. We've been really blessed that I've been able to be here this long with you guys."

I've been able to lead a wonderful life. I will always be very thankful for the big hits that I got, some of the big hits that got me, the victories, the celebrations afterwards, and all that stuff. I'll always remember that.

Pro Football Hall Of Fame Induction
The day I was notified that I was going into the Hall of Fame, I had an idea. People told me that I was up for it that year, but I was at my ranch. I had a pair of bib overalls on, and I was all full of dust and dirt. I guess it was in January when they made the

announcement that I made it. I raise walnuts and I have thousands of walnut trees. I just was going to work like I normally would, even on the day of the selection. I just went to the ranch and did some work.

The phone rang at my ranch manager's house and his wife came out and said, "Mr. Otto, you're wanted on the phone." So I went to the phone and there they were and they said, "Jim Otto, you've been selected to the Pro Football Hall of Fame." I said, "Oh, boy. Wow, what do I do now?"

Anyway, they made arrangements for my wife and everybody so we could go to Hawaii where they would make the announcement. It was very, very exciting for a kid that was told that he couldn't make it in the pros because he was too small. I went out to prove that I could do it. It was a very, very exciting time.

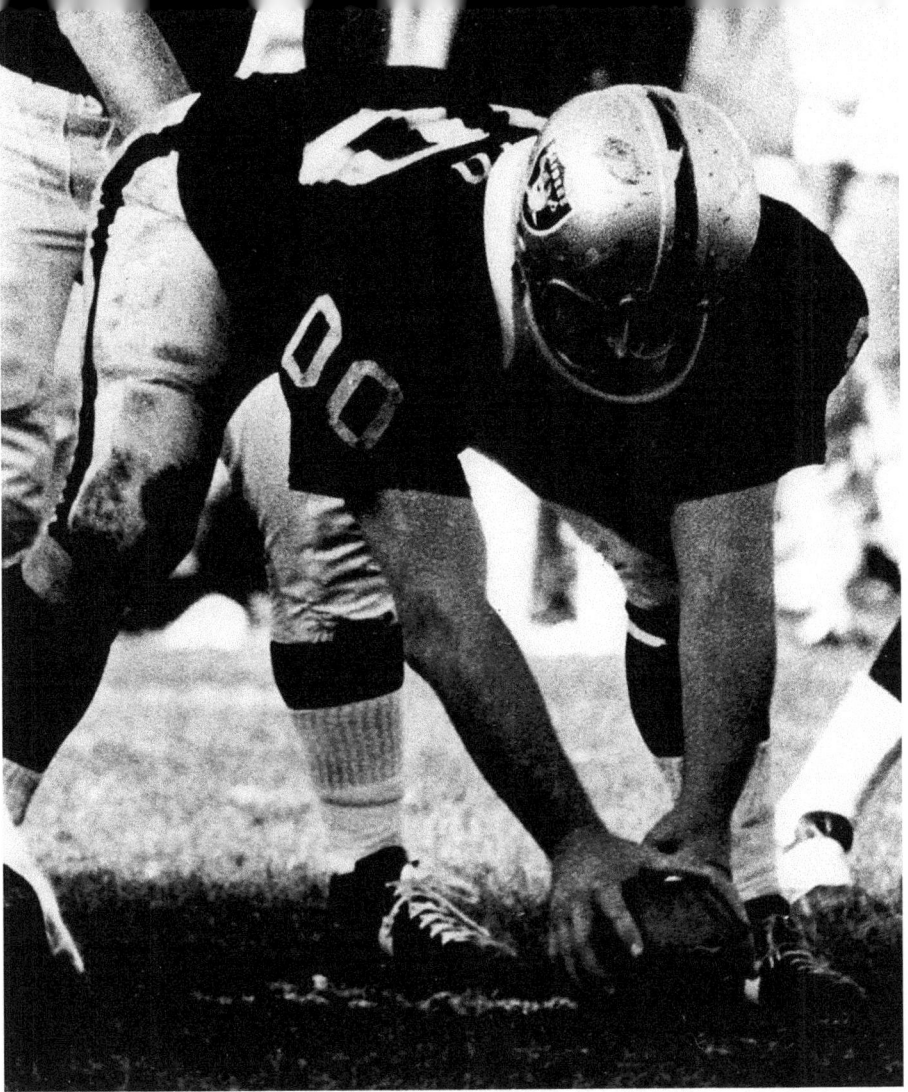

Photograph copyright Associated Press

Chapter 2

Ron Mix

College:
USC

Career History:
1960–1969 Los Angeles/San Diego Chargers
1971 Oakland Raiders

1979 Inductee Pro Football Hall of Fame

College Choice
My first choice was UCLA, but only USC offered me a football
scholarship, so the decision was easy. Parents who are raising
teenagers should just encourage them that if they are really
falling in the love with the sport and you put the time in, good
things will happen. It doesn't necessarily mean you end up in the
Pro Football Hall of Fame, but you'll be very pleased with
yourself.

In high school I was a very late developer. I didn't become a
starter until my senior year because the starting end was injured.
I really liked the game, though, so I decided I was going to keep
trying and I came up with a plan. I was going to start working
out right away, as soon as the season was over. The plan was to
go to a Junior College for two years and then go to UCLA. That
was my dream school. It just happened.

Our league was playing an All-Star game against another league,
and the head coach of the All-Star game from our league was my
football coach. All of the really good ends that year were juniors.
The coach was literally stuck with me. I bet he thought he'd
never see the words All-Star and Ron Mix in the same sentence.

I had been working out for months since the football season ended. I grew taller, I gained weight, my speed increased, and I started lifting weights. Lifting weights was something all coaches frowned on, but I couldn't understand how it could be bad to be strong. I was really one of the few people that were lifting. By the time of the All-Star game that summer, I was the star of that team. USC happened to see me and offered me a scholarship. I was so thrilled. I couldn't believe I got a scholarship to USC. I was almost embarrassed because every one of my high school teammates during my Senior year were better football players than me prior to my improvement. I told myself I was going to make USC look good. I was going to work out year round. I was going to moderate my life on and off the field to become a great football player.

My plan included lifting weights year round; something that really nobody was doing. I wasn't going to have a single alcoholic drink. I wasn't going to eat any sweets, because at that time, coaches said sweets were very bad for you, and no soft drinks. I didn't do any of that stuff.

I know objectively that I could have had a beer now and then. I could certainly have candy now and then. Every time I consciously refused to do it reminded me of what my goal was. I continued to progress and finally my senior year I was Captain of the team, made All-American, and was the number one draft choice of the Baltimore Colts. The Boston team had also chosen me in the new league. They traded me to the Los Angeles Chargers because I said if I had to go back East, I definitely wanted to play for the Colts, not a new league.

Willie Wood
It was interesting. You've got to remember the times those were. This was in the late '50s. Willie and I were Captains of the team at a time when 99 ½% of the fraternities would not permit us to be members because of Willie being black and me being Jewish. Our white Christian teammates decided we were the right guys to lead them and made us their captains. It's an example of how sports have been one of the most influential reasons for race and religions barriers falling down.

Al Davis and Mel Hein at USC

I was an end my first two years at Southern Cal and Al Davis was my position coach at end. Then my eyes started going bad so I couldn't see the ball. Not a good thing for an end. They switched me to tackle and my coach was a Hall of Fame center from the New York Giants, named Mel Hein. He was great.

Coaches at that time acted like mad fools. Everyone was screaming and yelling. There were no limits to the amount of time you could be on the practice field in those days. We were on the practice field 2 ½ to 3 hours. Every drill was full speed contact. Coaches screaming and yelling all the time; except for Mel Hein and to a lesser degree Al Davis. They were a little more cool and collected.

Notre Dame

To show you how petty I am, when I was at USC we lost to Notre Dame all three years. I still can't get over it. I root for them to lose at everything. I still can't get over it. I'm Exhibit A that men never grow up.

Monte Clark

Monte Clark was a terrific guy, an outstanding football player, and extremely funny. Back then he could do impressions. He did Al Davis perfectly. Monte was a pleasure to have as a teammate.

Al Davis Not Being Hired As USC Coach

I would think Al Davis was probably upset. He had a grand opinion of himself but it was justified. He was an outstanding coach even then; he was so young. When I first met Al it was in the locker room and I was doing leg lifts on the bench. I was standing on the bench and going up and down to build up my legs. Al came over and said, "Do you lift weights too?" I said, "Yes I do, although the coaches don't recommend it, but I think it's important." He said, "I do too." I thought he was a player. He looked that young. Then he introduced himself as the coach and it surprised me.

Al was a terrific, terrific guy. He did more for former players than all other owners combined. That's not an exaggeration. He gave more former players jobs in coaching, in scouting, and in the front office, than any other owners combined. There was never a time when I brought it to his attention that one of his former players needed some financial help, that he didn't come through.

Mike & Marlin McKeever

I could not tell the McKeever twins apart. They were truly great football players. The McKeever twins and I were the only ones who were lifting weights on that team. USC didn't even have a weight room. We worked out at a gym in Inglewood, California, which is about 15 miles away from the USC campus.

This is going to seem so immodest but we were so much stronger than everybody else, including anybody we played against. It was like a total mismatch. It was unbelievable. We could military press over our heads 300 pounds. We all weighed about 225. Guys we'd play against would be anywhere from 190 to 250. What a bunch of confidence it is to know that if you wanted to, you could pick them up and military press them.

Being Drafted By the Baltimore Colts In the NFL Draft And Not Signing

I wanted to stay on the West Coast. That was my preference. I wanted to start off in the NFL not the AFL. I think I could have broken the starting lineup with the Baltimore team. I'm very confident that I could have.

I only intended to play a couple of years to get enough money to buy a car and a house. The USC practices were 2 ½ to 3 hours; constant contact, all sorts of pressure all of the time. I didn't play a skill position so I never touched the ball. It's not like you're having fun. All you get out of the game is the satisfaction of doing a good job. My gosh, it was so difficult. I decided I was going to play two more years in the game.

Then in the NFL, both leagues, you no longer played both ways. You didn't play the whole game. It was so easy. Playing offensive tackle was honestly just so easy that I couldn't believe it. Also, because I worked out year round I was in great shape. Anyway, I found the joy in the game again.

1963 AFL Championship Game

You know what? The score was misleading. We beat them worse than that. The game wasn't that close. It was complete domination. What's interesting is that everybody played his "A" game. You don't get that. It was unbelievable. Keith Lincoln had something like 347 total yards running and catching passes. Lance Alworth had about 120 yards receiving. Paul Lowe had over a hundred yards rushing. It was just amazing what we did.

The defense was unreal. We had two defensive linemen that really don't get enough historic attention, Earl Faison and Ernie Ladd. For about a four-year period of time those guys played the game in their positions as well as anybody has ever played and I mean right up to the present day. Ernie Ladd was 6'9" and 340; Earl was 6'5", 280 and they were great, great athletes. Absent injuries cutting short their effective careers, they'd both be in the Pro Football Hall of Fame.

Nickname "The Intellectual Assassin?"

I got that nickname from my offensive line coach, Joe Madro. He came up with it because I was going to law school at night while I was playing and I had an aggressive style of playing for an offensive lineman. I did a lot more attacking than just dropping back. At the time I thought it was kind of silly and contrived. Now I really like it.

Only Two Holding Calls In Entire Career

I didn't hold. I really didn't. I really wasn't being facetious when I asked those referees how they made the mistake. Those were two bad calls. Here's the thing, this will sound holier than thou, but I don't know how you can take satisfaction in doing a good job if you cheat. That's the way I felt.

Joe Madro, my line coach, used to tell his offensive linemen when anybody held, "You know what? You're never going to make 15 yards on offense in your whole life. You never touch the football!" That was always ringing in my ear. I'd never really gain 15 yards so I shouldn't cause the team to lose 15 yards.

Deacon Jones
We played against each other three times. The first time I give to him, but then the next two times I give to me. I think I figured out the head slap. I figured out when he'd reach out to slap or attack. The next two times I thought I played very well against him. In fact, after the second time I played against him, the Cleveland Browns played the Rams the next week. Monte Clark saw the films and called me. He said, "Ron, that's the best I've ever seen anybody play against Deacon Jones." Deacon would never concede that he was beat.

I heard him on the radio once and they asked him who was the toughest offensive lineman he ever faced? He said, "I don't know because I never faced just one. They always put two people on me."

Deacon was such a terrific and funny guy, but he'd never admit that anyone ever beat him.

Jack Kemp
Jack Kemp was a terrific quarterback and he did a great job. Jack was an interesting guy. He became a U.S. Congressman and he was on the ticket to be elected Vice President of the United States. When I played with Jack, he was far more conservative than he eventually turned out to be as his thoughts progressed. For instance, he believed that we should do away with Social Security. People should just take care of themselves.

I remember Jack and I had as discussion about that. I said, "Jack, it just doesn't work. My Mom and Dad were divorced when I was four and my brother was five. We were on welfare the whole time. When my Mom did work, it was making twenty-five cents an hour as a waitress. Are you telling me that if someone like her had a chance to spend a dime on her kids or put it away for her retirement, she should put it away for her retirement? It wouldn't happen."

Anyway, Sunday comes and we were playing the Houston Oilers. It was 98 degrees in San Diego. It was hot and they were a tough team. At halftime, we're walking to the locker room and I hear Jack say, "Ron! Ron I want to talk to you." I think he's going to ask me something about the game. Instead he's says, "I've been thinking about what you said and you're right about Social Security." I said, "Jack, we're in the middle of the game. I'm exhausted. What are you talking about?" He was so obsessed with politics and public affairs. That was like Exhibit "A" of how obsessed he was. It was the middle of a football game he's thinking about our discussion.

Tobin Rote

Tobin Rote had an immediate grasp of the game and was so slick. His arm was going away. He made Lance Alworth famous because he'd throw those big floaters that would fall short and Lance would have to come back and jump like a deer. Dare I say jump like Bambi, which was Lance's nickname, to catch the balls. By the next year Tobin's arm was just completely gone and John Hadl had to take over. John needed that year to develop.

Sid Gillman was a brilliant coach. John Hadl just had it and Sid saw enough of him in college that he felt he could play quarterback. John's passing skills just developed and kept improving every year. It was my recollection of how John developed into a quarterback that made me think Tim Tebow would develop into one. Boy was I wrong. The guy can't throw.

Toughest Defensive Lineman

Deacon Jones was as great player. Bubba Smith was outstanding. Kansas City had a terrific guy named Jerry Mays. The New York Jets had a terrific end named Gerry Philbin. For a short period of time, Denver had a terrific end named, get this, Rich "Tombstone" Jackson. You know what? The truth is everybody's tough. Football is the hurt business. It's impossible not to have a giant collision on every play. Everybody's tough.

Sid Gillman

It was thrilling because we felt we'd score any time. We had explosive people like Lance Alworth, Don Norton, Keith Lincoln, Paul Lowe; gosh I can't even remember everyone. And there were terrific running backs, like Dickie Post and Brad Hubbard. At all times we had the threat of the deep pass because of Sid Gillman's offense.

My San Diego Chargers Number Being Unretired By Gene Klein When I Went To Raiders

I complained to Pete Rozelle and Pete ordered them to re-retire it. Then two years later they brought it back and by then I was tired of the whole thing so I didn't do anything about it.

Pro Football Hall Of Fame Induction

I'm not sure I really appreciated it immediately. When I was first called up about it I was just thinking another honor. That's somewhat blasé but I didn't really think about it. I didn't really understand it. I didn't have a full appreciation for it until that first luncheon took place when I was inducted.

Every year there's a luncheon just for the players. The players stand up and say something about themselves and talk about interesting things in their lives and what was important to them. To hear the guys talk so elegantly. Great legends of professional football, like Gino Marchetti and Paul Hornung, there are so many of them. It just came to life for me. I thought wow; I'm in the Pro Football Hall Of Fame with Jim Brown, Gino Marchetti, Bob Waterfield, and Norm Van Brocklin. I must be as good as them. There's not that many of us in there.

USC Treatment Of Athletes During His Time

I think USC started flirting with that preferential treatment again after those penalties. Let's see if we can get away with something. I know we'll give certain guys the cool jobs during the summer. The McKeever twins' jobs were at the studios. They were the most recruited two players in America. Their jobs were at the studios. The rest of us were called "Plunking Iron." We were working construction. We would carry these very heavy iron bars that would then be set to tie in grids before they laid the cement. They treated us a little differently than McKeever twins.

Photograph copyright Associated Press

Chapter 3

Larry Wilson

College:
Utah

Career History:
St. Louis Cardinals (1960-1972)
As coach/executive:
St. Louis Cardinals (1973-1976)
(Director of Scouting)
St. Louis Cardinals (1977-1987)
(Director of Personnel)
St. Louis Cardinals (1979)
(Interim Head Coach)
Phoenix Cardinals (1988-1993)
(VP and General Manager)
Arizona Cardinals (1994-2002)
(VP)

1978 Inductee Pro Football Hall of Fame

College Choice
Well, I'm really closer to Utah than I was to any place in Idaho.
It was a situation where my father felt like I would do better at
Utah, as far as getting an education, and we went that way.
I really didn't care to get too far away from home.

NFL Draft
It was an exciting time. That's quite a few years ago now. Back
then, the draft was not that big a deal. They called you and said
that you were drafted. I was excited about it. I was very happy
that things worked out. Actually, the Buffalo Bills and the
Cardinals drafted me. I signed with Cardinals for five hundred
dollars more.

My whole career, we trained in Lake Forest. They kept our training camp there so we were around Chicago. We always scrimmaged the Bears a couple of times. We also played in the Armed Forces game all the time and a Pre-Season Game with the Bears.

First Training Camp
I really didn't have expectations, to tell you the truth; I kept my suitcase packed all the time. I was drafted as a Running Back. They had John David Crow, and we had a crew of running backs. They traded Dick 'Night Train' Lane to Detroit, and that made a spot open in the Secondary. So I got moved over there, bounced around, and then they moved Jimmy Hill out to the corner. I got to play safety, and things worked out pretty darn well.

Safety Blitz
We played a lot of man for man defenses. We blitzed a lot and the coach always tried to come up with one extra guy they could block. I remember when we first did it back in New York. The coach said, "Larry, when you get in there, jump up, cover up your number, and run back to huddle, so they won't know who you are. Red Dog was just blitzing the outside linebackers. We were called the Wild Cat … kind of got that nickname.

Jim Brown
Well, the key was to get on Jim Brown and hold on. You never worried about getting hurt with Jim Brown. He was a guy who could slip and slide. Since he had a great running ability, you really never got a clear shot at him, and so you never worried about getting hurt by him.

Jim Brown, to me, was the epitome of football then. He just did so many things, and he is one of the guys that really made the game great.

St. Louis Cardinals Rivals
Back then we were in a Division with Philadelphia, New York, Cleveland, and Dallas, so we had some pretty good rivals. I think that our main one was Dallas. When they came in, it was always a big game for us. And, we loved playing in New York too.

Favorite Interception Of His 52

I wish I could remember that far back. I was a running back when I was drafted. I enjoyed getting the ball and running with it. I think what it proved was that I was on the right side of the ball; or I couldn't have been a running back in the League.

St. Louis Cardinals Secondary

Our secondary, I think, was one of the better ones in the business with Roger Wehrli, Jerry Stovall, Jimmy Hill, and Billy Stacy. We had some good defensive backs. Back then you played man for man most of the time. We played very little zone, so it was a challenge for everyone; but overall, I thought we had as fine a secondary as it was in the league.

Johnny Roland

Johnny Roland was one super football player and just a marvel. You're really fortunate to get a good guy like Roland who really wants to play the game, enjoys playing, has fun, and is a part of the team. That's the whole key to all of this, getting it all together, and doing your job.

Johnny Unitas

I think Johnny Unitas was absolutely a phenomenal player. I sit back and marvel, and think about the times that I got to play against him. He was as good as everybody said he was. I think that there were a lot of fine people. You're talking about the Jim Browns, and the whole slew of them.

Best Receiver

The best pass receiver that I ever played against was Paul Warfield. Paul could play in today's game and be a superstar like he was when he played. I just think he is a phenomenal guy and what a great player he was. He was very quick, had good size, and I tell you what, he was a mean bugger. All those things added together made him a real problem when he was out there. We spent a lot of time trying to figure out how to cover him. We got it done now and then, but most of the time he whopped us.

I think back to that time. We didn't get a chance to play against a lot of people in the American Conference, but at the end of my career, we were playing against the Miami Dolphins, and we had a change in coaches. We were playing against the Dolphins and a guy by the name of Larry Csonka who was a big fullback at that time, and our coach said, "We've got to stop Warfield." They had Larry Csonka carry the ball. I tell you what, he ran over me so many times, I couldn't count them.

Jim Hart

Jim Hart was a tremendous quarterback; he had some size and could really throw the ball well. I don't think he got the credit that he was due. We had another guy who played early on, but when Jim came in he just took over and made our team a much better football team.

Joining Front Office

After 13 years I was beat up bad. I thought there's got to be something else to do in this world, so I knew it was time to quit.

I always wanted to coach, and I got an opportunity a couple of times, but overall the Front Office was also an interesting situation. It was the time when computers were starting to move into the game, and getting those set up, getting the scouting program in, and taking the coach's work and getting it computerized, was always something that I was interested in. I enjoyed my time in the Front Office.

The draft has become a circus right now. There are so many things going on, they know everything about you. The thing they can't do though, is really tell what kind of a player you are going to be when you get there. That's all in the heart, and boy, the hardest thing to do is to figure out which guy is going to be the guy that goes out and gets to be a part of the team, and makes a real impact for you.

The toughest job of all is to predict which guy is going to come in and be the player that he should be. The guy who is willing to pay the price, to be a part of the team, to know that he's one of 11, not just one out there. Then, you have to put together a team that plays together and plays hard together; that's the real key to getting some success. You've got to have guys that can do their job and do it well.

Raymond Berry & Johnny Unitas

Raymond Berry was another guy that you just marvel about. He didn't have the great speed, but he certainly would run his routes well. He took advantage of everything, and could catch the football. He and Johnny Unitas were a part of unit that played exceptionally well together, and consequently they were winners.

Cardinals Move To Arizona

It was slow to start with. Arizona was basically a Dallas Cowboy area for television, so there were a lot of Cowboy fans here. I was amazed at how quickly they accepted us, and supported the team out here. The greatest thing that happened there is when we got our own stadium. We have a beautiful stadium here and one that, I think, everyone in the community enjoys. I just think people enjoy coming out and watching the game.

The interesting thing here is that this city is about 90 percent Chicagoans and 10 percent Minnesotans, so we have to win them over. I was just laughing because the neighbor next door has got a cockeyed Chicago Bear flag hanging in her yard, and I'm always on her about getting it out of there.

Pro Football Hall Of Fame Induction

I was so excited I was flabbergasted, and I enjoyed that. That is one of the real highlights of my career; I'm so gratified by being there.

Photograph copyright Associated Press

Chapter 4

Deacon Jones

College:
South Carolina State
Mississippi Valley State

Career History
Los Angeles Rams (1961-1971)
San Diego Chargers (1972-1973)
Washington Redskins (1974)

1980 Inductee Pro Football Hall of Fame

Best Defensive Lineman Of All Time

That's a question that's, I guess, forever in the people's mind about who's that and who's this. But I think if you get down to a situation where you could put the actual facts in the middle of the table, you'd understand, I'm talking about facts on everybody, not just the guys that they decided to talk about in 1982. You put my facts down the way they were accounted for, and you'll find out who the best ever was.

NFL Not Keeping Sack Totals Until 1982

It always upset me because every team in the National Football League kept their own stats. They started on a league level recording sacks officially in 1982, which I think is embarrassing. The point is they got the facts in the book. We got them in the book.

I got my facts right here in George Allen's 1967-68 playbook. I was paid per sack; they didn't let me count. I tore this league apart for six years straight. I mean total domination. I'll go right there. I'll give them the rest. I'll take six years out of the mid part of my career in the 1960s and I'll go with those numbers. I'll go with those numbers and I'll tell you what, you'll make them fold that stuff up and burn it up. Because if you're going to measure it on total sacks, total pressure, total tackles, there isn't anyone real close to me.

1967 & 1968 Seasons
Well, I don't think that anybody ever had a performance like me. I also had six sacks in 1967 in the postseason and you add that together. That's total domination.

I backed that up the next year with 24 sacks. These are stats that the world hasn't heard about. You look at me in 1967 and '68, and see if anybody ever totally dominated the game with pressure on the quarterback. I had 100 unassisted tackles that year, along with 26 sacks. Now tell me that doesn't scare some people.

Also, I got paid $500 a sack. So I made my money. I didn't even discuss my years I had 10 sacks or 12 sacks. I would have been embarrassed to go ask the man for any money.

Draft
They made you earn the money. It wasn't given up front. My rookie year, I was probably in the best condition I've ever been in. I was really scared to death when I came up here. I had never played against a white guy before. I had never played integrated football. So I had all these fears. I had the fear of going someplace that I had never been, which was that level of football. So I had all that pressure on my mind and I was a 14th round draft choice. After I got there I found out that the Rams draft people who were on the freeway going home when they drafted me. So I walked into camp with one thing on my mind man. I'm going to whip some heads. That was all I had going for me. I got to run everywhere on this football field. When the coaches blew the whistle, I got to run. I got to get in front in every drill. I got to get in front, and then get back in line, then get in front again. I got to make somebody see me. That violence in my game came out because of that. I learned the tougher you are out here, the better football player you are.

Accomplishment

One thing is certain. I got a chance to get all the frustration out man. I have no reason to be covered in anything anymore. When I left the game man, I stayed until I wanted to get out and I felt like I had done what I had to do.

Photograph copyright Associated Press

Chapter 5

Billy Shaw

College:
Georgia Tech

Career History:
Buffalo Bills (1961-1969)

1999 Inductee Pro Football Hall of Fame

College Choice
I was born in Natchez but I was raised in Vicksburg. My parents moved to Vicksburg before I was two years old, and my idol in grammar school was a high school player by the name of George Morris. George Morris was Mr. Football in Mississippi. George Morris went to Georgia Tech and he became an All-American. Coach Dodd said that he was the best football player that he ever coached. George Morris got into my life while I was in high school, and he led me in that direction. That's how I got from Mississippi to Georgia Tech.

Cookie Gilchrist
Cookie Gilchrist was probably the best football player I ever played with, not the best athlete, but what a great football player he was. He did some placekicking and it was in a pinch in 1962.

Cookie was one of those rare individuals as far as a football player. He could have played guard, because he was our size. He could have played linebacker, he could have played anywhere on the defensive line. Just a phenomenal player, and he took that competitiveness in his lifestyle outside of football. You didn't push him around.

NFL vs. AFL

The caliber of the player was certainly different. My situation, going to Buffalo, was similar to college because we were not one of those AFL teams that threw the ball. We ran the ball possibly two out of three times. We were more like an NFL team back in that day. We weren't like the San Diego teams or the Denver teams, and later on in Namath's career, the New York teams that threw the ball all the time. I did not regret not playing in the NFL.

Draft

My last year in college was 1960, and my coach was Bobby Dodd. The Bills of the AFL drafted me number two. I was talking to the NFL, particularly Gil Brandt of the Dallas Cowboys. They wanted to play me at linebacker, but I'd never played linebacker. Of course, I would never have been picked ahead of Bob Lilly, who was their first choice, and a great, great, great player.

I went to Coach Dodd to get his advice and he told me sign with the AFL. You're going to be playing the position either on the defensive side or the offensive side of the ball that you are used to, and that's where he thought that my career should be. I actually signed with the AFL before the NFL draft. The Dallas Cowboys went ahead and drafted me anyway, I think in the 14th round, 184th player picked, thinking that the AFL was going to fold and they would have my rights. I never, ever looked back. I enjoyed playing in the AFL. As time went on, the teams got better, the league got better, and I just enjoyed it.

Jack Kemp

Jack Kemp took command. You didn't cough or sneeze in that huddle. Jack came to us in the latter part of 1962, and we knew immediately that he was a different guy. He was one of the most intelligent people I've ever been around. His conversation was always geared toward the political arena, and we knew that he was going to be special.

I believed in Jack. At that particular time in my life, I was not a Republican. I was a Democrat, and we never argued about it. We talked at length about what one party believed and then what the other party believed. He was an intelligent person.

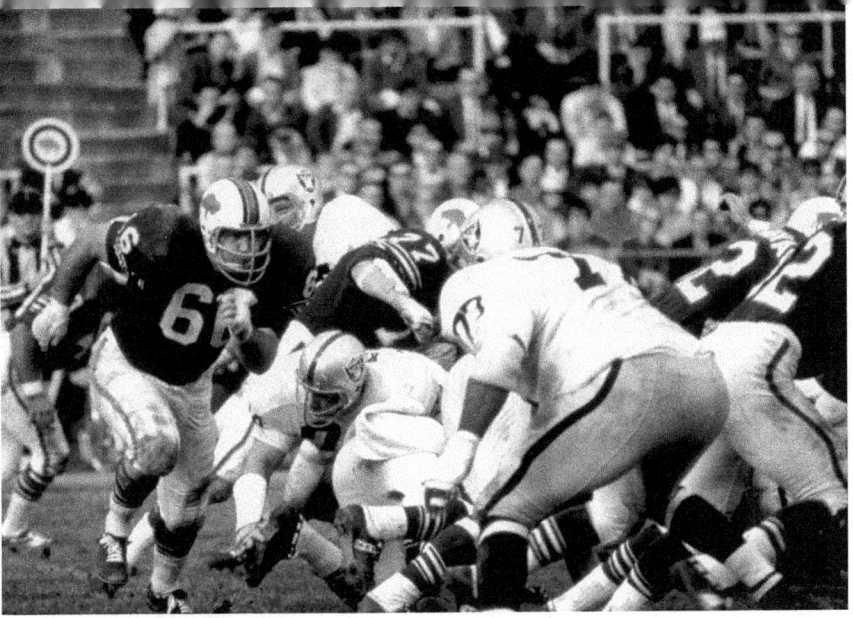

Photograph copyright Associated Press

Chapter 6

Herb Adderley

College:
Michigan State

Career History:
Green Bay Packers (1961-1969)
Dallas Cowboys (1970-1972)

1980 Inductee Pro Football Hall of Fame

Vince Lombardi Not Being Named New York Giants Head Coach

The New York Giants hired Allie Sherman. They said that Vince Lombardi applied for the job. For some reason they bypassed him and decided to hire Allie Sherman and got Lombardi a job in Siberia. That's what they called Green Bay at the time. They sent him up to Green Bay. I think Green Bay had only won maybe one or two games previous to Lombardi getting there.

Tom Landry

Tom Landry made a lot of coaching decisions that cost the Cowboy games. Not only with his play calling but also with the personnel. In the Cotton Bowl, Don Perkins was running like Jim Brown. We couldn't stop Perkins. Perkins was running inside the tackles. He didn't even come around my side, he would run inside the tackles and he got the ball down to the 20-yard line. All of the sudden, Landry decided to take Perkins out of the game and put in Dan Reeves. Reeves had two bad knees and I could walk faster than Reeves could run. Landry changed his game plan and started throwing the ball instead of running. If Perkins had stayed there, I guarantee you, that game would have been tied. We would have gone into overtime, and it might have been a different outcome. Because of Landry's coaching, decisions, and his personnel moves, it cost them games before I got there and it cost them games by the time I got there. I saw it firsthand.

Dave Robinson
The first time that Dave Robinson met Vince Lombardi was after the All-Star game when the All-Stars played against the Pro Champions at Soldier Field. When Dave was on that team, they'd beat us in that game. Lombardi was livid, man. Dave had time to take a shower, get dressed, and come over to our locker room.

He was feeling good with a big grin on his face coming to the locker room, and he heard Lombardi chewing us out. We didn't even have time to take our pads and stuff off because Lombardi was chewing us out for that game. This went on for about 45 minutes. I don't know what Dave was thinking when he came in, but that was his first encounter with Lombardi.

The College All Stars had a good team. They had some great players on that team. I don't think we took anybody for granted. It's just a case of them making some good plays. I guess you could say they won the game or maybe they outplayed us.

Move To Defensive Back With Packers
When I was at Michigan State, I was the number one draft choice as a running back out of all the Big 10 running backs. When I got to the Packers, Paul Hornung (a Hall of Famer), Jim Taylor (a Hall of Famer), and Tom Moore (drafted out of Vanderbilt), were all there. The year I got there, Elijah Pitts came along with me. We had four or five running backs. Lew Carpenter was also there. With all of those running backs, and I knew my chances were almost nil. I played special teams and played behind Boyd Dowler at wide receiver and at running back a little bit too in practice.

In Detroit on Thanksgiving Day of my rookie year, Hank Gremminger got hurt in the second quarter. At halftime Vince Lombardi said, "We got an emergency situation and we're going to put our best athlete out to play the left corner." I'm just sitting on the bench thinking about running the kickoff back in the second half. He comes over, puts his hand on my shoulder and said, "Herb, just do the best you can."

43

I looked at him and I say, "Who, me?" He said, "Yes." By that time, everybody was getting up and walking out of the locker room for the second half of the game. I didn't even have time to find my helmet. I was so nervous that I had to go back and get my helmet.

I had never practiced the position, and end up intercepting a pass and setting up the winning touchdown. I guess that's when he thought that I could play defense, because I could play both sides of the ball, and I went right back to offense. I never played another down on defense until the Championship Game when we beat the New York Giants, 37 to nothing. The last two minutes, he told me again, "Go out there for Jesse Whittenton." This was on the right corner. I intercepted a pass. The only two times I played as a defensive back I intercepted a pass, so I guess he decided in 1962 that he'd switch me over.

It takes a lot of athletic ability. I have God given athletic ability. I played four sports in high school. Basketball was my favorite sport. It wasn't any problem for me to make the adjustment. All I had to do was learn how to tackle.

College Choice
Number one, Clarence Peaks was my idol when I was in high school. I only played two years of football in high school because I played basketball. It was my favorite sport. I ended up playing football for a couple of years and my high school coach said, "Hey look, you're going to have the ability dude. Go to a big time school and maybe get yourself a scholarship." He started to ask me during my senior year, where I wanted to go and I told him about Clarence Peaks at Michigan State. He said, "Look, I know Duffy Daugherty." He knew Duffy from some coaching clinics they were having around the country. He said, "The only thing I can do is give him a call and let him know I got a blue chip ball player and let's see what he says." That's how the whole thing got started. I wanted to go to Michigan State because of Clarence Peaks. That's where the number 26 originated.

He was my idol. When I got there, he met me at the airport, and showed me around. He was a senior. In fact, he was the number one draft choice of the Philadelphia Eagles, my hometown. When I got to Michigan State, for some reason, they gave me 26. I said, "Hey, if you can emulate Clarence Peaks, you're going to be a great player." That's how the whole thing started with Michigan State. I went on as a walk-on. I had to make the team. I didn't get a scholarship.

I went to all integrated schools in Philly. My elementary school was Fitler Elementary School was an all integrated school. I also went to Roosevelt Junior High School. It was also integrated, and there were never any problems. Then I attended an all-boys high school in Philly, Northeast High School. We had a variety of ethnic groups playing sports.

Michigan State had probably more black All-Americans than any school in the country. You had Don Coleman, Clarence Peaks, Leroy Bolden, Ellis Duckett, and Jim Ellis just to name a few. All these guys were All-Americans, and they had a chance to play because Michigan State didn't go for segregation. They wanted to play the best ballplayers.

Segregation At Michigan State & Green Bay
The first time I really experienced segregation after coming out of Philly was in East Lansing, Michigan, because they didn't allow black people to live in East Lansing. All the black people that lived off campus had to live 10 miles down the road in Lansing, which is the state capital. That included the professors at Michigan State University also. I think it was in 1959, that the NAACP started picketing, but eventually it got to be okay. My senior year, I lived right on the street, Grand River Avenue in East Lansing, where the school's located, so things changed.

When I got to Green Bay, it was an all white town. It really wasn't a big deal because that's the way East Lansing was when I got there. There were fewer people in East Lansing than the 68,000 people in Green Bay. I really didn't have to make an adjustment. The small town blues didn't get me, coming from Philly with millions of people then going to East Lansing, a small town. Green Bay was easy for me to make the adjustment to.

45

There wasn't any social life at all in Green Bay. The social life at Michigan State, because they had quite a few black co-eds, wasn't a problem. In Green Bay, being single, your social life was just socializing with the guys or just going out to Speeds or to Tropicana or my brother's place and having a Budweiser or your adult beverage of choice.

We had to drive 112 miles to get a haircut in Milwaukee because Vince Lombardi didn't allow any facial hair or long hair, whether you were black or white. We had to keep ourselves in good physical shape and looking well, suit and tie on the road all the time. That's the way it was.

Being out at restaurants or wherever in a small town, people will come over and say hello and ask for your autograph. Nobody ever came to me and said, "We don't want you dating white women. Or, we don't want you talking white women." That never happened the whole time I was there for nine years.

Dallas Cowboys
When I got to Dallas, they had Mel Renfro, Cornell Green, and Jethro Pugh on defense. They had three black guys on defense. With Green Bay, we had seven on defense. In Dallas, they moved me to the corner; put Cornell Green at strong safety. Mel Renfro would have been the greatest free safety of all time because of his speed, his athletic ability to play free safety, and to help the cornerbacks. Tom Landry didn't want Mel playing free safety because he wanted Charlie Waters or Cliff Harris, two white guys in there to play free safety.

Mark Washington was drafted out of Morgan State. Mark was a great athlete and a natural cornerback. Mark could have played the right corner with the help of Cornell, Mel, and me. We would have had four black guys for the first time in history in the NFL secondary, but Landry didn't want to get that in his legacy. He didn't want any part of that.

In other words, Landry didn't want to put the best players on the field. I think that he made the choices because of the color of skin rather than the contents of the character and athletic ability.

It cost him some games before I got there and it cost him some games while I was there.

Man, I don't know what they would have done to him. I know one thing, the president of the United States got shot down there and killed. No telling what might have happened.

Bill Cosby
Bill Cosby and I grew up together in Philly, and he did the forward in my book. We're still friends to this day.

Fat Albert was a guy that we grew up with by the name of Bobby Martin, and he came to Green Bay a couple of times. He's about 350. He did play football in high school but he kept getting heavier and heavier, and he could hardly carry his weight around.

Man, we did all kinds of things in the neighborhood. Most of Bill Cosby's act comes from just the natural stuff that happened in the neighborhood when we were growing up. When Bill Cosby was a student at Temple University, they had a standup comic contest at a place called Underground in Philly. It was Underground because you had to go down steps, like if you're going down for the Subway.

Johnny Carson was doing "The Tonight Show" at that time, and he just happened to be at the Underground and he heard Cos. Then Cos got his break because Carson called him and said, "Look, why won't you come over to the show." That's when Cosby got started with a standup comic act. Fat Albert is still showing all around the world in different languages.

Cosby was a natural athlete in high school just like me, and we competed against each other. We went to different high schools. He went to Germantown High School, but we competed against each other in track, basketball, and baseball, and we played on the same local basketball team at the Boys Club. There's a picture of us. Cos was 16 and I was 14. We played on the same team. There's a picture in my book and, it points out Cosby and I being friends back in the day.

I was all-city in every sport. I don't think Cos was all-city in any of the sports, but he was a good athlete. In fact, he played halfback at Temple.

Mike Ditka

My senior year at Michigan State, we played Pitt in Pitt Stadium and Mike Ditka was on that team. Mike Ditka went both ways. He was a great athlete from Aliquippa, Pennsylvania. I was a running back like I had mentioned, and Mike Ditka was like a spy. He was playing linebacker and defense depending on where I lined up. He was hitting me on every play where I had the ball that night.

Finally, I think it was in the third quarter, I told Fred Arbanas, "Look. Next time Ditka does that, I'm going after him." He said, "I'm with you." Ditka did it one more time. As he was walking away, I hit him in the back of the head with a forearm and it started a brawl. Both benches emptied. Mike Ditka and I both got thrown out of that game along with a few other guys because the coaches and everybody were on the field trying to break us up. The game was on national TV, my senior year in 1960, and the game ended up in 7-7 tie. From that day on, I had no respect or love for Mike Ditka.

When he got with the Bears it even lessened because the Bears were our most hated rival. Ditka and I never forgot what happened at Michigan State in the Pitt game. We used to be going after each other when we were playing against each other in the pros.

When I got traded to Dallas, we ended up being teammates for three years. Obviously we spoke, but we never got to be great friends. He never invited me over for dinner. I couldn't tell you his wife's name. He never introduced me to her. We didn't socialize or anything, but we got along. That's about all I can say as far as Ditka is concerned.

Green Bay Packer Herb Adderley prepares to hit Dallas Cowboy
running back Don Perkins
Photograph copyright Associated Press

Chapter 7

Bob Lilly

College:
Texas Christian

Career History:
Dallas Cowboys (1961-1974)

1980 Inductee Pro Football Hall of Fame

College Choice

I grew up about 100 miles west of Fort Worth, where TCU is located. My dad's hero was Sammy Baugh, who grew up pretty near where I grew up. When dad was a young man, he went to watch Sammy Baugh. Dad started taking me down when I was in about the eighth grade. We went to a couple of games a year. Even though I visited many other campuses, for some reason, I guess because of my dad's love for TCU, I went to TCU.

We had a seven-year drought in Throckmorton that started in 1950. We were farmers, basically. Dad also had some bulldozers, which he used to build ponds, terraces, oil field roads, and things like that. By 1955, we were on the verge of being totally broke. In fact, I think we were, but Dad still worked. He had to go out of state to work.

In 1956, my mother and dad had called all of the relatives we had all over the country for work. My mother had some kinfolk in Oregon. Her cousin found Dad a job up there, so we sold everything we had. We had a 1952 Studebaker and a homemade trailer and we put what we could get on it, and moved. We were like the Beverly Hillbillies going to Oregon.

I went to Pendleton my senior year. It was a much bigger school, a 4A school, rather than a 1A. We went to the semi-finals in football, basketball, and I went to state in track. I think I made All-State in football and Second Team All-State in basketball. It turned out to be a blessing in disguise. I didn't really want to leave my kinfolk and my friends. It was kind of a lonely ride to Oregon.

I got a postcard from Allie White, who was an assistant under Coach Abe Martin. We didn't have a phone, so they had to call the coach. I visited schools in the Northwest, but when I got the one-cent postcard, they offered me a four-year scholarship to TCU with 10 dollars a month for laundry.

My dad had a mild heart attack by that time. I heard him talking about coming back and I think that's another reason I wanted to go to TCU. My grandmother was still alive, and they came back. My dad convalesced with Mom and they lived with my grandmother for about a year until Dad got well. Anyway, I started my career at TCU.

Draft

My senior year in college, I made All-American and the Dallas Cowboys, Dallas Texans, and Houston Oilers came into existence. I was drafted by the Cowboys and the Texans.

I asked Coach Martin what I should do. He said, "I like the people that own both teams. They're very nice people. But the NFL has been around quite a while and I think you would be wise to go with them if the money's about the same."

It didn't make a lot of difference. I think my salary was $11,500, or maybe it was $10,500. I can't remember. For the first two or three years that I was with the Cowboys, I thought, "I can't believe I'm getting paid to do something I really love."

I thought of signing with Lamar Hunt and the Texans at first, because when they started the AFL, they had a different way of drafting people. They tried to draft locally so they would have a lot of interest. There were a lot of Southwest Conference players that I knew personally and knew them well. Some All-Americans signed with the Texans.

I really didn't have any close friends other than Glynn Gregory, whom I had played against at SMU. Don Meredith was there; I played against Don. I used to go out and eat hamburgers with the Texans more than I did with the Cowboys the first couple of years.

The Cowboys didn't have a draft the first year, which was my senior year in college. They did have a draft the next year, and I was fortunate to be the number one draft pick.

I am very happy that I stayed in Dallas. I'm happy that I went to TCU. My dad and mother got to come down with my brother and sister, to watch the college games. They also were able to come to Dallas to watch the Cowboy games at home. I had extra tickets sometimes. My dad would bring my uncles too, which was nice. I really enjoyed that. I'm happy that that's the way things worked out.

Positions
I started out as defensive end. Tom Landry wanted me to play left defensive end, because I was really quick off the ball and I was left-handed. He just thought that would be ideal, but I had never played defensive end. I always played defensive tackle. Playing defensive tackle is kind of like playing middle linebacker. There's somebody who's going to hit you every play. It's really a perfect position for people who are very quick and strong enough to withstand the zone blocks and the double-team blocks. I fit right in there.

I moved during the middle of my third year, to defensive tackle. I went to the Pro Bowl after my second year as a defensive end, but I didn't like it. I hated it. There was no action. It was like you just sat waiting around out there, but in the middle, you've got to be alert or get killed.

Early Years Of Cowboys

We had training camp a long way from home all the years that I played with the Cowboys. The first year, I think we went up to Minnesota, to St. Olaf College. We had training camp there for seven weeks, but two of those weeks I was in Chicago at the All-Star game. The next year, we went somewhere up in Michigan and had frost every morning. We were also gaining weight. Tom Landry was working us to death and we were gaining weight anyway. Then we moved from there to Thousand Oaks California for my last 12 years.

We were always gone six weeks. It was quite an adjustment to leave your family and everything. The first few years in California, up until we started making money, nobody had enough money to rent a TV or a car. Maybe one or two of the guys would rent a car and we'd all cram in there as best we could. We only had Sundays off, so Saturday nights you could go to a movie and could be in at midnight. The rest of the time, it was 11 o'clock lights out with coaches checking the rooms.

It was a $100 fine if you were late turning your lights out. If broke a rule again, your fine doubled. If you were overweight a pound, it was 25 bucks. If you were overweight a pound the next time, it was 50 bucks. That's the way it was back then, as far as our living conditions. We had good food and dorm rooms the whole time I played. It was pretty austere.

By the time we were under Coach Landry for a couple of years, we were always early. Willie Townes, who I really felt sorry for, had a glandular problem and a weight problem. Sometimes they fined him as much as he made in the game when he was weighing in. There were little fines. Most people didn't really get fined that much.

One time Jerry Tubbs, who was our linebacker and eventually became our linebackers' coach, was fined. Jerry was from the neighborhood where I grew up. Jerry lived in Plano, and he came not far from where we were practicing. They had a power outage in Plano and Jerry had an electric clock like everybody else did. Jerry was a player coach at the time, so here he comes, late.

Coach Landry said, "Jerry, I'm sorry, but I'm going to have to fine you 50 bucks."

Jerry said, "Coach, I don't think that's right. Our power went off." Coach Landry said, "I'm sorry, but you guys need to go buy a mechanical clock as well as electric."

One time, Craig Morton had a wreck. He missed practice or he was late for the bus to go out of town to play. Coach Landry fined him for being late. He said, "Coach, I had a wreck, I couldn't do anything." Coach said, "You need to start earlier."

Coach Landry wasn't a mean person. He was a very nice person, but he meant what he said. Whenever he said something, that's the way it was. I think for that era, it was a good way to do it.

Transformation To Super Bowl Champion
It was a transformation and it was a long process, but my first year, I didn't know what to expect. We had some good players that they'd gotten out of the pools, but they didn't have a draft. Meredith was there, and so was Eddie LeBaron. He was very good and very smart. We had some other players that were also good. Most of them were toward the end of their playing careers. We didn't have the speed that we got in the next few years.

The draft my second year was a really good draft. We drafted a lot of good players, Cornell Green, George Andrie, and Dave Edwards. All of those guys played about 14 years. I don't even remember who they all were, but anyway, a bunch of really good football players. We had Meredith and Perkins already, and then we started getting people like Mel Renfro in about 1963, and Lee Roy Jordan somewhere around 1964. We started building a team.

By 1963, our defense was planned pretty well. Our offense was still sputtering a little, but by 1965, we had a seven and seven record. We lost up in Pittsburgh in the seventh game. We played 14 league games. In the seventh game, Coach Landry ordered everybody out of the locker room, and told us that he was proud of our 110 percent effort. Landry was proud of us as people, because we'd done everything he'd asked. He said, "I thought I would be a good coach in the NFL, but maybe I'm not a good coach." Then he teared up and said, "I love you guys."

That was the last year that we didn't perform well. We had a winning season every year from then on. The next year we had the opportunity to go to our first Super Bowl. We played Green Bay and lost. We had the ball on the one-foot line, had a penalty, and Don had an interception. We lost our shot at that. The next year was the Ice Bowl. Then we had three years where Cleveland beat us. Then we came back and went to the Super Bowl and got beat by Baltimore.

Finally, the 1971 team went to Super Bowl VI. I think it was in New Orleans, and it was in January. That was really a highlight. We had gradually and slowly built a team that was performing on a championship level, but we just couldn't quite seem to get the job done. We had all kinds of names that people gave us, like "Next Year's Champions" and "Bridesmaids of the NFL", and I don't know what else. There were several. "Can't win the big ones," or "Cowboys can't win the big ones."

But we finally did it that 1971 season. It was like we'd had a 100 pound weight lifted off each other's back. I'd never seen people so happy. It was a great experience. Roger Staubach had come and taken over as quarterback. He was a great leader. He guided the Cowboys for several more years. Anyway, it was just a wonderful evolution. I'm really happy that I got to go through that, because it made me understand a lot more about how hard it is to be successful in life and in other things besides football.

Coach Landry taught us a lot of things in a business way, because he had several degrees. He was very smart, but he was also a businessman. We had goals and we set goals. We learned how to do all this. If we had some faction of our game, or some element of it that was going downhill, then that's when we stayed after practice and we worked on it for 30 minutes. In a few weeks we had that corrected.

We were a good team. We weren't a dynasty, but we were in the playoffs a lot of years. The Cowboys went to three more Super Bowls after I left. They won one of them and lost two to Pittsburgh.

29 Yard Yack Of Bob Griese In Super Bowl

It seemed to me all I was doing was chasing Bob Griese from behind and Larry Cole was kind of helping me a little. Then, finally I caught him because I could outrun Larry and Bob. I'm not sure I could outrun Bob Griese, but I think I could. Anyway, it was a big play. I don't think it really affected the outcome of the game that much. It was a big play for me, because I'd never had a sack that long before.

Super Bowl VI

The Miami Dolphins had a great team. I'll never forget watching them. We watched hours and hours of games. We were very worried about the running game. The thing was, we had the flex defense. We could stop the run pretty well, but we didn't know if we could stop them, because they were running the ball about 65 percent of the time. They were making about 240 yards a game and wearing everybody out. They had a great team. Of course, the next year they proved it when they won all of the games.

It wasn't as easy as it looked. They had opportunities. We took it away from them and shut their running game down. Then they had to go to the passing game. They just weren't used to being a passing team, and our coverage was good enough to stop Warfield and some of the other guys,

Career

I really enjoyed my career. I think it was a perfect setup to go to TCU and then go 30 miles away and play the rest of my career. That was 18 years of my life right there in Fort Worth and Dallas. You establish a lot of friends. Your kids grow up in a pretty stable situation, where they don't have to move around all the time. I think I've been blessed.

Induction Cowboys Ring of Honor

I didn't know anything about it. I knew that they were going to have a Bob Lilly Day, and at halftime they sent me back out to the middle of the field. I thought, "They're probably just going to give me a plaque." I had no idea. I went out there and all my teammates were down there on one side. They had a brand new Pontiac station wagon. Our team doctor had given me a bird dog with a cage, and my teammates gave me a Browning shotgun because they knew I loved hunting birds.

Then they made big speeches, and they pulled a flag off of the top of the stadium. There was a blue stripe running around Texas Stadium. Finally, they got the rope loose, and there it was. Bob Lilly, had number 74, and I don't know what else. They announced the Ring of Honor, which was a shock to me. I was shocked to get a shotgun, a dog, and a Pontiac station wagon, and then be in the Ring of Honor.

Nickname Mr. Cowboy

Roger Staubach was the one that pinned that on me. I asked Roger one time, and I think what he told me was he was watching our films quite a bit. Whenever we played the game, it was filmed very inclusive, it wasn't split up defensive and offense like it is now. He would watch offense and he would watch the defense. One day after a couple of years, he said, "I think you're Mr. Cowboy," and that's how it got started, as far as I know. I didn't have anything to do with it.

Dallas Cowboys, America's Team

Being America's Team was the worst thing that ever happened to us. Because where we went, people were trying to kill us. We hated that name. We hated for the Cowboys to be called America's Team, and I'm glad that I was toward the end of my career when I started getting the nickname Mr. Cowboy, but it has grown on me since then.

End of Career

Actually, I don't think I ever felt like I was slowing down. I knew that I was breaking in guys like Harvey Martin and Ed Jones, and I loved them; they were great defensive ends. George Andrie was a great defensive end in my opinion. Larry Cole was a great football player. We had really good athletes, but these guys were just getting bigger and faster.

I hurt my neck probably about the seventh or eighth game of my 14th year. I woke up thinking it was a crick, but it ended up that I had a bulge disc, and I couldn't sleep at night. I was taking aspirins and I got a bad ulcer. I couldn't hit anybody with my head. It just hurt too much. I figured I don't want to go out of this league on a sorry note. I played and started all the games that year, but I wanted to leave while I was ahead, while I was on top, and I did. That's the reason I quit after 14 years.

Coach Landry tried to get me to come back but I told him, "Coach, I wouldn't be very good. I'd be an embarrassment." He said, "You can help these younger guys." I said, "I don't think so. I physically can't do it." That's the reason I quit.

I finally explained that to him. My wife helped me. He used to come by and have coffee with us in the morning and talk about it. I knew better. I'm glad I did what I did. It has never quit hurting, either.

Tom Landry
Coach Landry was very stable. He never had what you called real highs or real lows. He was always businesslike and everything, but he had his principles, and I don't think I ever heard him say a curse word. A lot of coaches will cuss the players or they will cuss something, which is fine. That is part of football. That's just the way it is. He was a good example to all the guys. All the guys that played a long time for Coach Landry, I think he made better people out of them. I think they had a lot better sense of how to accomplish things, like how to actually start a business and how to set it up.

Also, he was very successful in business in the Dallas area, and we saw that. Back in those days, it might have just been the era, but I think because he was a Christian man and he controlled himself, that we had that same type of control among the players. There weren't many prejudices. There just wasn't a lot of friction or conflicts.

In the meetings, we always watched the film together, because it wasn't split up. It was all on one reel. We would watch the game and the kicking team they had a separate camera for the kicking team, so we did get to see that separately.

Anyway, when we had a really bad game, he would come in and he would be very serious. We knew that we were going to be running a lot of wind sprints. He would run that film back and forth. If he had a good game he would praise you some times and if you had some bad plays he would get on you for that as well. If we lost as a team and we didn't do very well at all, we made a lot of errors—that's what he really hated, was errors.

He would run that play back and forth about 20 times. We hated that more than anything, because our teammates watched us get flattened or something. That was his way of getting out of control. If you were creating problems as far as being part of the team, he would call you in and tell you about it, not get mad, just tell you bluntly. He would say, "This has got to stop, or you're going to have to move on."

He was very good with players when they would get toward the end of their career too. He would want to keep them around another year to train the younger people coming up. A lot of guys got to play another year probably after they should have quit, like I could have done. I just didn't feel right about it. I knew that I wouldn't be able to help my teammates.

Anyway, Coach was a wonderful man. He was very involved with the City of Dallas, in the Fellowship of Christian Athletes in Dallas, as well as other business, and all kinds of charitable things with his wife Alicia. Both of them were involved. They were wonderful people. Coach Landry was a wonderful man. After we all retired from football, I would go see him from time to time or be in a golf tournament with him or something like that. He was so down to earth and so nice and pretty glib, but when you were playing football for him, it was a little more serious.

59

Jerry Jones

I think most of the players were shocked that Jerry Jones didn't notify Tom Landry prior to hiring Jimmy Johnson. What I found out later was that Jerry ended up having to negotiate with Bum Bright, who was the owner after I'd gone. I didn't know Mr. Bright very well. I think what happened was Jerry was negotiating with Bum Bright and they made a handshake deal. The snake had got out because Jimmy Johnson had come to town and they were eating in a restaurant in Dallas, and the people put two and two together with the media there.

Sure enough, there had been a handshake sale, and he went ahead and hired Jimmy Johnson. That was announced. Then somebody said, "Nobody's told Coach Landry." Jerry said, "Oh my goodness," so he flew down and told Coach Landry. I'd never heard Coach Landry say one bad word. I heard him say, "I wish I'd had known this a while back because I have put so much effort into this next season and I hate to miss it." That was about it. He said, "I've been ready to retire for two years. I knew that the ownership can change at any time, and things like this are possible." Jerry came down and apologized for the way it was handled, and that's fine with me. He never said another word.

Being Called Greatest Defensive Tackle in NFL History

I don't get a big head, because I don't think I was. I think there's been many, but it is a compliment. I appreciate it, but I don't think about it. I don't dwell on things like that. There's too many different circumstances. I think there have been many great tackles, so we'll just let it go with that.

Interest In Photography

My senior year in college, I was on the Coaches All-American Team, which was sponsored by Kodak back then. They gave each of us a camera and film. By the way, there were only about 13 guys on the team back then because we played both ways. They usually had a couple of guys like the kicker and somebody else who would be a backup for the quarterback to play on defense or something. Anyway, I got an automatic camera. They

60

also gave us 200 rolls of film with mailers to send them back to Kodak, and they would send us the pictures free.

After that, I got to go to several All-Star games, the Hula Bowl being one of them. I took a lot of pictures over there. I wish I could find them, because I actually took some pretty nice pictures. I took some at the Shrine Game, and then some in Buffalo. I played an All-Star game up there. I went to Chicago and played in that game. We played the winners of the seasons before, the College All-Stars versus the pros. I took my camera with me.

My second year, I had dark room. I had a real dark room from that point until about 1992, when we moved and I didn't want to build another one. I started going digital, although I still went down to the camera store to print my own prints on their equipment and paid them for the use of the equipment. I do it all digitally now, and I really enjoy it. It's a fun thing to do. I'm getting older and I don't do it as much as I used to, but it's been a really nice hobby for me throughout the years. I took all my teammates and their children's pictures. Some of my teammates have come back and told me they wouldn't have had any pictures of their kids if it hadn't been for me. Anyway, it worked out pretty good.

Dallas Cowboy Bob Lilly takes on Los Angeles Ram Tom Mack
Photograph copyright Associated Press

Chapter 8

Mike Ditka

College:
Pittsburgh

Career History:

As Player:
Chicago Bears (1961-1966)
Philadelphia Eagles (1967-1968)
Dallas Cowboys (1969-1972)

As Coach:
Dallas Cowboys (Asst. Coach) (1973-1981)
Chicago Bears (1982-1992)
New Orleans Saints (1997-1999)

1988 Inductee Pro Football Hall of Fame

College Choice
I visited Notre Dame; I visited a lot of places but really I wanted to be a dentist and that's what my high school coach wanted me to be. That's why I went to Pittsburgh. They had one of the best dental schools in the country and they had a great football program. They'd play Michigan State, Syracuse, Penn State, Miami, and Notre Dame. They played them all. We had a national schedule that we would play all the best teams. That's why I went. That really is the main reason.

College Stats vs. Rookie Year With Chicago Bears
My first year in pro football, I caught 56 passes for over 1,000 yards. You know, it's crazy. What'd I have, 12 touchdowns? I don't know what it was, but it was crazy. I caught 12 passes my senior year in college and I caught 56, I think, my first year in pro football. That's a pretty big jump.

College All Star Game
My head coach for the College All Star Game was Otto Graham. He coached a number of the All Stars in those years and he had a really good staff. Dick Stanfel, who coached for me with the Bears, was on it. A lot of good guys were on it. It was really a good staff. They were good people.

Pittsburgh
We dodged Syracuse. It was close, it really was. We couldn't score a lot of points. We had a good defense, we played hard on special teams, and we ran the football on offense, but we just couldn't score a lot of points. We weren't a high scoring offense, so if we were going to beat somebody, we were probably going to beat them seven to nothing or fourteen to seven or ten to seven, or something like that. That's basically what it was. We ended up with four wins, three ties, and three losses one year. The losses were by five points or something, not very much. I think Penn State beat us the last game, thirteen to three. That's basically all I remember.

We had a lot of good players. That recruiting class that came into Pit when I was a freshman was one of the best recruiting classes ever. We had a different quarterback every year. We never had one quarterback all three years. It was hard because there was not a whole lot of stability to that position, but they didn't put a lot of emphasis on that position really, because all we did was hand the ball off.

Draft
Houston offered me a lot of money at that time. Here is what it came down to. I had a great respect for George Blanda and the Houston Oilers and the whole AFL, but I said, "If I'm going to play football, I'm going to play in the best league there is. I'm going to play in the National Football League," and I did. That was my decision. I went to the Bears. I'll never have any regrets about it ever.

I talked to the 49ers a lot, I talked to the Redskins a lot, and I talked to Pittsburgh. If I were to have played for any of those teams I would have been a linebacker, no question about it.

When the Bears drafted me and I went to Chicago and was told that I was going to play tight end. You had to say what the heck is a tight end because most people didn't know and they never really used them to catch the football. Because of a guy named Luke Johnsos, who was the position coach for me with the Bears, and George Halas they really created that position and they got me to play it and a lot of good plays were set up for me.

We had a great outside receiver, Johnny Morris, myself, and we had a great running back in the beginning with Willie Galimore. We had some good players, we really did. We were a pretty darn good football team, but don't forget in the early '60s. The Packers were really great. In 1963, we broke through and we won the Championship and that was a big deal. I feel I played against some of the greatest teams in NFL football, including the Packers in the '60s.

Rick Casares

Rick Casares was pretty special, I mean, I've never seen someone play a game with a broken bone in his ankle. He taped it up. I don't know how he did it, but he played, and he played really good. He was a fullback, nothing flashy. He would knock you right on your back. He could run, he could catch, and he was just a great football player. We had Willie Galimore and Casares in the same backfield. We had Billy Wade at quarterback. He played great quarterback for us in those days. He had been with the Rams earlier but he came to us and he played great. He was a great guy.

I look at our defense and we had Doug Atkins, Stan Jones, and Bill George. They're all in the Hall of Fame. We had Richie Petitbon, Larry Morris, Joe Fortunato, and Fred Williams. We loved him. All of these guys can't be in the Hall of Fame. We had a great group of guys. I can't remember them all now because I'm getting old. We had J.C. Caroline who played for us at that time. He was a cornerback. Bennie McRae came in and played cornerback for us and he was really good.

We had Bill Brown who was drafted number two. I was drafted number one by the Bears. He played with the Bears before he went to Minnesota. The reason he could play was because of Casares. Bill Brown was a great football player, a great professional football player for the Vikings.

Chicago Bears Winning 1963 NFL Championship

You think there would be a lot more championships, but there aren't. A lot of the other teams stepped up and became very good, the Colts especially, there were other teams too, like the Browns. You're always caught in the moment. I mean you don't look to the future but you always say well, there'll be a lot more good years, but there aren't. It was the same when I coached. When you hit that magic moment, you think there's going to be more of these, but there's no guarantee about anything. The fact that we won one was great. We had the critics that said we should have won more than one. We probably should have, but we didn't. We were a good football team. We won a lot of football games but we only won one championship. In life, you're judged on your championships, not your wins.

1963 NFL Championship Game Between The Chicago Bears & New York Giants

Well, it was bad field, but both teams played on it. There's no question about that. Were the Giants a good team? Yeah. Were they a better team than us? They had a better offensive team than we did, we were a better defensive team and defense wins football games. The field just wasn't good. I mean none of the fields were good at that time of the year anyway. The grass was all gone. You were playing on dirt. In this case, we were playing on mud and dirt. It wasn't very good, that's true, but it was a very good football game. I think that year our offense had an average score of fourteen points a game and we won the Championship. Our defense on average was giving up ten points a game. The score that game was fourteen to ten. That's pretty crazy, but that's basically what it was. We might have scored maybe a few more points and made it to seventeen, but that game was very close, very hard played. It came down to our defense making a couple of big plays, interceptions, and knocking Tittle out of the game. There were a lot of interesting things that happened in that game.

George Halas

You've got to understand that George Halas and George Preston Marshall, these guys started the National Football League. They persevered. They robbed Peter to pay Paul. They didn't make any money in those days. Then they developed it and created a great, great sport.

Halas persevered through a lot of things. He had another business on the side. George was old school, he was tough, he was tight, and he should have been. I mean that's just the way it was. It was his money, he made it, and he had a right to spend it the way he wanted to. He wasn't a guy who was going to throw it around needlessly or overcompensate players, that's for sure.

I got along with him in the beginning. I really did, but after a while he got tired of my act and shipped me off to Philadelphia. That was okay. I have no apologies for anything that I did in Chicago. I enjoyed all those years. I played as hard as I could for the Bears.

Trade To Dallas Cowboys

My life changed when I went to Dallas, I'll be honest with you, when I met Tom Landry it really resurrected my career, resurrected my life as a person, and I really learned to play the game the right way in Dallas because they played as a team. As a member of the team, there was no ego involved in Dallas. I was just trying to help the football team win games. Anybody who says that there's no ego involved in sports is lying because we all have one. I can honestly say that in Dallas, it all changed because of Coach Landry. I spent four wonderful years playing there, then spent ten more years there, as an assistant coach. That's where I really learned the game of football.

Tom Landry

Tom Landry was a Christian. He and Lombardi were so similar. They were two people who were driven by three things: faith, family, and football. They were both the same. Both were very devout religious men, with strong beliefs, who were also big family people. I mean tremendously they're families are first and then football. That's basically their life. They didn't have a whole lot of other things going on outside of that. That's why they were good at what they did. Tom would never swear, but I did hear one slip out when I was an assistant coach.

Roger Staubach
Roger Staubach was a winner, period. He's a leader, he's a winner; he was a guy that should have been a quarterback and he finally did get to quarterback and we finally did win the Super Bowl. That's as simple as I can put it. When it comes to leadership and the guy you want to go into battle with, you want to go in with Roger.

When you talk about what a quarterback is, I don't care about raw emotions. I don't want to hear that. I want to hear about your leadership. I want to hear how you play under pressure, the respect you get from your teammates by the way you play the game. Staubach had all that.

New York Giants Not Hiring Vince Lombardi As Head Coach
It was New York's loss and Green Bay's gain. I think it was meant to be. Vince Lombardi was meant to go to Green Bay, Wisconsin, the smallest NFL city in the country, and win, and win big. He made many fans from all over the country. I still go everywhere and people still say, "You know, I'm still a Packer fan." I understand that.

Revolutionizing Tight End Position
I didn't revolutionize anything. All I did was play the position and they threw me the football. I really loved to run with the football after I caught it. I had a lot of success doing that. I'd run up over people stiff-armed. I didn't care. I was having fun. They just started throwing the ball to the tight end at that time and I happened to be the guy in Chicago they were throwing it to. After that, the tight end became a very integral part of every offense because people would double on the outside guy and there you'd end up with a linebacker on you, basically, as a tight end. If you couldn't beat a linebacker, you shouldn't have been playing.

Process Of Being Hired As Chicago Bears Head Coach

In 1982, Tom Landry called me in and said, "Mike, Coach Halas wants to see you." I said, "What about?" He said, "I think he wants to hire you to coach the Bears." That's what really happened. I said, "What do you think?" to Tom. Tom said, "I think you're ready." That's basically all we said. He said, "Good luck!"

Process Of Being Hired As An Assistant With Dallas Cowboys

I was in a business in Dallas with some guys and we were making pretty good money. We had a couple of nightclubs. We opened one in Houston, one in Shreveport, and one in Oklahoma City. We were making good money at that time and we were pretty successful. That's what I thought I was going to end up doing.

I was in this place in Dallas when Tom Landry called me and he said, "Can you come in and talk to me?" I said, "Sure, coach." I drove up there to talk to him. He said, "Have you ever thought about coaching." I replied "I have to be honest with you, I never thought about coaching ever! Not for one minute, not for one second. I never thought about it." He said, "Well, I think you'll make a good coach. I'd like to hire you to coach the special teams and the receivers." I said, "Okay, oh boy."

Now I've got to make a decision and give up all this whatever you call life it was. It didn't take me long to make the decision, though. I made that decision and I went to work for I think, the greatest man I've ever known, I really do. It was the best decision I've ever made. I'm so fortunate to have been in that position, to meet somebody like that, and then do something like that.

Drafting Jim McMahon

Actually, when we were drafting him, George Halas said, "Why do you want to draft him?" I said, "Because he's a good leader, he's a great quarterback, and he's smart." He said, "He's got no arm. He's small and he can't see out of one eye." I'm telling you, he said all this. I said, "Coach, I still want him." He said, "Okay, you want him, we'll draft him." Then we drafted him.

Whether you like him or you don't, Jim McMahon was the best thing we did at that time with the quarterback position. He played the position with courage, with brains, and he was a leader of our offense. That's as simple as I can put it.

Jerry Vainisi & Bill Tobin

Jerry Vainisi, Bill Tobin, and I worked together. Bill was our Director of Player Personnel, Jerry was our General Manager, and I was a Coach. We worked together. We drafted and put in place what we thought we needed for that football team to make it successful. I'm very proud of that.

I love Jerry Vainisi. Did he have the football background? No. Was he a football man? Yes, and George Halas knew that. That's why he hired him.

Sustaining Only Loss During 1985 Season To Miami Dolphins

Play every game one at a time. You don't worry about that stuff. You just play them one at a time. We played Miami and we got beat. We got beat by a better team. We got beat by a better coach that night. There's no question about it. But we learned from it. We could have fallen apart, but we learned. We learned that we had to do certain things a certain way. We went down to Miami with a pretty cocky attitude and they just whipped us, period. That caused us to refocus, and as a result of that, I think we became a much better football team to finish out the year. The records in the playoffs show that. We were pretty dominant.

George Halas Retaining Buddy Ryan As Defensive Coordinator When Hiring Mike Ditka As Head Coach

There was a transition and I couldn't control that. Buddy Ryan wanted to keep the defensive staff, and I said fine. I hired the offensive staff. Buddy was a great coach. He was great for our defense. Our players loved him and he was the reason we had a great defense. It was Buddy. I'm not going to blow any smoke at anybody. There was some animosity, but I think a lot of that was a little overstated. There was none on my part; I know that. Anyway, when we won, we won. I knew when we won that Buddy was going to leave. I knew that. He should have had a chance to have a head job, and he did. Did the Bears miss him? Heck yes, they missed him. His players really related to him.

Walter Payton Not Scoring A Touchdown During Super Bowl
I realized it after the game, not during the game. That's something I regret. Walter Payton was probably the greatest football player I've ever seen. I said I scored a touchdown in the Super Bowl, he can have mine, and I really mean that. It doesn't mean anything. In the end, the only thing that matters is if you win or lose. It hurt him. It was my fault. It was an oversight on my part because it would have been very easy to hand him the football, just as well as the other guy.

Comparing Jim Brown & Walter Payton
I didn't play with Jim Brown; I played against him. Was he great? Absolutely. He was probably as great as anybody. I can only deal with what I know, and I know that the way Walter Payton was on and off the field, the leadership and camaraderie he provided for his teammates, and the way he treated the fans and the media, he was special.

Now, I think the whole package is what counts. Was Jim Brown a bigger back? Yeah. Was he stronger back? No. Did he have bigger heart? No. Maybe he did some things better than Walter, but I don't know what they would've been. I've always said that Gale Sayers was as good as anybody who ever played the game. Don't forget he only played six years and then he got hurt. I mean my goodness; there are a lot of great running backs. I don't even want to get into all that, but I'd say, in my opinion, I've been around some of the greatest ones. How good was Paul Hornung? How good was Jim Taylor? These guys were great football players. They were versatile; they did everything. I don't know that Jim Brown handled a football. Walter walked, caught, and ran … everything. I'm not knocking anybody. Believe me, I have the utmost respect for Jim Brown. I think he's maybe one of the top three players that ever played the game. I'm just saying, I was close to somebody that I thought was the epitome of greatness, and that was Walter.

Pro Football Hall Of Fame Induction

I'm very honored to be in the Hall of Fame. I have so much respect for the Hall of Fame, what it stands for, and the guys in it. It wouldn't have changed my career if I didn't make it into the Hall of Fame. I played the game the only way I knew how and I enjoyed it. Some people may not have enjoyed the way I played it. I can't help that. I played as hard as I could for as long as I could. It's a wonderful reward. Were there better tight end receivers? Yes, absolutely. Were there better blockers? Yes. I did both of them pretty well.

Mike Ditka looks over film with University of Pittsburgh Coach
Johnny Michelosen Photograph copyright Associated Press

Chapter 9

Jackie Smith

College:
Northwestern State

Career History:
St. Louis Cardinals (1963-1977)
Dallas Cowboys (1978)

1994 Inductee Pro Football Hall of Fame

College Choice
I wasn't recruited at all to play football. I went up there to run track and they said they couldn't give me a full scholarship for track. They said if you just go out for football and don't quit then we can give you a full scholarship. That's how I got into football. I ran the high and low hurdles, mile relay, javelin, and the discus.

Transition From Track To Football
At times I did both track and football but you benefit from one to the other as far as the workouts. The type of condition that you get from the workouts really carries over. It was nice to be able to do both because one sort of complimented the other and helped me stay in shape for each sport. It was tough to do it.

The last year I was there during track, I worked on getting in shape and trying to do things more directed towards football. I found a guy who played football at Northwestern State, named Charlie Hennigan, who had gone on to play with the Houston Oilers of the American Football League. I went to a camp he was running when I was drafted and had him help me. I worked out with him in the afternoons.

I didn't miss much of spring football practice. I didn't miss much of anything. They found some way to make it work because there were a lot of guys that played football and ran track. It wasn't a very big school, so everybody had to do everything if we were going to have a team at all. That's sort of the way it went.

Charlie Hennigan

Charlie Hennigan taught me the basic fundamentals of running a pass pattern. At that time the League was running mostly man-for-man defense so it necessitated the receiver being able to run straight at that guy and beat him on a pass pattern. That's really what we concentrated on. The efficiency of those steps that Charlie taught me really worked well throughout my whole career. What Charlie taught me really allowed me to make the Cardinals.

I see him periodically when I get back to Northwestern at some events. I always make sure that he knows how much I appreciate him. He was the reason I made the Cardinals, with his expertise and his ability to teach me to run those patterns and teach me a little bit about them as far as the footwork was concerned. That's the truth because they make it on such a slim edge sometimes every little bit helps.

I continually talk to people about how Charlie Hennigan should be in the Pro Football Hall Of Fame, but he played such a long time ago. He still has some records in his name that he did back then as a receiver. A lot of people have never seen him. I'm not going to stop putting in my two cents worth about him and about his contribution to the League. I'm hoping somebody will listen one day.

Draft

I didn't expect to get drafted by either the NFL or AFL. I was surprised as hell. I was like, what are you talking about I got drafted in the tenth round? I was the most surprised guy in the world when that happened. I thought they had made a mistake and so that's how we left it. But it worked out okay.

Being Named A Starter With St. Louis Cardinals
Taz Anderson got hurt and that's when I got to play. Tight ends were bigger then and I was only 205 pounds. So I was really a receiver

and that was the reason I got to stay there. I could jump in at tight end if need be, but I was really a receiver so that's actually what happened. When Anderson got hurt I got in there and got massacred for the rest of the season and figured I'd have to gain weight or get a gun or something to keep on playing.

Evolution Of Tight End Position
It has definitely changed. It's a different deal than it was. Now tight ends take a five or ten yard split with nobody in front of them. They have a wide-open look at the defense and a quick read on where they're going. I think even as old and beat up as I am, I could run a couple of pass patterns today. I'm even more scared now than I was then, so I would be running like hell.

Playing For St. Louis Cardinals
It was fun. It was a great time to play because of the time and place it was. Nowadays I wouldn't even know if I would've made the team because they have so many ready-made tight ends coming out of school that are used to playing the same type of offense formations. I'm lucky to have done it when I did.

I didn't care what I did. I just wanted to make the team. I wasn't really that concerned. I was also damn surprised. I was in shock for the first year that I even made the team so that was a surprise to me. I was willing to do most anything just to stay around.

Head Coach Wally Lemm
Wally was fine. He wasn't a big fan of mine. He didn't think that I should have made the team but the offensive coach at the time, begged him to let me stay. He said that I think I can make a tight end out of him sooner or later. Thanks to him I was able to stick around for a little while until I could get my bearings in the league.

Head Coach Charley Winner
Charley was just glad to be there. He was glad to be there and he's a nice guy.

Head Coach Don Coryell
He made a difference and made some changes that really modified our offense. We were glad he came along; really glad he came along.

He'd already been established. That's the reason we got him. Then he brought some good guys with him who went on to be successful in their own rights.

Cardinals Drafting Joe Namath
The Cardinals management didn't ask us to be involved in the negotiating process, but Mr. Bidwell was not about to pay the asking price for us to get Joe Namath. Mr. Bidwell almost had a heart attack when he heard it. That was just the Cardinals. That's the way the Cardinals operated.

Playing Philosophy
Listen, any of those guys can hit. If they couldn't hit they wouldn't be there. It's a question of just giving them a chance to do that and it's much better to be the hitter instead of the one getting hit.

The trick is not to give them a good shot and then trying to hit them as hard as they hit you so that you kind of neutralize them a little bit. I'm certain there are plenty of guys that could tackle me. I'm sure that there were. That did happen a lot. Well, I tried not to let it happen. I just wanted to make sure I got in as much as I could out of each play. That was really my driving shield.

Pro Football Hall Of Fame Induction
I was elated. I was surprised and it was under some interesting circumstances, but I was really very elated and so was my family. They were tickled to death about it. It was a nice thing to happen.

Photograph copyright Associated Press

Chapter 10

Mick Tingelhoff

College:
Nebraska

Career History:
Minnesota Vikings (1962–1978)

2015 Inductee Pro Football Hall of Fame

College Choice
I grew up on a farm in Nebraska. The only school that gave me a scholarship was the University of Nebraska.

Nebraska
I played my sophomore year some, and then I think I started my junior and senior years.

We ran the ball a lot and yeah, it was fun. We won quite a few.

NFL Draft
The Vikings were the only pro team that contacted me. I was very happy that they did and they wanted me to move to Minneapolis and play for the Vikings. I said, "Fine, I will."

First Training Camp
I had just gotten married. We drove out there together and looked at the stadium and around the area. I came from a very small town in Nebraska and we were in the big city in Minneapolis. There were a lot of things to look at.

Coach Norm Van Brocklin

He was a very good coach. You didn't want to make him mad, though. His nickname was Stormin' Norman. He got mad all the time, and he was real strict coach.

Fran Tarkenton

Fran the Man is what we called him. He was from Georgia. He was very good. He could run. Fran could really run. We'd have the guys blocked. It was good playing with him because he was a very smart guy, too. He's really fast and quick.

Coach Bud Grant

Bud was a very good coach and when he came in, he did it his way. Bud was a real strict coach. I don't think he ever smiled.

Minnesota Vikings Defense

The Vikings defense was very good. They were great defensive guys and we had a real good defense. We had a real good team, actually.

Vikings Super Bowls

I wish we had won one. We didn't, but we made it to the Super Bowl. I think we beat some of the teams we played in the Super Bowl in the regular season, but we didn't beat them that day.

Dick Butkus

We called Dick Butkus "Dickie Doo" to try to tease him. You didn't want to tease him too much because he would get mad. He was a very good player and we roomed together during the Pro Bowl out in LA one year. Dick was a good guy, a very good guy.

Playing In 240 Consecutive Games

I was lucky. I never got hurt. No one was hitting me. I was going after them and I was trying to block so no one was trying to block me. I think that's one of the reasons.

Photograph copyright Associated Press

Chapter 11

Bobby Bell

College:
Minnesota

Career History:
AFL Kansas City Chiefs (1963-1969)
NFL Kansas City Chiefs (1970-1974)

1983 Inductee Pro Football Hall of Fame

College Choice
The thing is, Minnesota did not recruit me. I wanted to go to
North Carolina but at that time, blacks could not go to North
Carolina. I played in the All Star Game as the quarterback. I was
a quarterback in high school. When I went to the All Star Game
for the black schools in Greensboro, some of the coaches from
North Carolina and up North, like Michigan and Notre Dame,
came to watch us play. Jim Tatum, the head coach from North
Carolina, saw me play.

When I went in to the game to play, the guy already had three
good quarterbacks from Triple A schools. He said, "Well, you
can play." They had me playing halfback. When they finally put
me in the middle of the first quarter and I started running the
ball, I think I scored at least two or three touchdowns, and I got
Most Valuable Player of the game. He ended up calling Coach
Warmath at Minnesota and said, "Hey, there's a kid here who
lives next to the mountain in Shelby, that's a hell of a football
player. You need to put him up there. I guarantee he'll make it."
I didn't know this until after the fact that he made a promise to
Coach if they'd take me. They'd never seen me. I found out
years later that he told the coach if I couldn't make the team he
would pay for the scholarship.

As a freshman at Minnesota, I played quarterback. Then, I was moved to offensive tackle and defensive end. I went both ways.

It was a culture change, a big culture change for me when I ended up in Minneapolis, Minnesota. Back then it was probably two percent black in the whole state of Minnesota. I went from one culture in North Carolina, to Minnesota where I'd walk around campus and didn't see anybody black except Sandy Stephens, Judge Dickson, Bill Munsey, and Bob McNeill. We had five black players on the team. That's all I had socially with blacks at that time. It was a big shock.

The thing is, when I went to Minnesota, I wanted to play baseball. I was a better baseball player than I was a football player. At that time, Minnesota was a Big Ten champ and a National Champion in baseball. I wanted to play baseball. When I ended up going there and getting off the plane for the first time, I asked the football coach "Can I play baseball too?" He said, "Oh, yeah." I told my Dad, I would love to go to Minnesota.

Going to high school and elementary school, the whole school was 168 students and I'm going to a big university. At that time I guess it was 35,000 students. I'd never seen that many people in one place. I told my Dad, "Listen, I would like to go here." He said, "Hey, if that's what you want, go for it." I say this all the time; my dad is the one that drove me. He just kept saying, "Son, you can do it. You can do it."

Back then, most of the people in Shelby graduated from high school, went to college for a couple of years, came back and got a 40 hour job, got married, had a family, and that was it. That's what they were doing, but I wanted to do something better. I wanted to go beyond that. My dad worked at a textile mill in Shelby where they would take cotton and turn it into yarn, then turn it into cloth.

The owners of the mill lived up at the country club. I used to cut their grass and take care of their house. Their kids went to military school, and when they'd come back, they'd invite me into the house. I'd go in there and look at the yearbooks. I thought that was the greatest thing in the world.

My dad never finished school, he just barely went to three grades and that was it. He worked. I always went back to him and said, "Dad, you should see this book, man, this yearbook and stuff. You think that I will be able to do that some day?" My dad always said, "Yeah, you can do it, son. Go for it."

People always ask me, "What's the biggest thing that ever happened to you, Bobby? Was it going into the Hall of Fame? Going into the College Hall of Fame? Being the Outland Trophy? Being third in Heisman?"

I say, "Well, no the Pro Football Hall of Fame, that's the top of the pyramid." I say, "The biggest thing for me, guys, is that you know my dad always was a driver of me. He was always on my side. He told me to go for it. The biggest thing is that the first time that I played varsity football at Minnesota and they had Father's Day there, my dad and mom came to the school. He had an opportunity to see his son play in front of 65,000 people. It was a nationally televised game; it was like my dad went to school there. For him, that's one of the highlights of my life, of playing. I had the opportunity to go to school and my parents got to come see me play like the other kids. The people from the mill, the owners of the mill, saw I had the opportunity to go to a big school."

My father always walked up the street and back, and people would holler, "Pink, saw your son on national TV, on the Johnny Carson show, on the Ed Sullivan Show, man, the Big Ten Champs, man he's awesome, he's awesome." My dad walked down the street, just like a king. So for him to see that and for me to have that opportunity for him do that, to go to Minnesota, to go to the Rose Bowl and see it, the biggest game in the country, that is the top of my pyramid. The other stuff, the awards, is good too but to have the opportunity to see my parents come to Minnesota, on Father's Day at Minnesota, it was just awesome.

My Dad passed away but I still can see him walking that day with his big coat, his hat on, and an overcoat on. It was just unbelievable.

Shelby was a small town. I played six-man football. We didn't even have enough men to play eleven-man. Nobody really saw me play in high school until I got to the All Star Game and these coaches saw me play. You've got Shelby tucked next to the mountain, right in the mountains there; you played little bitty towns, that was it. You didn't get exposed like some of these other players did. I saw Grambling play at A&T one time in college in North Carolina but I wasn't exposed to a lot of that stuff.

I played basketball and I played football. We played basketball and football in high school. That's it, no baseball. We had a baseball boys club and I had a chance to play with the White Sox on their farm team. They came through Charlotte and I was playing up there on a field. They wanted to offer me a baseball contact. My dad said, "I thought you wanted to go off to college."

Nobody actually saw me. When I got really exposed was when the late Jim Tatum from North Carolina saw me and called coach Warmath. Coach Warmath brought me to the campus. They hadn't seen me play one down. He went on the word of him and that's what happened.

College Career

Sandy Stephens was a quarterback from Uniontown. He was the first black All-American quarterback. The whole thing is Coach Warmath, God rest his soul. He brought me into his office my sophomore year. At that time, freshmen could not play varsity football. He had me running the freshman year at quarterback and the next year he brought me in the office and said, "Hey listen, this is what I got to do. We've been losing, losing, losing, but I want eleven of my best players on the field at the same time. I want you to be part of that." I said, "Hey coach, not a problem." I'd have played any position. Then he said, "I'm moving you to offensive tackle." I laughed at him and said, "Oh come on, coach." He said, "Yeah, I'm moving you to offensive tackle." I said, "Wait a minute." I laughed. I thought he was kidding and the nose guard joked. He said, "That's what I want to do because I want my best players all up on the field at the same time. Now we can go both ways." I said, "Well, are you serious?" He said, "Yeah." I turned around and I looked at him and I said, "Ok, coach. I've never played tackle but I'm coachable. If you've got somebody to teach me how to play tackle, I'll play tackle." That's how it happened.

I was so nervous when I went out to play my sophomore year, I didn't see my name. We had 13 teams suited up. I walked out and I looked down there. I figured he's got to be kidding; I might be an end. I looked down there and I didn't see an end. My name was nowhere on the charts. Halfback, no name, quarterback, that was out. We had three quarterbacks. I looked there for four. I was sitting there and Coach Crawford, who was the line coach, came out and said, "What's wrong with you?"

My heart was beating out of my chest because I thought maybe he'd let me go and send me back home. I thought I was gone. I said, "Coach, my name. You forgot to put my name. Am I on anybody's team?" He said, "Well, hell bell, look over there on the tackles." I went down to tackles and I went all the way down to the thirteenth team. I was on the thirteenth team tackle. I went out there and I had no idea what I was doing.

For the first three or four days I was getting beat like a pom-pom. Then I told the coach, "You got to stay out here and tell me, show me, coach me. Teach me how to play tackle because I'm going to play it." At that time, my sophomore year, it was all junior and senior teams. The first two teams were juniors and seniors. They said there wouldn't be a sophomore that makes the team. I said, "I'm going to make the team." On the first day we played, I was the only sophomore. I started at offensive tackle and defensive end and never gave up the whole time. It was one of those things. I could have been a quarterback or a running back; I didn't care what it was. I wasn't going home. I'd have played any position I told him. I probably played every position out there. I even centered the ball. I even centered the ball on field goals and extra points. I also did that in the pros, too. I centered the ball for the extra point on center relief. I snapped the ball for Joe Wilson. I had to stay. I wanted to play.

The more you play, the more you're involved in the game. From us, blacks going to Minnesota, it was a moving thing for the blacks across the South. Everybody started watching us play at

Minnesota, the Big Ten, we were on national TV all the time. We won the Rose Bowl two years in a row, National Champs, and Big Ten Champs. We were on TV and everybody was trying to figure out this all black backfield. It was all black. How'd they win the National Championship? They said we couldn't do it. Rose Bowls and Big Ten Champs ... they can't do it. We had a pow wow. We were beating everybody.

From that we started the next year by kind of recruiting Carl Eller from North Carolina & Lou Hudson for basketball. I was the first black basketball player at the University of Minnesota. A lot of people didn't know that.

Draft
At that time I'd have said the Vikings were after me. They were saying that I was too small to play offensive tackle and defensive end. They said I was too small. Minnesota drafted me in the second round and Kansas City got me in the seventh round. Montreal drafted me also. Everybody thought I was going to go to Minnesota because I played at the University of Minnesota. Minnesota drafted me, but at that time, Norm Van Brocklin was the coach there and I was telling him, "Hey, I'd like to play here but I want a three-year contract. You've got to give me a chance. Not a one-year, I want a three-year." I wanted him to guarantee it because I didn't want to be jacked around. He kept saying, "Yeah, we're going to give you a three-year and they didn't." They wanted to give me a one-year, two-year, three-year contract, but they didn't want to guarantee me.

Lamar Hunt came up, but I never talked to any of the coaches from Kansas City. Lamar came to Minnesota and met with me. I took him out and to get some ice cream. He wanted to know where he could get some good ice cream. I took him down to the University to a good ice cream place and he told me, "Hey, I'd like for you to be part of my organization." He asked me what it was going to take and we went back and forth and I said, "I don't know. If you want to sign me, just tell me."

I ended up signing with Kansas City but my contract was written down as Texas. That was the year they moved, 1963. I asked him, "Hey, we aren't even going down there, aren't we even talking to the coach?" When we came to terms it was a long-term contract. He didn't have the contract at the time we agreed; he shook my hand. The next morning I was flying to New York to be on the Johnny Carson and Ed Sullivan shows for the All-American thing and shook his hand. Lamar went with me to New York.

That's how it started with Lamar. Everybody thought I was going to the Vikings. I'm kind of glad I did go with the Chiefs. People ask me tall the time if I would change anything going from Shelby and the high school six-man football team. I wouldn't change anything. That ride from Shelby to Greensboro, Greensboro to Minneapolis, I wouldn't change anything there. How many guys can say that they won the state championship in football and basketball in high school? How many guys can say they won the American Championship and Big Ten Champs? How many can say that they were a College All-Star in 1963? The College All-Stars beat the Green Bay Packers in '63. I was on that team.

College All-Star Game
When I got out of college and went to the All-Star Game, I went up there as a defensive end and offensive tackle. Otto Graham was the coach. For some reason he called the Minnesota Viking Coach, Norm Van Brocklin, and said, "This Bobby Bell's not a tackler. He weighs about 215, 218 soaking wet. This guy can't play."

He made me leave the offense and defensive end. He told me to go down there with the linebackers. He said, "You can't play up here, man, go down there." I changed again. I changed positions like toilet paper. I went down to the linebacker crew. The linebacker crew was Lee Roy Jordan, Dave Robinson, and Lee Roy Caffey. I went down there and had no idea what the hell I was doing. I went down there and played linebacker. I ended up starting as a linebacker for the first time.

I must have pissed him off or something. I have no idea why he sent me down there. I sat there and watched those guys and learned what to do. That's how I learned and got in the game. I almost got Most Valuable Player.

I don't know what I did to piss him off, but he swore up and down. One of the things that bothered him was that I got a no-cut contract with the Chiefs. Back then a lot of coaches didn't like that. They didn't give out no-cuts. Van Brocklin wouldn't do that.

Even after I ended up playing left linebacker, Lee Roy played the middle and Dave Robinson played the right, we all kind of changed positions but we ended up playing linebacker. Right before the game started, they go to introduce the Green Bay offense and they said, "Oh, we wanted to introduce you all to defense." We lined up on the sidelines and the coach came up to me and said, "Hey, Caffey's going to be in and he's should be standing here." I said, "Oh, I thought I was on the starting defensive linebackers." He said, "Yeah, but Otto said he wanted Caffey to be in." They introduced him. He goes out there and he plays three plays and the coach says, "Man, you got to get in there. I played the rest of the game."

It's just strange the way things happen. For a long time, Otto didn't say much to me. Then he came when I was playing with the Chiefs, against the Jets. Otto was coaching the military. After the game Otto walked into the locker room straight to my locker and said, "Hey Bell, I wanted to apologize to you about some things. I want to let you know that you are a hell of a football player." I said, "Thank you." He turned around and walked away. That was it. From that moment on, every time I saw him at a function or something like that he would acknowledge me. He'd be the first one to come up to me, and say, "Hey Bell, come here, I want to introduce you to somebody."

That was my trail, my learning process from high school learning how to adjust, and learning how to change with the different organizations. I learned a lot. By playing quarterback, I learned how to play defense. I talked to Willie Lanier. We talked all the time when we were in the game. We were like coaches on the field. When we played defense we didn't have a platoon. We had eleven guys out there. The offense came out and changed the formation. We'd check off and we'd have to play. That's why I ended up playing defensive end at times, then I moved back and played linebacker. I could play route cornerback or I could play safety, it didn't make any difference. We just used the personnel that we had on the field.

Black Football Players
Willie Lanier was the first black middle linebacker. We had a lot of firsts. We were just awesome. Yeah, he was the first middle linebacker, and they said he couldn't do that. That's what a lot of black quarterbacks who played college ball heard. When I was at Minnesota, we recruited Tony Dungy. Jimmy Raye went to Michigan. A lot of these guys came to Big Ten schools because they saw us play back in the '60s. We got a lot of players to come out of the south and go up north to start playing at the big schools. That's when they started branching out all over the country.

Hank Stram
Coach Stram was an awesome, great coach. He was, as they say, before his time. He had the offense, the defense, big players, small players, wide players, and quick players. He wanted to win. He was a coach that didn't care whether you were blue, black, green, orange, or white. He just wanted to know if you could play football. That's the way he was. He cared about you as a man. He looked at you like a man. He respected you and you respected him.

I talked to him up until the day he passed away. The first thing he'd ask me was, "How are you doing? How's your family doing?" That was the type of coach. I would go down and visit him at his place and I'd be in his swimming pool.

After he left the Chiefs and went to New Orleans, he kept in contact with all of his players from Kansas City. I talked to him once or twice a month all the time. That's the way the coach was. If he found out a player living in Kansas City had a problem, he would call me or somebody in Kansas City and say, "Hey guys, you need to check on so and so. I heard that so and so might ..." That's the way he was until he passed away. He was the coach.

If you had a problem, you could go into his office and talk with him. If something came up, he'd call you in his office and ask you point blank, "What's the deal here? Let's straighten this out." That's the way he was. He was a hands-on coach.

We came out with the spread offense and everybody thought, you can't run that stuff, you can't do that. We came out with the triple stack, three lineman and four linebackers, and we were told we couldn't do that stuff. Everybody wanted to run the 4-3. The spread offense, they had to rename it, was called the West Coast. We were running all that stuff back then.

When we came out in the first Super Bowl, the coach said, "Hey, we can beat these guys. The only reason we lost that first game is because we turned the ball over to Green Bay." We turned the ball over twice in that fourteen-point loss. That was the game right there. You can't do that with a veteran team like Green Bay.

We just wanted an opportunity to come back and play in another Super Bowl. We knew we had a great team. That's when we played against the Minnesota Vikings and we were the underdog by 17 points. We felt like, hey, no way. Coach said, "They're good, but we can beat them. We got a better team." We were the wild card that year. We went back to New York and beat the Jets. The Jets thought that they were going to go back to the Super Bowl.

Oakland beat us twice that year. Stram said, "We beat the Jets and we got to go back and beat Oakland. There's no way they going to beat us a third time. We had too good of a team."

Coach, always came up with something new. He always felt like he had to keep everybody fresh and strong. We were the first team, I think, with Gatorade; we were the first team that had a weight coach.

Coach Stram had everybody lifting weights and stretching. We had quick guys. We had strong people. That's why we ended up playing Minnesota. We basically crossed the line and man-held the guys up there. We had running backs that were bench-pressing 250, 240, 260.

Coach Stram was just out in front of everybody. If there was anything new, he wanted to experiment with it. He wanted quick guys. We had a racquetball court inside the stadium. He said, "I want you guys to learn how to play this game." I already knew how to play racquetball from Minnesota. He had lineman in there because you're moving quick, quick steps. He had us playing tournaments and stuff like that. He came up with stretches, all kinds of different things like that. If it was out there, he wanted to know about it.

Max McGee in Super Bowl I

Fred Williamson was our left cornerback and I was a left linebacker. I asked, "Fred, why are you running your mouth?" He was just talking, "I want to do this and do that."

Freddy knew that I was a linebacker. If any plays came my way he knew I was going to take it out. Freddy would come up and jump on the pile or something. One time I cleaned out everything, but then Donny Anderson hit Freddy in the head and knocked him out. I went over to him and said, "Freddy, hey man, get up." He said, "Man, leave me alone." He was taken over to the sideline. I said, "Hey Freddy, what's up, man?" I know Freddy. I see him all the time. I talk to him a lot. He tells everybody he broke his leg or something like that.

That wasn't the problem. We lost that game because of the two turnovers. One was an interception and then a fumble or something. They got the two turnovers and 14 points, and that was the game. Going into halftime we were ahead and we turned it over.

Super Bowl IV

We went into that fourth Super Bowl and there was no way we were going to lose. There was no way. We were going to shut them down. We felt we had the best defense and they could not keep up with Mike Garrett, Wendell Hayes, Frank Pitts, and Otis Taylor. Those guys were so quick and fast, man, they were like horses when they ran, like thoroughbreds all over. Minnesota started off getting beat, and we hit them with the short stuff. If they wanted to pitch on the quarterback, we would do the in around reverse on them. We would keep them off balance all the time. That's what the coach wanted.

Coach Stram was a great coach. He should have gone into the Hall of Fame a long time before he did. Everybody thought that he made fun of the team by calling the plays on the sideline. The NFL film brought cameras down there. Bud Grant said he wasn't going to put the stuff on. They went over to Coach Stram and asked, "Can we mic you up? We want to tape everything. We got cameras here, and we want to use them." Coach said, "Do it. Don't tell anybody." He called the plays off the sideline, sent them in with the clock running and all. A sixty-five-toss sweep is in there, like it was a script. He called the play and it worked. Everything he used, worked.

Kansas City Chiefs Players
I'm kind of prejudice. I think we had the best linebackers. If I had a choice of picking people, I wouldn't change it. I would pick Willie Lanier and Jim Lynch in a heartbeat. If I picked a linebacker, that's who I would pick. Unbelievable. I loved it. We got to the point where we knew each other. We knew the capability of Willie and Willie knew the capability of Jim Lynch and me. We knew what we could and couldn't do. We compensated for each other. That's what you do, you compensate.

Same way with the defensive cornerbacks, Jimmy Marsalis, Emmitt Thomas, Jim Kearney, and Johnny Robinson. It was like having five or six coaches on the field. We'd come up to the line and look around. You wouldn't have to call a time out. You'd check out, say hey man, check out, man, man. We talked to each other.

1969 AFL Divisional Game Versus Jets
They had Matt Snell coming in there and Joe Namath takes it in there and pulls it out. Joe says, oh no, he's going to go for this fake; he's going for it. He came out of there and I said, nope, here I am, Joe. I stopped him right there on the seven, eight line. He came up to me and said, "God damn it, Bell. There's no way. How do you?" He just got the ball out, didn't even give it to us. He was just going to drop it. We stopped them and we beat them. That was a big play right there. Lanier would stop and say, "Hey man, we can't let them score. We can't let them score."

Joe Namath
Actually he was one hell of a quarterback as far as I'm concerned. He came to Kansas City one time and it stands out in my mind. He threw the ball three times, the same way. We didn't stop the ball twice on it. Same play. The third time, it's a touchdown. He said, "God darn it, I knew that thing would work." I mean, he sat there and picked them out. He called the plays up there; he'd pick them out. I don't know what he was thinking about or what they'd seen, but here's a guy saying that hey man.

Let's go back one step and say that's one of the things about quarterbacks. Peyton Manning right now, kind of reminds me of Joe Namath. He'd come up to the line and he'd chill out. Peyton Manning comes up and looks at it and studies things. He thinks oh this isn't going to work here, and he tells everybody. That's the guy. I would have loved to play with Peyton Manning, Joe Namath, and Johnny Unitas.

I played against Johnny Unitas and I thought he was a good. I think I made the first sack on Monday Night Football against Johnny Unitas. Joe Namath, I tell you he's one of the greatest quarterbacks in the Hall of Fame.

Approach To The Game
I approached the game in the same way that I did my homework. I'd know some of the things that a player liked to do.

Every time I got a new contract, I'd always end up playing maybe two years of the contract duration and they'd extend it. I always walked into his office and say, "Coach, the reason I want you to pay me is because I'm going to give you the ball two and a half times a game, with a turnover. You hear me? I'm going to give you the ball. I'm going to get an interception, make a fumble, or create a fumble or two interceptions, a game. I'm going to turn the ball over to you. My goal is to give it to you two and a half times a game. Some games I might get three, one game I might get less. But, I'm going to average two and a half times."

I said to the Coach, "You need to get another player to do that. If you're doing that, making a turnover four times a game you'll win the game." I walked out of his office.

Pro Football Hall of Fame Induction

At that time, back in 1983, I didn't even know I was up for it. Pete Elliot, who played against me in college when he was at Michigan, was President of the Pro Football Hall of Fame. I didn't even go to the Super Bowl that year. That was the one year I missed going to the Super Bowl. Pete Elliot called me to let me know they voted on it. The way they do it now, everybody knows for almost a whole year that is up for going into the Hall of Fame. Back then, you didn't know. They went into a room to decide. They'd go in and say this is this and you wouldn't even know until Saturday who was eligible for it and then they'd pick.

I had no idea until I got a message from Pete. My son, Bobby Junior, was playing at Missouri. I called him up and said, "Bobby, are you sitting down? I just got a call from Pete Elliot and he said I've been inducted into the Pro Football Hall of Fame." Bobby's roommate at Missouri was Willie Davis, the son of Willie Davis who played for the Packers. Willie went into the Hall of Fame the year before me. Bobby Junior and Willie Junior were roommates at Missouri and played football at Missouri.

That's how I found out. Pete wouldn't let anybody else call me because he was a friend. He said he wanted to call me.

I went in 30 years ago and I got the opportunity to meet a lot of the guys that I read about in books. I got to meet them, personally. Marion Motley and I became great friends. John Henry Johnson, Joe Perry, and I did so much as a family. We got to know each other and our friendship is unbelievable. It's a fraternity that we join. We're all here together, we played against each other; we had a lot of fun, now we're on the same team. You're on a team now that you can't be trade from and they can't cut you from. We're all the same. It's not one is better than the other; we're all the same and that's how we try to treat it. We're all Hall of Famers.

Kansas City Chief Bobby Bell grabs Buffalo Bill Cookie Gilchrist
Photograph copyright Associated Press

Chapter 12

Lance Alworth

College:
Arkansas

Career History
San Diego Chargers (1962–1970)
Dallas Cowboys (1971–1972)

1978 Inductee Pro Football Hall of Fame

College Choice
I was going to Ole Miss. I got married and they told me I had to come on a baseball scholarship rather than a football scholarship, so I decided to go to Arkansas.

Baseball was an awful lot of fun. I enjoyed playing it, but football was, particularly playing outside receiver, a lot of fun.

In baseball they give you a glove to catch with. It's a lot of fun. I played center field and enjoyed it. At that time I think the Yankees, and a couple of other teams were interested. I almost signed during the summer but my dad said, "No, you need to go get a college education." He was smart and right. My hat goes off to him. He was a great father.

Arkansas
It was a different type of football than people see these days. We didn't throw the ball very much. It was just a running game and a defensive game. Coach Frank Broyles started smaller teams, playing with smaller guys even up in the front. We were quick and fast, but not big. Whenever we ran into a big team that was fast, sometimes we had a lot of problems.

Other than that, it was great. It was a great time. I think we won or shared three Southwest Conference Championships in a row. I can't complain. It was a great life.

I went to law school for a couple of years. I just decided I didn't want to be an attorney after seeing how much time you had to spend in the library.

Coach Frank Broyles
He's a great guy, a great coach, and I really enjoyed playing for him. Whatever honors they gave him, he deserves more than that.

He had a big stand out in the middle of the field, where practice was filmed from everyday. I think he's the one that started that. He really coached from up there.

We had a lot of outstanding coaches on the field, but Coach Broyles was the mastermind. He stayed away from the guys a little bit.

Ron Mix
Ron's certainly a great attorney, but he had a lot more patience than I did in law school. I was ready to get in and get out. Ron was always right there, very studious, very strong, a great teammate, and a great football player.

Pro Football Draft
The Chargers drafted me. I was their number two draft choice I think, and they traded for me. I was drafted number one in San Francisco, and I can't say that I talked to them one time. At that time you didn't have any agents. I met with the San Francisco people on my way back home.

First thing the San Francisco people asked me was, "What do you want?" I said, "I talked with the AFL guys. I'd like a no-cut contract." They said, "We don't give no-cut contracts." I said, "Thank you very much." I walked out of there and never talked to them again.

When I signed that year, I signed with the Chargers. Al Davis was really the reason that I ended up in San Diego. He recruited me to San Diego and I loved him. I still love him to this day. He was a great man and a great coach. I have nothing but positive things to say about him. They gave me a $10,000 bonus and $20,000 a year for 2 years. A lot of money, huh?

Move To Wide Receiver With Chargers
When I came in, that's what they wanted me to play. It was really funny because when they started the draft, Kansas City had called me and said, "Look, we'd like to draft you. We want you to play defensive back." I said, "Hmm-mm. I'm going to law school if you draft me to play defensive back. I don't want to play defensive back." They didn't draft me but the Chargers did, so I got a chance to play the outside receiver.

"Bambi" Nickname
Charlie Flowers, a guy from Ole Miss walked in to training camp. He walked around a little bit, went out and practiced a bit, came back in and said, "Well, you know you got big brown eyes, you run like a deer, you got short brown hair. We're going to call you Bambi." I just ignored it because I didn't like it, but it sort of stuck. For the first couple of years they called me Bambi. Then for three or four years they called me Bam; Bam this, Bam that. In my seventh year when they called me Mr. Alworth, I knew that I was an older player. That's really how it happened.

Sid Gillman
Sid was a genius. He was an offensive coach. All the stuff that you see today, and all the stuff that was run by San Francisco and San Diego in the '70s and '80s was all from Sid Gillman. He invented the West Coast offense. They didn't call it that at the time, but he's the guy that was responsible for it.

Differences Between AFL vs. NFL
We didn't throw the ball very much. Nobody did in those days. I think if you look back in history, it shows you that the AFL probably threw more than the NFL did in those days.

I wish I were playing now because they throw almost every down and I love it. That's fabulous. I love watching it. They used to be able to hold a little bit more.

Toughest Cornerback
Willie Brown from Oakland was like 6'2" or 6'3" and he was fast. He played hands on. He could come up and play right in front of me. He could hound you from the moment you left the line of scrimmage. He was just fast. I really enjoyed playing against him. He was a great player.

John Hadl
John had a great arm. Unfortunately, John hasn't gotten into the Hall of Fame. If anybody deserves to be there, he does. You check his stats against people that are in there now and he's right in the middle of the stats. It's really a shame that he hasn't. John had great timing. He was a great athlete, a great guy, and a great leader. I had to tell him all the time I was open, but I think all receivers say that.

Al Davis
Al Davis called me one training camp when I was trying to get a raise of $5,000, from $30,000 to $35,000. He said, "Hey, I just traded for you. Sid Gillman will be calling." I'd been going before and Sid had given me all kinds of problems about a $5K raise. He said, "What kind of raise do you want?" I said, "Five grand." He said, "No problem. I'm trading for you."

I expected to have Sid come up and call me for my playbook. A guy came up and called me and I went in to see Sid. Sid looked up at me and said, "What did you want?" I said, "Thirty-five thousand." He said, "You got it." He didn't trade me. He didn't take the trade.

I don't think he would've traded me. At that point in time I was right in the middle of my career and I was doing pretty well.

1963 Championship Game
It was a game during the season we played the Boston Patriots who beat us I think, 7-6 or 10-7, or something like that. Sid Gillman put together a great game plan for the Championship Game. We went in

and played and almost ran them off the field because of the great game plan that Sid had. It was all based around our fullback and Keith Lincoln. Keith had a fabulous game; one of the best of all time. I have to say the 1963 team was probably the best team I played on during my career.

We offered to play the Chicago Bears who won the NFL Championship. They wouldn't play us. I think we could've beaten them.

Dallas Cowboys
It was pretty different. When I got there, Coach Landry told me, "I traded for you to block. If you block, we'll win the Super Bowl." I said I would. I did and we won the Super Bowl.

It was a big change for me. It looked like on paper that the Cowboys threw the ball a lot, but they threw to backs and tight ends. They very seldom threw to outside receivers. It was a real adjustment for me mentally trying to get ready to play the game.

That was the reason why I retired after two years. I couldn't get myself to go work out during the offseason because there wasn't anything to work for. All I did was block. I enjoyed doing it because it was part of the game, but it wasn't the real reason for playing.

I went back one time and told Coach Landry, "Look, all I have to do is look like I'm going to run and turn and run straight down the field and we'll got a touchdown." He looked at me and he said, "When I go deep, I'm going with Bob Hayes." I looked at him and never spoke to him again about being open.

Roger Staubach
Roger was a great quarterback. Roger was a lot like the kid going to the Browns, Johnny Football. Roger was that type of football player. He was a great one. I can't say anything but good things about him.

Having Al Davis Present Him At Hall Of Fame Induction
I wouldn't have had anybody else. Al was a special guy in my life. He was the real reason I went to the AFL. He was the one guy in pro football that I respected more than anything. To this day, I hold that respect and awe for him and appreciate all that he did for not only me, but for everybody that played for him. He was just a super, super guy and meant a lot to me in my life.

Pro Football Hall Of Fame Induction
It's really funny because I got a call five years after I played. I was out trying to make a living and doing things and they called to tell me I was voted into the Hall of Fame. I thought they were just calling to tell me that I was on the list or something. I hung up the phone and told my wife at the time. I said, "Let me call my dad and tell him." I called my mom and dad and I realized at that moment what it meant because I couldn't get it out to tell them. It meant so much to me. All of a sudden I realized that all my life I had spent trying to prove to my dad that I was that good. My dad always told me no matter how good you are there's always somebody better and don't forget it.

Wide Receiver Position
When I played, it was sort of a new position. There wasn't anybody you looked at who ran patterns or watched that closely because there wasn't that much of it at the time. It's not like it is today.

Most 200 Yard Receiving Games In A Row
That's a long time ago so I should be real proud of that record, I guess. We didn't throw that much, but when we threw it we did it pretty well. We had great players and great coaches. We had some great guys, an outstanding quarterback, and the system made it work.

AFL Players Who Should Be In Hall Of Fame
We've been trying to get John Hadl in. Nobody seems to back us up and that's really a shame when you look at all his stats. Charlie Hennigan's should be in too.

The thing about it is now we're getting where we put too many people in. There are a lot of those guys who deserve it, too. There are just too many. There are just an awful lot of people getting in.

Left New York Jet Joe Namath talks to San Diego Charger Lance Alworth Photograph copyright Associated Press

Chapter 13

Willie Brown

College:
Grambling State

Career History:

As Player:
Denver Broncos (1963–1966)
Oakland Raiders (1967–1978)

As Coach:
Oakland Raiders (1979–1988)
Long Beach State 49ers (NCAA) (1991)
Jordan High School (Los Angeles) (1994)

As Administrator:
Oakland Raiders (1995–present)

1984 Inductee Pro Football Hall of Fame

Al Davis' Loyalty To Former Players
At one time we had 15 former players employed by the Raiders.
That is one thing about Al Davis; he always took care of his
players. He'd make sure they were okay and he'd find a position
for them. I think it's great. I've been here 41 years, and
everything is fine with the organization and me. I'm pretty sure
we'll be the same with Mark Davis. Mark Davis understands the
process and what Al was doing. He knows how Al handled the
players and Mark feels the same way.

When you play for the Raiders you feel right at home.
Everybody in the organization understands once a Raider always
a Raider, and that's the thing we like to live by. When you've
been in this organization, you understand the organization. You

understood Al Davis when he said certain things and did certain things.

Eddie Robinson

Eddie Robinson was demanding and understood the game of football, period. He taught you to play many positions. When I was at Grambling I was a starting tight end or a starting linebacker. Sometimes he would put me at halfback, and sometimes he would put me at wide receiver. He was very aware. He had the knowledge to see and understand that the players he brought into Grambling had a lot of talent, and they could play at that level. I've told a lot of guys that the starting team from Grambling for three or four years was really great. The starting team that I played on was bigger than any pro team.

Not Being Drafted

Not being drafted really wasn't difficult. I never had my eyes set on playing pro ball. I had other goals in mind. Number one was to get my education, get my degree, and coach in high school. That was my main goal, to go back and to start coaching in high school. We had so many great ballplayers on the team my senior year, that a team was coming in trying to sign whoever they could sign. Buck Buchanan was the number one draft choice that year. So I knew that if I wanted to play, I had an opportunity to play. The Houston Oilers came in and offered me a contract. It wasn't much of course. I believe they only offered me ten thousand dollars and I signed. I saw the competition that I was matched up against playing the defensive back position when I got there. I had played college football as a linebacker, and as a tight end. My first day of training camp, they stuck me outside on the corner. I didn't know anything about playing corner of course. But I picked it up fast.

Interception Of Fran Tarkenton's Pass In The Super Bowl

I got winded after I got into the end zone with all the players rushing onto the field, patting me on the back, throwing me around, and jumping up and down. That's when I really got tired. The run wasn't bad because I was in pretty good shape at the time. You know it's a thing that you do every day in practice.

Toughest Receiver

People always ask me who the tougher receiver was. I tend to look at the guys that I played against who are in the Hall of Fame, of course. Guys like Paul Warfield, Lance Alworth, and Charlie Hennigan. I have a lot of respect for those particular guys. When I played against Lance, he was a guy who hustled on every play. He would do the same thing, so you had to pay attention to him because he was tough. Paul Warfield ran very good yards. One time I was covering Paul and he jumped up in the air and changed directions while he was up in the air. I was like man, what in the world are you doing to stop him. So I stopped playing tight cover. I was the first one to start playing bump and run because I knew the receivers couldn't get by me because of my size. I was just as fast as they were, so I decided to play end tight. That's how I played Paul.

Fred Biletnikoff

I covered Fred Biletnikoff. Fred stayed away from me because he knew I could beat the hell out of him when I played bump and run. So Fred stayed on the other side. He didn't want any part of me and I probably didn't want any part of him either. Fred was small, but he had very big, good hands. That was the thing about Fred, if you threw it anywhere near him, you knew that he was going to catch it. So yeah, we had many battles in practice but the majority of the time Fred stayed away from me. He stayed on the opposite side from me.

Favorite Moment In Career

I have a lot of favorite moments because my career was good. I mean every game, every week; I had something good happen to me. So I guess to cap it off, it would probably be the Super Bowl when I ran an interception back for 75 yards to score a touchdown. That was probably one of my highlights. The other time was when I intercepted four passes in one game and I had one other, which would have been five, but the referee called roughing the passer or something like that. Things like that kind of stick out.

Houston Oiler Ken Burrough hangs on to Oakland Raider
Willie Brown Photograph copyright Associated Press

Chapter 14

Nick Buoniconti

College:
Notre Dame

Career History
Boston Patriots (1962–1968)
Miami Dolphins (1969–1976)

2001 Inductee Pro Football Hall of Fame

College Choice
I had a couple of good influences for that. One was Angelo
Bertelli who was the Heisman Trophy winner I guess in the '40s.
He was from West Springfield, Massachusetts, went to my high
school, and lived nearby. He was just a great all-around athlete.
There was another man who went to my high school, who
graduated two years before me. His name was Joe Scibelli. Joe
ended up not finishing at Notre Dame, but he influenced me to at
least take a visit out there. Being a small kid from an Italian
family, living in an all-Italian neighborhood and not really being
exposed socially to some of the finer things in life, I was really
enamored when my father and I took a trip out there. I just
became enamored with the entire situation, the history of Notre
Dame and the boundaries of it. My father saw it and the thing
that sort of captured us was the golden dome. My father saw the
golden dome in all it's splendor and the beautiful bay, and he
said, "This is where you're going to school," and he helped me
make the decision and I never regretted it.

College Coaches
My freshman year, I was recruited by Terry Brennan and his
staff. He had a great bunch of assistant coaches too. At
Christmas time of my freshman year though, they let Terry
Brennan go. I felt this was not a great decision on the part of the
university because I thought Terry Brennan was a very good

coach and I really liked his assistants. I really enjoyed being with those people.

The university went out and hired Joe Kuharich, an excellent Notre Dame guy. He had been coaching with the Washington Redskins. The next three years under Kuharich were probably as grim as anybody could ever have in major college football. He just didn't understand how to coach young players. He tried to bring a pro system into a college atmosphere. His work ethic was demeaning of the players and it was not a pleasant experience. Our record showed it, too. In the three years that I played under Kuharich, I think we won 12 games. Winning 12 out of 30 is not a great record.

The great thing that Notre Dame did for me was something that can never be replaced. It gave me the opportunity to grow socially, but at the same time, to respect how my family brought me up. I was taught to respect my elders and enjoy life. My time at Notre Dame also taught me social graces. It was a great experience.

You build friendships at school that never go away. Not only that, you're part of the Notre Dame family. When you're part of the Notre Dame family, you are a part of that family for life. That's why when good things happen for Notre Dame we all rejoice. It is a great school. The great tradition lives on; it's just a wonderful.

College Positions
Notre Dame had me playing offensive guard because we had to go both ways back then. You had to be able to play both offense and defense. So I played offensive guard and linebacker and every once in awhile I would go down in the three-point stance to make the defense calls. I normally played linebacker for ND and unfortunately at the time, I was the only All-American my senior year on the team. It was the College Football Coaches All-American Team and wasn't the Kodak Team. Since it wasn't the Kodak, team I'll never forget it. I was passed over for guy from Colorado, who had a 4.0 average and was an engineer. That kept me out of the College Football Hall of Fame. That's the only Hall of Fame that I'm not in. I was a first team All-American, but it wasn't on the Kodak team.

Draft

I had the choice to go to the Patriots in Boston, which was 90 miles from my home, or go to Calgary, which was 3,500 miles from my home. It was not a difficult decision to make. Number one I didn't want play in the Canadian Football League, and number two I got to be close to home.

I was drafted in the 13th round by the Patriots so it was not like I had a layup going there. I had to make the team. It was a long climb, but obviously I got lucky and I made the team. I spent seven great years there. I love Boston and I love the people. Everybody still thinks I'm coming back. They still can't believe that I'm living in Miami. It's remarkable. I made such great friends on the Patriots, Gino Cappelletti, Larry Eisenhauer, Houston Antwine, Jimmy Hunt, Bob Dee, Babe Parilli, Larry Garron, and Ron Burton. It was just a great team. It was just a really solid bunch of guys and it was just wonderful to be part of it.

Trade To Miami Dolphins

Obviously what ended up happening was Mike Holovak was fired and they brought Clive Rush in from the New York Jets. Clive's claim to fame was that he coached Joe Namath and Namath beat the Baltimore Colts in the Super Bowl. He said that I was making too much money. I think I was making, $30,000 a year and I was going to law school at night. I was going to get my degree in 1968. After got my law degree, he got there and said to me, "What we really don't need is an attorney for the defense." He basically traded me for nothing. He traded me for Kim Hammond, John Bramlett, and a fifth round draft choice. I was one of the best players on the team. He got nothing for me.

Don Shula

I was there one year before Don Shula. George Wilson was the coach. Things didn't change until Shula got there. When he became coach, things dramatically changed.

He had unbelievable assistant coaches. The assistant coaches were Monte Clark on the offensive line, Bill Arnsparger as the defensive coordinator, Mike Scarry as the defensive line coach,

Tom Keane as defensive back coach, and Howard Schnellenberger as the receivers' coach. It was a super bunch of assistant coaches. You put all those guys together in one room and you're going to come up with a good game plan every game. You may not win every game, but it's not because of the game plan. Maybe we didn't execute the game plan, but it was just a stellar group of assistant coaches. The great thing about Don Shula is that not only did I learn a lot about football from Don, but also he really is the most highly principled individual I've ever been around in the game of football. I took those principles into my business life and it really helped me succeed. He's just a super, super leader.

Joe Thomas

Joe Thomas traded for me. He traded for Paul Warfield. He made the Larry Little trade. Then you follow him up with Bobby Beathard and then George Young. If you look at the transition within the Dolphin franchise, you can understand why during those years the team was so good.

Joe also traded for Marv Fleming. He picked up Wayne Moore on waivers. He picked up Jim Langer on waivers. He picked up Bob Kuechenberg on waivers. You've got Langer, a Hall of Famer, and Kuechenberg who should be in the Hall of Fame. It's a travesty that he's not in the Hall of Fame. I still to this day don't understand that. Then you have Wayne Moore who was just a great tackle for us. Along the way he picked up Doug Swift, our stunning linebacker, Mike Kolen was drafted. All in all it was a pretty good way to reap the harvest.

The No-Name Defense

Tom Landry was preparing for the Super Bowl against us and he looked at the roster and said, "You know, these guys are nothing but a bunch of no names." Someone picked it up in the paper and that's how we got tagged with "The No-Name Defense". We really embraced it because we weren't the Purple People Eaters and we weren't the Fearsome Foursome. We were The No-Name Defense and it was something that I think we all embraced.

1972 Miami Dolphins

No one expected us to go undefeated. That was not our goal. Our goal was to get back to the Super Bowl. We had embarrassed ourselves so much the year before getting slaughtered by the Dallas Cowboys. I believe it was 24 to 6 or something like. It was very embarrassing, so our whole objective was to get back to the Super Bowl and the wins just sort of happened. The key to any team having a great record is having someone, either offensively or defensively, step up to make an incredible play and that's what happened to us game after game. Someone stepped up. Manny Fernandez kicks off the ball, takes the ball from the quarterback from the Bills and helps win the game. I intercept Joe Namath on the goal line to help win the game. Paul Warfield makes a great catch against Cleveland in the playoff game that sets up the winning touchdown. I can go on and on about every game that we played. Someone stepped up and made an incredible play to help us win. All of a sudden you look up and you're 14 and O, and you're in the playoffs. It really wasn't something that we played for; it's just something that just happened.

Pro Football Hall Of Fame

When you're talking about 273 players who played the game being in the Hall of Fame, that's the epitome of success. That's recognition by your peers. You were good enough to be in a select group. I'm in the Patriots Hall of Fame. I'm in the Dolphins Hall of Fame. I'm the Italian Hall of Fame in Chicago, which is an honor, but the NFL Hall of Fame is the epitome of success.

Miami Dolphin quarterback Bob Griese, left, and Nick Buoniconti
Photograph courtesy Associated Press

Chapter 15

Dave Robinson

College:
Penn State

Career History:
1963-1972 Green Bay Packers
1973-1974 Washington Redskins

2013 Inductee Pro Football Hall of Fame

Vince Lombardi
Vince Lombardi Jr. said that Wellington Mara and his dad were very close. Marie Lombardi, Vince Lombardi's wife told me Wellington Mara called Vince in his office and said, "Vince, I know what you want to do. I'll tell you what. New York City is not ready for an Italian head coach. If I were you, I'd take the job in Green Bay." She said that Vince vowed at that time never to lose to the New York Giants, and he never did. That was the end.

The other thing he told him was Allie Sherman was going to be the next head coach. He was of after Tom Landry left being an assistant coach.

I don't know how the true this story is because I've heard it about three or four times in different places, but the Giants received a kickoff in overtime and they went down the field. It was fourth and one. Lombardi told Jim Lee Howell, the Giants Head Coach, "We should go for it. Any good team can make one yard." Tom Landry said, "The odds are against it. We should punt the ball and let my defense hold them." Vince was adamant they should go for it. Jim Lee Howell went with Landry and they punted the ball. The other team got the ball, marched down the field, scored and beat them. Lombardi always felt that he was right.

Fast-forward another 18 or 19 years. On December 31, 1967, we were on the one-yard line, third and goal, with 16 seconds to go in the game. We call timeout; Lombardi goes in and tells Bart Starr to go for it. Mel Renfro told me that Tom Landry told him, "Play the outside. The only play they could run is a bootleg or a pitch out or an option play. They got to have something where they can throw the ball to kill the clock."

Some of the defensive guys from Dallas were playing to the outside, soft, which made the block a lot easier on Jethro Pugh, who was trying to get outside to stop a sweep that was going to come right up the middle. We made it. Vince Lombardi felt vindicated at that moment. He beat the Dallas Cowboys right up the middle. That's how it was.

One of my greatest plays happened the year before that down in Dallas. They had fourth and two with 52 seconds left. What did he run? He ran a bootleg with Don Meredith. Similar situation there, but thank God Meredith was slow enough that I caught him and it was no problem. That's how we maintained a lead of 34-27 and won the game, which allowed us to go to Super Bowl I. I think Vince was very, very happy with those two victories, because it proved his point to Tom Landry.

It was true euphoria when I got to Green Bay in 1963. I'd been moving around in a lot of positions after the All-Star game, defensive end, offensive end, and then finally linebacker. When I got there, he felt obligated to tell me what the problem was. He said, "You'd be a great linebacker. We won in 1961 and 1962. Our goal is to win three consecutive World Championships. No one has done this since play was initiated. I don't want any distractions. You'll be the first black starting linebacker in the National Football League. I don't want any newspaper articles or anything else. If anyone asks you about this, tell them to see me." I told them to see Vincent and that was it.

In 1967, he won a third consecutive World Championship. How would you feel if your goal in life was to win an Emmy or something for radio and all of a sudden you've got it not once, not twice, but three years in a row? That's how Vince Lombardi felt about winning three consecutive world championships. We were all so close to our coach that if he was happy, we were ecstatic.

College All Star Game
We never thought we stood a chance. We went into the locker room with 10-10 at halftime. You have to remember that Ray Nitschke didn't play at all. They had Urban Henry out there at defensive end, and he was kind of weak. Urban Henry was not the greatest defensive end in the world.

On top of that, Otto Graham did some things most coaches never do. We went for it on fourth down on our own 30-yard line and stuff like that; crazy moves like that. See, everybody expected him to lose. Otto Graham just made ridiculous calls. We were lucky enough that they worked.

Everything had to fall in place for the All-Stars to win. Later, Vince told me, "If I could have got that All-Star team, the whole team as it was and kept them together, I could win a Championship in three years." Back in 1967, I knew that Vince Lombardi would have kept that team. It was a great team. Guys on that team started all over the league, both in the AFL and NFL. If he could have got them together and trained them, I think he could have won a championship with that team.

Comparison Of Football In 1960s and Today
One thing you've got to remember is that there were only 12 teams in the league. It went to 14 teams later on. They only took the draft choices and the top 20 guys, so they only had 36 people on a team. My rookie year it went to 38. There were only 38 men per team, on 14 teams. You could take the cream of the crop and get them into the league.

Now you have 32 teams with 53 men per team. The problem is, you don't get ball players who are well rounded like Herb Adderley, who played four sports. I think he could have done it all, play running back or defense or anything. Thank God he was my corner. I loved that.

Ballplayers are hard to come by now because there are so many specialists. These guys specialize in high school and they only know one part of the game.

In college, we had to learn both positions, offense and defense. College kids today play offense or defense. Some can switch over, but when they do they have to learn all over again. It was a whole different time, a whole different era. I think when I played it really was the golden age of football. I'm just happy to have played during that time.

When I came up, I was the fourth linebacker, the swingman, until Ray Nitschke broke his arm. Like I always told Nitschke, "Bad break for you, good break for me." That's when I started.

When I was in college, there was an article in Sports Illustrated by Dan Currie about how to key in pro football. I read it, and I didn't really understand what keying was in college. I went to Penn State, a great school, but they hadn't really taught me the keys. I took that article and I carried it with me for six to eight weeks. I idolized Dan Currie. I walked on the field the first day, and who's the starting left linebacker for the Green Bay Packers I'm trying to win a position with? Dan Currie. That team was so good, so many good ballplayers, that when you came in as a rookie you knew you had to be able to do everything.

One last point, I was going along fine during my rookie year. I was the number one draft choice. My wife was home pregnant with twins. I was laughing one day about how Jerry Kramer was kicking off and couldn't get the ball past the 20-yard line. Someone told Vince Lombardi that I'd kicked off at Penn State. He came to me and put his arm on my shoulder and said, "I hear you kicked off at Penn State." I said, "Yes, sir." He said, "Why aren't you kicking off here?" I said, "Well coach, I'm playing the new position of linebacker and I want to practice so hard and study my book, and I want to be the best linebacker in the National Football League." He said, "Well son, your best chance to make this team is as a kicker."

I kicked off because Paul Hornung was gone, so we didn't have a kickoff man. I kicked until I got hurt. That's how it was. There were great men at every position. If you weren't multifaceted, if you didn't have more than one talent, you weren't going to make the Green Bay Packers.

First Black Outside Starting Linebacker In NFL
Now Bobby Bell and I came in the same year. He went to the other league, the AFL. The AFL was a funny league. The AFL brought more black ball players in. I don't know if this is necessarily true but the NFL had sucked up just about all the good white ballplayers in the country. The only white ballplayers that were getting into the AFL were guys who were played out and their career was over. Guys who were cut by an NFL team, they would raid off the cut list.

The AFL needed ballplayers badly. They went down to the black colleges and got that. They were really pioneers in fully integrating the game of football. But there were none in the NFL. I was a first-round draft choice. Herb Adderley was the first black man to be drafted in the first round by the Green Bay Packers, ever, and I was the second. That shows how things have changed. Now, everything is so different.

Racial Climate In Green Bay In 1960s
My roommate had come from Utah State. At Utah State he started dating a Mormon girl who happened to be white of course. All Mormons were white in those days. They were dating and they wanted to get married, her parents were going to disinherit her and everything else.

Word got out that they wanted to get married. Word got back to Vince Lombardi that he was bringing this white woman to Green Bay and cohabitating with her. Vince called him in and said, "What are your intentions?" He said, "I'd like to marry her. I don't want to get blackballed." Vince told him, "You marry her and make an honest woman of her. Let me take care of all that."

Pete Rozelle came all the way to Green Bay to tell Vince, "Do not let this happen." There were no white and black marriages,

124

he thought, in the league. Vince told Pete Rozelle, "You run the NFL and I run the Green Bay Packers."

Nobody who was married to a white woman, no matter what the team, brought his wife to camp. You have to understand, we're talking about pre-civil rights. The Civil Rights Act was in 1964. People denied you rooms in Green Bay. That was perfectly legal. That was their right. People denied you service in a restaurant. It was their right. They were not breaking the law.

Vince Lombardi would not take any kind of guff. Vince would react the same way if you had a white wife or with anybody else. He had a zero tolerance for racism and he felt as though any type of discrimination was wrong. Now Pete Rozelle, it was none of his business as to whom anybody was going to marry. To me, it was like a racism thing for him to come in and try to stop something like that. At the same time, Rozelle knew that there was racism going on in NFL that he did nothing about.

Cookie Gilchrist was a great running back, but he was dating a white girl or married to her, I'm not sure which. He was blackballed out of the league. He had to go to Canada where he played his best football. In his later years when he came back with the Buffalo Bills he was still good enough to make the all-AFL team.

When Vince got to Green Bay in 1959, there were only two African-Americans on the team and they were banned from going to certain bars and restaurants in the city of Green Bay. The story I heard was that the owners of all those bars were invited into Vince's office and they sat down and they pleaded their case. We don't mind this, but our customers don't want to do it, blah, blah, blah, blah, blah. Vince was opposed to this and said, "Listen, you bought, worked, and earned those places. They're your places. You can serve or not serve anybody you want to. That's the American way. I'll go to war to defend your right to deny service to anybody you want to, and you have my word that as of this day, no black Green Bay Packers will go in any of your establishments. As a matter of fact, even white players won't be there because you're off limits." I heard the guy said, "You can't do that. You'll kill us if we can't have any ballplayers in our establishments. You can't do it." Vince said, "I just did." What happened next, as the story goes, was that the whole town instantly became integrated. This was before Herb Adderley got there. They instantly started allowing the black ballplayers to go wherever they wanted in Green Bay restaurants, bars, and anywhere else. The thing I admire the most about Vince Lombardi, there was no big paper, no big band, no NAACP had to come in and march, no Jesse Jackson or Al Sharpton came in with great speeches. One man, very quietly, in a room with seven or eight bar or restaurant owners integrated the whole city of Green Bay in a matter of minutes.

That is why he was a great football coach, a better than average football player, but his influence on that city, his influence on the National Football League and consequently, his influence on America is far more than anybody realizes. I think the world of Vince Lombardi, I really do.

I grew up in Mt. Laurel Township in Burlington County, where NFL Films is today. The difference between Green Bay and where I grew up is, to use an old term, night and day. The first time my wife came up with me to Green Bay we rented a two-bedroom house. It had two bedrooms, a living room, kitchen, and a bathroom, that's it. That was what we had. My landlord told me, "I know it's not much of a house, but it's probably a lot better than what you have to live in back in New Jersey."

That's when I realized, people in Wisconsin didn't understand. They thought that every black person in America, Philadelphia, New Jersey, and the East Coast, lived in roach infested, ghettos. I told him, "You know what, neither me nor my friends in New Jersey would live in your house." He was offended by it until my wife took out pictures and showed where we lived and our neighborhood.

I wouldn't say the people were biased, I think that they were uninformed. They truly felt, because of the news reports and the lack of black TV shows, that every black person in the East lived in some form of the ghetto. As you know, it wasn't right. I have no ill will toward the people. I know that they were uninformed, but that was what it was.

I got a house one year because the lady had an argument with the next-door neighbor. She said, "I'll get even with you. I'll rent to blacks."

Elijah Pitts brought his wife in during the preseason, and she was the only African-American woman in town except for a couple of people who came in, go-go dancers primarily. She couldn't take it; so she went back to Arkansas to student teach.

The next year, I tried to explain to my wife that none of the black wives were there, and she should just stay in New Jersey and I'd go to Green Bay. Her mother told her "A woman's place is with her husband." I had to go along with that, and she went with me. Once Pitts saw that my wife had moved in, he brought Ruth up. Ruth and Elaine, my wife, were really the first black Packers wives in the city of Green Bay. What they went through was horrendous.

First of all, they were attractive young ladies. Every young black lady in Green Bay at that time, besides them, were usually go-go dancers or prostitutes or something of that sort. They were approached every time they went downtown by the farmers coming into the city for the first time. Some of the things they said … it almost wasn't what they said but the way they said it. Even the way they said hello. They didn't think they were talking to a Packer wife or someone of stature. They thought there were talking to a low-life go-go dancer or prostitute. Many days, Ruth and Elaine came home upset with what was going on downtown. We were recognized downtown, but our wives were a different story.

The thing I regret the most is that my wife passed away five years ago, and she won't be standing there beside me when I get inducted into the Pro Football Hall Of Fame. She is the one who, in my opinion, was the real Hall of Famer for what she did, put up with, and the way she held our family together. I can't say enough about her.

Mike Ditka

I played against Mike Ditka at Penn State when Pitt was our archrival. I went to Penn State for one reason. I wanted to get an education and my mother couldn't afford to send me to school. I only played football in college because that's the way I got a scholarship. That's why I think Herb Adderely went there. We just wanted to get an education. I'm appalled now when kids are coming out of high school talking about what they are going to do with their bonus money when they sign in the National Football League. I never dreamed of playing in the National Football League. I just never had the desire to. I just want to get my degree and get out of school.

In my sophomore year, Mike Ditka was All-American. In the Pitt-Penn State game, I went up against Mike and had a decent game. I didn't crush Mike, but Mike didn't crush me either. The next year, Mike was NFL Rookie of the Year. I said to myself, if he is the best in the NFL, then I could play with those guys.

Not until the end of my junior year, did I even think about playing in the National Football League. I only thought about going there because I wanted to get married and I needed some money. I thought I would go in and play five years, get vested, and come out. The rest is all history.

George Preston Marshall

George Preston Marshall was a defined racist. He admitted to being a racist. He's the one who said that there's not a black man in America good enough to play on his team in 1961. That's why when they boycotted the Redskins at Washington Stadium, he finally succumbed and went out and drafted Ernie Davis. He then traded Ernie Davis to Cleveland for Bobby Mitchell, who was the first black to play on their team.

Also, the rumor until the day he died was there was a meeting in 1932 where George Preston Marshall told all the owners, "White people will not pay to see black people make money playing football." If you check the records, there were black players in 1932, but in 1933, there was not a black player on any team in the National Football League. They all deny that there was this agreement.

There were no more blacks until 1946 when the Cleveland Browns and the Los Angeles Rams integrated. This was two years before Jackie Robinson integrated baseball. There was black, then there was the white era from '33 to '46, and then there was the modern era. When it came back around, all of those different things about what black guys could do and couldn't do came around because our buddy once said that black guys could run. It can be real but they didn't have the heart to play defense.

You got guys like Jim Parker, the greatest offensive lineman the world ever saw, and they said he couldn't play defense. Willie Wood was a quarterback, a great quarterback at USC, but there was no question when he came to the NFL, he was going to play defense.

Pro Football Hall Of Fame Induction
My first experience with the Hall of Fame was in 1963, its first year. I used to have little quiet conversations with Vince Lombardi, and Vince Lombardi would tell me how much it meant to go there. We were one of the first teams to play in the Hall Of Fame Game. I loved this man. I started watching and I tell you, I can't even put into words what it would mean to me as a person, as a professional football player to be in the Hall of Fame.

Photograph courtesy Associated Press

Chapter 16

Chris Hanburger

College:
North Carolina

Career History:
Washington Redskins (1965-1978)

2011 Inductee Pro Football Hall of Fame

College Choice

I was in the Army right out of high school. The University of North Carolina stayed in touch with me while I was in the service. They even talked to me about getting out of the service early. I had signed up under a two-year program. It was referred to as a Federal Reserve program. It was two years of active duty and four years of reserve duty. They stayed in touch with me while I was in the military and of course, I didn't get out early. I told them, "Look, I agreed to two years of active duty. That's what I'm going to do. If you guys are still interested in me when my time's up, I'll look into it with you." That's what I did.

Of course, I had to go to summer camp for four years after I got out of the Army. I could file for educational interference while I was in college where I didn't have to attend monthly meetings and things like that. I just had to go to summer camp for two weeks. So it worked out pretty good. That's how I ended up at the University of North Carolina.

Favorite Team

It didn't make any difference. You played both ways then and the way they had it set up, on offense I was a center and we'd flip over on defense and I played linebacker. It didn't make much difference. You didn't get off the field very often, especially when we were all on special teams.

North Carolina

I enjoyed it. I looked at it just like I looked at pro football, a means to an end. I ended up getting a full scholarship. It paid for my education. I struggled since I'm not the brightest guy in the world. I ended up majoring in American History, which I've always been fascinated by. All my courses were from about the year 1700 up to the current times. I'm one of those nuts that drive down the road and when I see a historical marker, I'm going to pull over and read it.

It was a chance to get a college degree, which I had to struggle to do. I had to take courses that were related in some way or another so when I was studying for one, I was actually studying for two or three of them at the same time. It just made it a lot easier for me. In fact, when I was there I don't know of any athlete who got special treatment at all, none whatsoever.

I've never, even today, been a big football fan. People are probably bothered by me saying that, but when I was in college I knew about professional football, I just never watched it.

Draft

When the Redskins drafted me, I think I was away from college. I think it was over a weekend. When I came back some of the guys said, "Do you know you got drafted by the Redskins?" I said, "You've got to be kidding me?"

I didn't do anything and about it. Five days later I go a call from the Redskins go to D.C. to see about signing a contract. They were playing at home and gave me two tickets. My wife and I went looking to sign a contract. I didn't even go to the game. I think I gave the two tickets to a bellhop after I signed the contract. We jumped into the car and headed back down to Chapel Hill.

"The Hangman" Nickname

I don't know how I got the nickname, "The Hangman". It's just one of those weird things. I guess mainly because I tackled high most of my career until they ruled that you couldn't do that anymore. I always remember when I went to my first Pro Bowl. Kansas City had a cornerback called "The Hammer". He got his bell rung real early in the game. I thought man, nicknames sure aren't good to have.

First Training Camp
I just figured I'd go to training camp and do the best that I could. If it didn't work out, I thought I'd enjoy it and try to hook up with another club. Things happened to work out in my favor. You live in the dark when you're in training camp. You don't know what the heck's going on. I remember the equipment manager came to me after we had been in training camp for a while and he said, "Would you like to have the number you had in college?" That number was 55. I said, "If it's available, that's fine."

I guess it was about a day later Sam Huff came up to me and he said, "Look, you keep working hard on special-teams, I think you've got a good chance to make the club." That was the first time that I felt a little relaxed about everything. I just didn't let any of the guys there intimidate me. I was just going to do the best that I could, study, and just try to excel all the time.

Sam Huff and I ended up rooming together for a couple of years during training camp and on the road. I've always told Sam, "The only reason you got to play a couple extra years is because I took care of you. I had to babysit you."

Vince Lombardi
I don't think any of us knew what to expect from him. I had heard stories about him and I think we were all in awe of the fact that he was getting back into coaching. I remember in training camp he mentioned we needed to go around the practice field at least three times before practice started. I'm walking around the practice field and he pulls up in a little golf cart. I don't think he knew my name, but he said, "Mister, he called everybody Mister, how come you're walking around the field? All the other guys are jogging." I said, "Coach in the meeting all you said we had to go around the field. You didn't say how we had to go around." He put his head down and shook it back and forth and said, "My God, I have mellowed." I thought it was kind of neat and I said,

134

"Coach, I'll tell you what. I'll jog around this field three times from now on." That's what I started doing. Vince Lombardi worked you real hard, he really did.

Otto Graham was a fantastic player. He really was, but a head coach is only as good as the players he has and as good as his assistants are. It was a much more lax atmosphere with Otto Graham then it was with Coach Lombardi.

If I recall, I think he had gotten sick. He was in Georgetown hospital. I believe we were on strike at that time. Most of us who lived in the area would go to the Georgetown Athletic Field and practice on our own. Edward Bennett Williams was the owner of the club at that time and of course, he got chauffeured everywhere he went. All of a sudden we're on the field and a limousine pulls up with Coach Lombardi in it. He gets out and you could tell he was very weak.

We were just starting to get warmed up for practice and doing his famous, what he called, "ups and downs". He talked to us for a few minutes and you could just tell he was worn out. I think he wanted to stay and visit and talk some more, but he just got back in the car and left and that was the last time I ever saw him.

I think it affected everybody. We all had so much respect for him; we were all just hoping that he could pull through what he was fighting. It just didn't work out.

He had this crazy thing called "up and downs" where you had to jog in place and he would say, "Down, and you just collapsed on the ground." You know more than hit the ground, and he'd say, "Up, and you got to jump up and start running." He'd have you do 50, 60 of those crazy things. People would get sick, throwing up. Then he'd make you run toward one end of one of the field, and then he'd make you run all the way down the other end and around the goal post and back to where you had started.

I'll never forget one day we finished one of those things and he announced that would be the last day of it. He told Sonny Jurgensen, "Sonny, lead them down around the goal post." Sonny said, "I'll try coach. I'll try."

George Allen

It was really nice to have a head coach that was very defense-oriented and it was a wonderful system to operate under. We had a ton of defenses. We called all the defenses on the field. We didn't have to worry about watching the sidelines for signals or anything like that. The preparation was very extensive. Prior to him getting there, I know from my standpoint, there wasn't a whole lot of emphasis on defense. There wasn't a whole lot of emphasis on special teams either. He brought all that to the Redskins.

Of course, I think the defense got a little special treatment compared to the offense. When he came on board, Edward Bennett Williams always joked. He said, "I gave him an unlimited budget and he already exceeded it when he built Redskin Park." It was kind of funny. We started off in the initial building and we would meet there as a team. The defense got to stay in that main room and the offense guys had to break down into some of the real small offices that the offense coaches had.

All the offense guys started complaining. Next thing you know, Coach Allen is giving the offense the defense room and then he's having another addition put onto the building just for the defense. We couldn't even wear shoes in it. It had this real nice carpet in there. It was a great big old room, a real nice facility. Coach Allen really took care of the players. His preparation was just unbelievable as far as getting the club ready.

Deacon Jones

Deacon was a character. I remember going out to LA to play a game. I don't remember if it was an exhibition game or regular season game. Anyway, we get out there and Coach Allen appoints Deacon as one of the honorary captains for the game. We're in the locker room and Deacon gets up and gives a speech.

He says, "Follow me." He doesn't realize that we're in the visitor's locker room. He leads us down some hall that doesn't even go to the field. Now we finally get regrouped and get out and get introduced. They introduce Deacon and he runs out on the field. He gets to the sideline and he sits right down and hooks up to the oxygen tank.

Redskins Cowboys Rivalry
I think Coach Tom Landry and Coach George Allen had a tremendous amount of respect for each other. I don't think either one of them trusted each other at all. I think they were both paranoid about people spying on them. The press caused a lot of it. I'm sure Coach Allen put Diron Talbert up to saying things about Roger Staubach in the press and things like that. It's kind of funny. I never got caught up in all that. I think it was because I was fortunate enough to go to quite a few of the Pro Bowls. The Cowboys would always have a lot of players on the Pro Bowl squad, and I got to know a lot of them. It was just another game to me. I just never get caught up in all hoopla.

Super Bowl VII
As far as I was concerned it was just another game. You still played as hard as you could and you wanted to win. I know when we went to the Super Bowl in 1972, we weren't expected to go anywhere in the playoffs. We get to California and different manufacturers for shoes and apparel and stuff come by the hotel we're staying in to give us things. The stuff they wanted to give us was in Cowboy colors.

Everybody thought the Cowboys were going to go to the Super Bowl. The Super Bowl was just another game. We played Miami. That's the year they went undefeated. They had a heck of a football team. That was so long ago.

If I remember, the goal post hadn't been moved to the end of the end zone at that point. We had a couple of chances to offensively put some points on the board and just couldn't do it. The score probably should have been worse than it was. I think it ended up being 14-7. The only points we got were on a mishandled field-goal attempt, I think by the Dolphins. It just didn't work out in our favor.

Calling Signals

When Jack Pardee retired, it just became a natural thing for me to start calling plays and I didn't have any problem with it. Coach Allen had always been one to tell us we must take the film home, watch it, and study it. I had been doing that even before calling signals. When I started calling signals, everything just seemed to fit in. It was a lot of fun to control the game right there on the field.

We always had a defensive game plan with the defenses we wanted to use. If necessary, we could make the adjustments right away. We didn't have to wait until halftime or go to the sidelines. We could automatically audible if we saw something out there. If I saw something and felt pretty good about it, I could just audiblize real quick. I think we had close to 150 different audibles. It's just made it a lot of fun.

Pro Football Hall of Fame Induction

Well, I never even thought about it, to be very truthful with you, and I mean that sincerely. I played, and I enjoyed it. I've been out for like 33 years, and what's happened is just wonderful. I look back, and I've always thought there were a lot of great players that played before I did, that I played with and against, and guys that are playing now that will never get nominated, let alone get elected into the Hall of Fame. It's unfortunate. I guess I've been lucky all my life, and I feel like I've just been real lucky with what's happened.

I somebody asked me, "What was your reaction when you got the news that you'd been elected?" I say, "Well, truthfully I thought, here goes my normal routine. I've got to go get packed to go to Dallas to the Super Bowl."

It was kind of funny. When I was nominated, I just happened to be watching the news on TV that morning, and all of a sudden up on the TV screen, we've got one of those crazy systems where the ID caller thing flashes up there, and it had "HOF" and a number. I'm thinking what in the devil is that, so I answered the phone and of course it was the Hall of Fame. I hung up, and not five minutes later my son calls, and he said, "Dad, are you aware that you just got" ... and I said, "What are you talking about?" Of course I knew. He said, "I'm getting emails and phone calls from all over the country." I said, "Well, then you better start getting your speech ready."

I just decided that I wasn't going to say a whole lot. I wasn't going to pre-plan anything. I was just going to speak from the hip, keep it short and concise, and get the heck out of there. That's what I tried to do. In fact, the Hall of Fame called me and they wanted to know if I had written a speech. I said, "No." They said, "It's very intimidating to be up there", and I said, "I'm not worried about it. I'm not writing a speech." I said, "Some of these people get up there and talk a half hour, 45 minutes. That isn't me and it isn't going to happen." I didn't write anything down for the speech. I just got up there and talked. I think I was up there between seven and nine minutes at the most, and that was probably five minutes too many.

Greatest Asset
Ironically, it may have been my quickness and speed. I certainly didn't have a lot of size. I'd go to training camp maybe weighing 215 to 218, and toward the end of the season, I would be down to a couple of hundred pounds. We always had weigh-in one day a week. I didn't have an assigned weight, but I would put on a heavy sweatshirt, tape some two and a half pound weights around my waist, and jump up on the scale. They always thought I was a lot bigger than I was.

John Hannah Said You Were the Smartest Player He Ever Played Against
I've heard that and I appreciate him saying that. It's very nice of him to make a comment like that. I don't know why he would say something like that. We hardly ever played against them, but it was a nice compliment.

Conrad Dobler
I think he got a bad rap. He was just a very aggressive player. He probably made a few hits after the whistle blew, but that's football. As long as they were legal, that's part of the game. He was going to go 100% all the time no matter what, but I think he got a bad rap as being a dirty football player. I never thought of it that way.

Favorite Coach

Coach George Allen was my favorite coach, no question about it. He could be a pain in the tail at times, but he was a great coach to work with.

There were times during timeouts, whether we called them or the offensive team called them, I'd go over and see what he was thinking. He used to take and lick his thumb all the time. You'd say, "Coach, what have you got in mind?" He'd say, "Well I don't know," and he'd be licking that thumb. So, I'd just jog back into the huddle and call a defense.

Washington Redskin Chris Hanburger pressures Dallas
Cowboy Roger Staubach Photograph copyright Associated Press

Chapter 17

Charley Taylor

College:
Arizona State

Career History:
Washington Redskins (1964–1977)

1984 Inductee Pro Football Hall of Fame

College Choice
I really wanted to go to Prairie View, a black school down in Houston, but didn't get in there. I ended up going to USC. After two weeks and one day I went into the teams' office. I was like the 16th running back.

I immediately called Frank Kush at Arizona State and asked, "Is that deal still good?" He said yes, I thanked him, and that's how I ended up there.

Arizona State
Arizona State was great, Dear old Frank. Frank hadn't gone crazy yet. He was not that crazy. He was just a tough guy. He had that Lombardi thing going, and we all knew it wasn't him because after practice he would talk to you in a different voice.

On the field if you fumbled the ball you had to do laps. He would take the whole day to get through practice and meet and discuss. He was a character.

Frank would never give you a hard time if you did your job, took care of business, and played ball. That's all you had to do.

We practiced at night because it was so hot during the day. We had training camp in Basin, Arizona, up in the mountains. It was freezing up there. There were days we had to wear jackets to practice, because it was so cold. We had drinks all over the place, and the food was great.

NFL Draft
I thought I was definitely going to be a Cowboy, because Dallas was the only team that really showed interest in me. My roommate woke me up and said, "Hey man, come on get up, get up, you've been drafted by the Redskins." I knew absolutely nothing about the Redskins so I said, "Who?" He said, "The Redskins," and then Gil Brandt called me right after that. What happened was Dallas and the Redskins had the same record. They tied. They flipped a coin and Dallas lost. That's how I ended up going to Washington.

Switch From Running Back To Wide Receiver
After I got Washington, I was a running back for two years. When I was switched to receiver, having Bobby Mitchell as a teammate helped. I would ask him, "How do you do this? When do you do that?" It was a learning experience. It worked out, thank God.

We had two running backs Steve Thurlow and Joe Don Looney. Coach Otto Graham wanted to go with the big bull guys. He told me, "We're going to put you outside because we got the two guys in here." I understood that, not that they did any better, but he was happy.

Otto Graham coached me in the College All-Star Game and then two years later, he was my coach in Washington. He called me lazy before the College All-Star Game. I was the first one at practice, and I would leave first.

For him to tell the papers that I was lazy and I was the first one to leave practice was crazy. I was in Chicago. Who did I know in Chicago? Nobody.

Where was I going if I was leaving? I road the bus to practice. It was wild. Frank Kush wrote him a letter about it. Then two years later he's my coach in Washington. How about that?

I probably wouldn't have even been playing had the other running back not got hurt, and they needed a back. So he sent me in.

Vince Lombardi
I can see how those guys in Green Bay kind of loved him and hated him a little bit. He was tough, but he was also fair. He knew what he was doing; he knew how to win. He put together practice so you could win.

Playing Baseball At Arizona State
I played a little third base. I was there with Reggie Jackson. Frank Howard hit a ball off my knee and Frank Kush took me off the team. He said, "No more baseball for you sir." I played three games and that was it.

Sonny Jurgensen
It was a miracle man. Sonny was ahead of his time. The man could throw a ball with a hand behind his back. He was a great guy to work with.

George Allen
Vince Lombardi covered how to win. Then George Allen came in and gave us that little momentum to win. We cared about each other and we looked out for each other. That's what George did.

Billy Kilmer
He threw two spirals in his entire career. I couldn't believe it. I'm going down the sideline, I look back, and the ball is taking off. I go, "Whoa, I've got to go get this thing." He actually threw two spiral balls over thirty yards.

Jerry Smith
We had a tight end, a poor kid named Jerry Smith who also played with me in college. When they would double-team Bobby Mitchell, Roy Jefferson or me, then Jerry would kill them. He would score four or five times. So that took a little pressure off of me. They had to cover him a little bit.

Jerry was great. You know we lost him, but he was a heck of a friend. He was a little light for a tight end because he only weighed 217, but he was smart and we'd let him get the ball.

Was There Racial Tension?
No, not really. I didn't realize Washington had a problem with it until I got there because all our pre-season games were in Florida and places like that. In Virginia before a game, I went to Bobby Mitchell and he explained what was taking place. I had no idea.

Jack Kent Cooke
When Mr. Cooke took over, it was a whole different ballgame. He wanted to win. He was the right guy because he was at his best when we were losing games. He'd come in and half joke, "What are you on? You need something? We got it."

He was not afraid to spend money, but he'd spend it wisely. He'd always consult with the personnel people or the assistant coach. He would discuss it with everybody.

Deacon Jones
Deacon was unreal. You're talking about a guy who loved what he was doing. He was just unreal, a fast but big guy. I don't think we've seen anybody play the game as well as Deacon.

Joe Theisman
I played two years with Joe. Joe was just an athlete. He would go out there be it snowing, raining, whatever, and the ball never slipped out of his hand. He threw a tight spiral. He was just a great player. He just talked too much. He threw a strong ball.

Sam Huff
Sam taught me how to play the game. Sam taught me from the running back spot how the linebackers would take shots at you going across. He didn't tell me he was covering me until he knocked me out, then I had to knock him out. He was a tough guy, God bless him.

Coaching Art Monk, Gary Clark, Charlie Brown

Those guys made it easy. They were easy to work with. Their job was to just catch the ball. All I asked them to do was just catch the ball. We'll work on the rest of it; we could direct the rest of it. The only guy I had a little problem with was Desmond Howard. It took him a couple years to learn how to look at stuff up higher and reach. Good for him, he went to Green Bay and he was named MVP of the Super Bowl. You just have to be truthful with your players, and that's what I did. I would tell them you did it right or you did it wrong, one of the two. We corrected it if you did it wrong and kept on moving.

Doug Williams In Super Bowl

Doug is a tough guy because he had been in the hospital the night before. He came back and played the next day. Outstanding.

Pro Football Hall Of Fame Induction

I couldn't believe it. Of all the people who could call me, Bobby Mitchell was the guy to call me. I said, "You got to be kidding me." I knew I did fairly well, but I had no idea I had made that step being inducted into the hall. I thought I had to be pretty good to be with these guys.

Washington Redskin Charley Taylor left with Billy Kilmer right
Photograph courtesy Associated Press

Chapter 18

Bob Brown

College:
Nebraska

Career History:
Philadelphia Eagles (1964–1968)
Los Angeles Rams (1969–1970)
Oakland Raiders (1971–1973)

2004 Inductee Pro Football Hall of Fame

"Boomer" Nickname
When I was playing for the Eagles a defensive back friend of
mine, Joe Scarpati, started calling me "Boomer" our rookie year.
I was very, very attack oriented. It just stuck.

College Choice
It's a very interesting story. I wasn't really recruited by Ohio
State. I talked to Nebraska and I just liked how they talked to me
in terms of an opportunity to play. I didn't come from a great
high school program in Cleveland, Cleveland East Tech. It just
was a real good fit for me. I felt comfortable after talking with
the freshman coach out there and so I took a shot.

Bob Devaney
Bob Devaney was just a wonderful, wonderful man. People who
are too young don't remember the '60s. A lot of people forget
about the '60s, and the transition that the country was going
through. I couldn't have had a better coach, a guy whose door
was always open. There were a lot of social issues going on, as
you know in the country. He was just a top coach and maybe
even a better human being. He was just a wonderful, wonderful
man.

NFL Draft

I think I was talking to Charlie Taylor, and he said, "You know the 1964 class was quite a class," and I told him, "You're absolutely right." There were a lot of very talented guys who came out. It was a fabulous, fabulous class of guys.

I think I was the second guy picked in the National Football League, and I think I was the first guy picked in the AFL. I took the NFL because, at that time, I thought it was the best football in the world. I didn't want to be my age now, 70, and look back and think, "Did I go in the AFL because I didn't think I could dance at the big dance?"

As far as not being a Cleveland Brown, it was a lot of fun playing in Cleveland when I was with the Eagles. I would look up in the stands, because I'd have a lot of friends sitting in the bleachers, yelling at me. These were people that I played against in high school and some people I went to high school with, and they were actually there watching me. I thought that was really a big thing for a young guy.

Joining Philadelphia Eagles

Both teams I played with treated me great. Of course, Philadelphia fans are unique in the sense that they not only love their football, they know the game. I played five years in Philadelphia and was never booed. I don't think many guys can say that. The fans were knowledgeable. They could be critical, but if you gave them what they expected to see when they paid their money, they were great fans.

Racial Tension In Philadelphia

I played on teams with guys who had played in the Southeast and Southwest Conferences. I'm sure at no time during their careers that these young guys had ever played with or against any athletes of color. There were things said that would be considered inappropriate. It was not a great time to play on any NFL team, especially one that was integrated. You had some fellows who had never played in an integrated environment.

Jim Ringo

I don't know how many years he played with Green Bay, but he was a very steady influence. He made the offensive calls as the center. He was not a big guy, if you remember, but he had great technique and was extremely quick. He was a great teammate, a great center, and a great Hall of Famer.

Weight Lifting

Nebraska was always a very innovative place. We had a weight room. Not a large one, but we did have weights. There were guys who were into lifting, so I started lifting out there. As a matter of fact, I just finished my weight program for today. I do it to this day. It's one of those things. It's a part of my DNA now. I knew that it made a difference. I felt that a lot of guys around the National Football League weren't lifting, and so it was putting me one up on them. It did not affect my quickness and my speed, and I think that's been proven more, and more today. Most programs, probably all the programs, have weight-lifting programs. I was lucky. I was not an innovator but I was a guy who got onboard and stayed onboard.

Timmy Brown

Timmy was quite exceptional, a turn the corner type of halfback. We use to run a play in Philadelphia called the 21 flip. I like to think that he liked for me to lead it. I know that I liked for him to be behind me. It was a great play and we got a lot of mileage out of it. I did, however, have an opportunity to play with Timmy in a couple of Pro Bowls that I went to.

Joining Los Angeles Rams

It was different in the sense that, back in those days, everyone thought that the best football in the world was in the old bumps and bruises division, the Western Division of the NFL. Without getting into a long story about why I ended up being traded to the Rams on the other side of the world, to me it was all football. It didn't matter, of course. The great part about it is that I had an opportunity to work every day against the best defensive end ever, David Deacon Jones, and to work against guys like Merlin Olsen, Roger Brown, and Lamar Lundy. It only helped to put me in a situation where I was working against the very best linemen anywhere. We use to have some battles in practice. That was when one-on-one practice was a part of the daily routine. It was always a challenge, and it was always a good street fight.

George Allen

George would, with his first line guys, let us occasionally mix it up a bit. Basically George was a defensive genius. I believe he could design a defense to stop anything they're running today. George had a leaning toward the defensive guys. If there was water on the field he made sure that they quenched their thirst first. The rest of us had to push our way to the front of the line.

Pass And Run Blocking

I like to say I could do both well. I've always felt like, anything that was born from a woman, I can block. Short of being a transformer, I didn't care. It didn't matter if you called a 34-buck or a pass. I didn't have a preference. I was there to work. I was going to punch in and I was going to go to work.

Deacon Jones Claim He Was Best Defensive End Ever

I couldn't dispute it. I played during an era when I saw Carl Eller, Deacon Jones, Claude Humphrey, and L.C. Greenwood week in and week out. There was always a lot of talent out there.

Bob Lilly was like a cat. He was playing defensive tackle more then defensive end, so I didn't have that many experiences blocking Bob out. His record speaks for itself, but he was not playing defensive end when I was around.

Kenny Stabler

The thing that made Kenny so great is that he never complained. If someone brushed him, or touched him, or was in his face, he never said a word. I never believed that I needed a quarterback to be a leader. We were all out there getting paid. We were all professionals. Kenny never complained. If somebody touched him he never said, "Hey man, get these guys off me." He said, "Don't worry about it. We're going to win it."

Raiders Offensive Line

I played on a line alongside, Art Shell, a Hall of Famer, Gene Upshaw, a Hall of Famer, Jim Otto, a Hall of Famer, and George Buehler, a great guard. I don't know how many guys can say they played on a line that had four Hall of Famers at the same time. I don't know if that's ever happened.

Al Davis

I think the one great thing about Al is that you always knew where you stood with him. If he liked you I honestly believe he would go to the wall for you. If you didn't necessarily have a relationship with him, then that's just how that was too.

John Madden

The best experience I've had as a pro football player. He's everything he appears to be. He's nice, honorable, and funny. He knows when to get serious, too. He has great expectations of his players. He's the kind of a guy you want to give your best for, not only because you're being paid to, but because he's just a really, nice man.

The John you see on TV is pretty close to the John I know. He's just a funny guy. In Philadelphia, of course, I had great admiration and respect for Joe Kuharich, because he was my first coach. George Allen was the Ram experience, a different sort of experience. I would have to say that my Raider experience with John Madden was great. He made it a great experience, along with the guys on the team. The Raider guys were at one time, and maybe even today, a bunch of wild and crazy guys. It was a lot of fun in the locker room. We expected a lot from each other and we tried to truly be a band of brothers.

Ron Mix

Ron's a great weightlifter and a great tackle. He has great technique. We worked out together. The Raiders did not have the expensive weight room that they have now. When I started in Nebraska, weight lifting was not even in its infancy. We were probably one of the few schools doing it. The Raiders did not have an exceptional weight facility at all. I've always had Olympic weights at my house.

Induction Into Pro Football Hall Of Fame

The Hall Of Famers always have a bet to see who will be the first guy to cry at the induction. You've got to think about income tax, biting your lip, or something bad. I had to, at least, because it was such a touching moment for me. To be honest, I thought that I would have been in the Hall of Fame sooner. I'm being very honest. You know, it wouldn't have been nearly as sweet as it was had my son as an adult introduced me.

This was the pinnacle of everything that happened in my past, from Cleveland East Tech, to the University of Nebraska, the Eagles, the Rams, and the Raiders. What else could I ask for? This was everything.

In all honesty, my Hall of Fame was every game I played, every player I played against. I just wanted to be able to do it in a way, so when it was over, that I felt I worked hard enough and did enough to be in. I wanted them to say, "Man, Bob Brown's getting robbed." At the end of the day, that's what it was all about for me.

Willie Davis

I'll never forget, I was a high school student and I was at Garfield Park. I was just watching some of the Browns work out before the season. Willie Davis called me over and we were talking about Grambling. He said, "Let me show you some things."

I think that was a fabulous turning point for me. When I had the opportunity to play against Willie in Green Bay, and had a chance to talk to him before the game, that was very exciting for me. I was able to see someone who was kind to me, nice to me, and trying to introduce me to some techniques. Later during the course of the game, he said, "I didn't teach you that." I said, "Well, I picked up a few things along the way." That was a great moment for me.

Comparing Todays Players With His Generation

We didn't make a lot of money, but that's not to say that these guys today don't play as hard, and don't deserve the piece of the pie that they're getting. I don't want to be one of those old guys who say, "Oh, it was better when I was doing it." It's a great game. We've passed the baton on to some great young players. They might not be quite like us because the environment that they're dealing with isn't like it was when I was a young guy coming up. It's still a great game. I think that we handed it off to some great young guys.

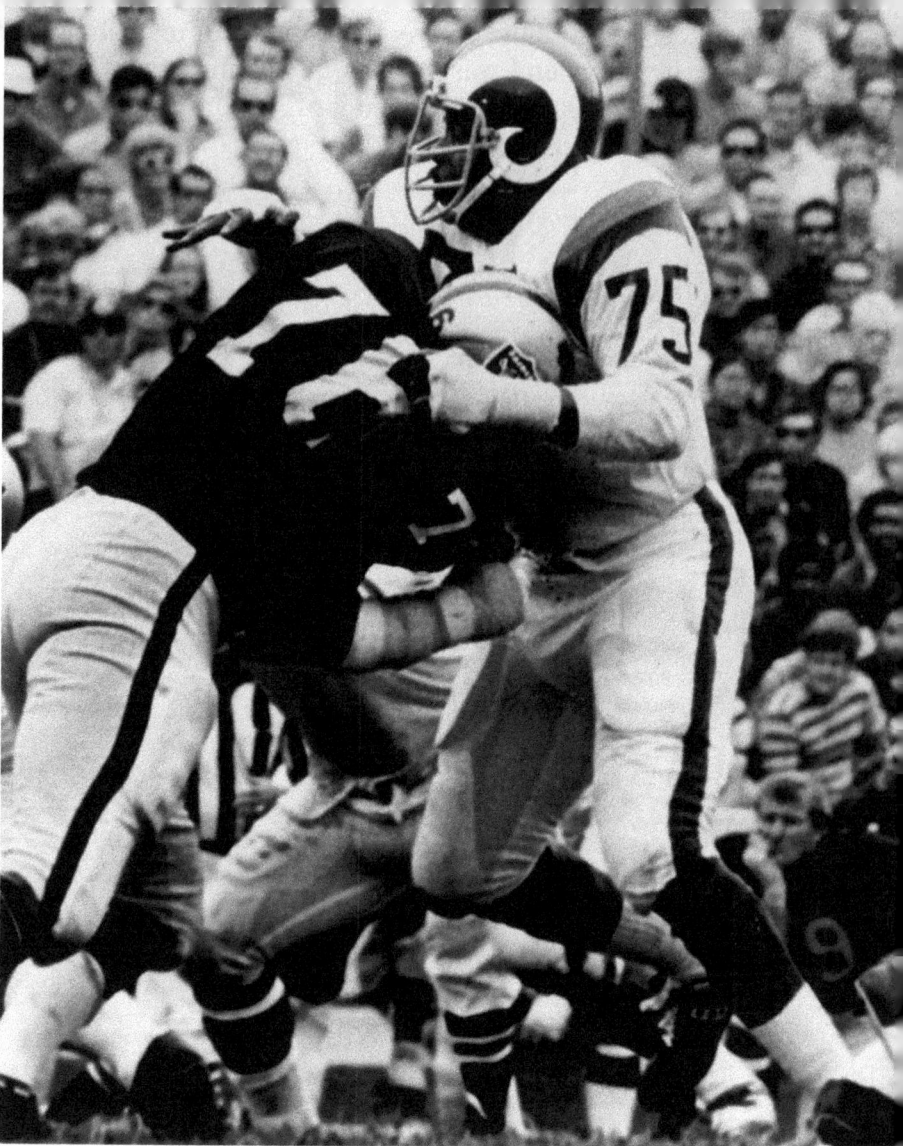

Oakland Raider Bob Brown takes on Los Angeles Ram

Deacon Jones Photograph courtesy Associated Press

Chapter 19

Mel Renfro

College:
Oregon

Career History
Dallas Cowboys (1964-1977)

1996 Inductee Pro Football Hall of Fame

College Choice
I was very versatile in high school. I played almost every position. My senior year, I played quarterback. It just came easy for me.

I was two weeks away from going to Oregon State. I had planned to go to Oregon State but two weeks before it was time to report, my parents sat me down and said, "You're not going to Oregon State. You're going to Oregon." I suppose Bill Bowerman, the Oregon track and field coach and future founder of Nike, got to my parents and convinced them that I should go to Oregon. I did what my parent's wished, so I ended up at Oregon.

Shoe Deal
Adidas came after me. They came to the Cowboys training camp and handed out a lot of free Adidas equipment. I wore a lot of those shoes and what not in my playing career. That's a little payback to Nike for not doing more for me when they had an opportunity.

Len Casanova
Len Casanova had an excellent group of coaches. Max Coley was my coach and Len was the boss, but Max taught us the ropes and told us what to do. He pretty much took care of us. Len was

a teacher and he was tough. He wanted you to do your job and do your job right. If you made a mistake and did something wrong, he'd come down on you no matter if you were one of the best or just a mediocre player. He didn't have any favorites. Len was a very fair guy and well liked as a coach.

1964 Olympics

The 1964 Olympics were on the table. As a matter of fact, I was training for the Decathlon, playing football, going to school, and raising a family. It was a little too much for me for me to handle at that time. I chose a pro contract in the National Football League rather than stay and train for the Olympics.

First Encounter With Racial Discrimination While Playing At Texas

It was the first time that I noticed and encountered racial discrimination. It was a situation where we were told what we could and couldn't do and where we could go. Len Casanova tried to keep everybody together as a team. We were very cautious about how we moved around as an entire team. It worked out okay. We had an outstanding game against the Texas Long Horns right up until late in the 3rd quarter, when I think we ran out of gas. We weren't used to that Texas heat. I think it was in the 90s at night. We were used to playing in 50- or 60-degree weather. We were leading, but we made some critical errors late in the 3rd quarter. They were rated number one in the nation that year. We had a good opportunity to beat them, but we let it slip away.

Ohio State

We played against Ohio State twice, my junior and senior year. When we got there and went into that stadium, there were 87,000 screaming Ohio fans. It was a hard challenge for us. We battled as hard as we could. I think I ended up with 15 unassisted tackles and 23 or 25 tackles all together. I planned free safety. I just remembered that big fullback coming up the middle. The first thing I saw were his knees coming at my head. It was a quite an experience but we had two great games against them. We battled them, but they were tough. We battled, and we gave it our all. We gave everything we had on the field.

Rice

The 1962 Rice game was very, very emotional for me. Being born in Houston and coming back and playing in an all white stadium was just remarkable. I had so much adrenaline. I was so pumped up. I probably had one of my best games ever. I think some of the news reports read, "Renfro Runs Rice Ragged." It was great to see. I can't remember how many of my relatives were there but I know my grandfather was there.

I didn't get to talk to him but I went over as close as I could get to the stands and waved to him. I think I probably teared up because of the special game I had. It was special to have relatives there that I hadn't seen in such a long time, watch me have such a great game. It was just a wonderful experience; something I'll never forget.

Oregon Teammates

We had great quarterbacks in Bob Berry and Doug Post. I was playing wide receiver, running back, and safety. I had my hands full back in those days. You didn't play just offense or defense; you played both. It was tough to do, but you stayed on the field the whole time. I was a punt returner, a kick-off returner, and played offense and defense without ever leaving the field. Sometimes, you were running an 80-yard touchdown, then you were out on the kick-off team, and then you end up on defense. That's the way it was. We had to do it; we had some great teams.

Draft

I thought maybe the Redskins or the 49ers were where I might go. I was passed over in the first round, because of the rumor that my hand was cut off or something. Dallas was the one that held up the draft for 8 or 10 hours. They passed over me and drafted Scott Appleton. Then, they traded him away before the draft was over. They immediately took me in the second round. I don't know what their theory was; maybe there was some deception. They ended up with a first round quality player in the second round.

Position Change In NFL

I came in as a running back and wide receiver, but they had a host of running backs and wide receivers. Tom Landry didn't feel like I would be able to start in my rookie year. He said, "I'm going to put you on defense and see what you do." Immediately, the defense improved tremendously. I was also returning punts and kick-offs. Actually, my first two years, I gained more yards returning kicks than the running backs gained. My first year I was at free safety, and my second year I was strong safety. I had such success returning kicks; Tom decided to move me to offense in my third year.

I started my third year at running back but was injured in the first league game. I broke a bone in my foot, so I didn't play for about 4 or 5 games. When I came back the foot wasn't right, I just couldn't make a cut. Tom decided to put me back on defense and put me back in at free safety. I played the rest of the year at free safety and still went to the Pro Bowl. The next year, they put me at cornerback and that's where I played for the next 10 years.

If I had stayed at free safety, I probably would have intercepted a hundred passes. I love the challenge at cornerback in man-to-man coverage. I was so good at it that in 1971, 1972, and 1973, I had almost no passes thrown in my direction. We'd play a game and they'd grade the film. They were only able to grade me on pursuit because the other team always threw the ball in the other direction. As a consequence, I didn't get the interceptions. After my 10th year, I wasn't able to earn Pro Bowl status because there was no just action over there. Not that I wasn't the same good cornerback. It's just that if you get no action, you get no statistics, and you're not going to end up in the Pro Bowl. Ten years was a good run and I appreciated that.

Bob Hayes

I had a technique where I was a reader. I would read the quarterback's steps, I knew the patterns, and I knew Bob Hayes' moves. I would just get back about 15 yards, wait for him to make his final moves, and then I'd go after him. One thing about me, I had tremendous quickness. I was running against Bob but between 60 and 80 yards, he'd go by me very easily. I really had a tough time

159

covering him in practice and the opponents had a difficult time covering him anytime.

You line up 15 yards deep and when you back up you try to read the quarterbacks drop. You just go for it. It helps to get some deep help.

Dallas Cowboys Defense
Bob Lilly was the number one player for us but the leader was Lee Roy Jordan. He was the team captain, the play caller, and was tough as nails in that huddle. I tell you, he growled and said, "Man, we're not letting them in the zone." He'd say that a hundred times a game. Before every play, we came up with a purpose to stop them, not let them score. Lee Roy was pretty much the trooper who got us going with that.

Favorite Punt Return
I would not say I had a favorite, but I had a one in the fourth quarter of the Pro Bowl in 1971. I ran back two punts for touchdowns. They named me Offensive Player of the Game, Offensive MVP as the Defensive Back. The first punt was a short kick but it started bouncing down around our 12- or 13-yard line. The other team kind of relaxed and I scooped it up. I went right up the middle 83 yards for a touchdown. Just a few minutes later on a short punt, I fielded it on our 44-yard line, cut left, then cut back right, and went 56 yards for another touchdown. That was interesting to be able to score twice on punt returns in one quarter.

Favorite Super Bowl
I have to say that my favorite would be Super Bowl VI, because we shut down Paul Warfield, Jim Kiick, Larry Csonka, Bob Griese, and everybody. Bob Lilly was all over Bob Griese. We had a reputation for not being able to win the big game. We finally won the big game and got the monkey off our backs. That was by far the most exciting, but Super Bowl XII was my last game. I had a bad knee that year and didn't play very much. As a matter of fact, I didn't play the last 6 or 7 games of the season. In the first quarter of that Super Bowl, I think Benny Barnes went down. Mark Washington was the back up and Mark was over

rubbing his knee, like he couldn't go. He said, "Fro", he called me his brother, Fro. He said, "Fro, can you go?" I went in early in the 2nd quarter and played three quarters of the game. We ended up winning. I was very thankful that I was able to play in that game because it was my last game. To win a World Championship in your last game and retire, it just doesn't get any better than that.

I kind of felt like it was my last game because my knee was totally gone. I had the cartilage removed, I think in April, just before training camp. I really wasn't supposed to play much and just wore out during the season. I felt like I couldn't play anymore unless they moved me inside to safety. They weren't going to do that because of Cliff Harris and Charlie Waters. Those guys were permanent fixtures there. Their number one draft choice was a cornerback and they wanted him to play. I felt like I was on my way out anyway.

Tom Landry
Tom Landry was a tough, smart coach. He left no stone unturned. He was a very strict, tough taskmaster, but he was fair. He was a great teacher. He taught us all how to play our positions as good as we could. Not only that, he taught us to be good football players and to work together. He also taught us to be better people, better men.

After we retired, most of us realized the influence he had on our lives. We give Tom Landry a lot of credit for the way that we turned out as men after retiring. He strengthened us in faith and consistency. He was just a great man and a great individual. We all loved him dearly.

One time during practice he was demonstrating a linebacker move, and he tripped and fell. He got up and said, "Gosh, darn." Everybody just broke up. The closest he came to a curse was, Gosh, darn.

Although he came up as a defensive back and was a defensive coach, he concentrated on the offense, in multiple sets, multiple posts, and all the movements. Dick Nolan was a great defensive back coach who did a great job. Tom kept an eye on the defense to make sure that everything was in order.

Toughest Receiver

Paul Warfield was good. I learned Paul's routes, his tendencies, and I was able to cover him well. Roy Jefferson was good when he was with Pittsburgh, then the Redskins. Cliff Branch could flat out fly. I bet he could even run as fast as Bob Hayes. Guys who could run really fast gave me problems. I didn't have too much difficulty in covering them.

Favorite Quarterback To Compete Against

I loved to go up against Sonny Jurgensen. The guy could throw the ball extremely well. I think in my rookie year, I picked him off twice. In the first game that we played, I ran it in for a touchdown. Then in the Pro Bowl at the end of the year, I picked him off and again ran in for a touchdown. He was a great passer, easy to key, but he could throw the ball extremely accurate. He loved to pass.

I played against Joe Namath one time. I thought he was a very good passer. He was at the end of his career when I played against him, but I thought he was excellent quarterback in his heyday. I loved Johnny Unitas. I grew up watching him and fortunately, my rookie year, I intercepted a couple of passes against him in Baltimore. I will always remember Johnny U. as being one of the greatest. I just admired him. Of course being able to play against him was just kind of a dream come true.

1970 Dallas Cowboys vs. St. Louis Cardinals

It was probably the worst experience we ever had. The Vikings beat us in the preseason like, 53 to 14, but we came back that year and did extremely well. The Cardinal game was a nightmare. I think it was on national TV, but we didn't lose a game after that.

We all had different attitudes toward practice and meetings. Coach Landry kind of loosened up a little bit, telling us to relax. I think we were like 4 and 3 at the time. To him, that was like the season's about over. He relaxed and we never lost another game, we went right on to the Super Bowl.

Jim Brown

I think Jim Brown is the greatest running back who ever played the game. I tried to tackle him. I hit him as hard as I could and he ran right over the top of me. A guy that big … nobody ever ran him down from behind in his career, except me. One time in the Cotton Bowl, I chased him 73 yards and he said, "Mel, you're the only guy after I broke loose that has ever run me down." I appreciated that compliment coming from the guy who I thought was the greatest running back who ever played a game.

I grew up watching him. It was a highlight for me to be able to play against him and then to play with him in two Pro Bowls. Spending quality time with him at the Pro Bowl was really exciting for me.

You would hit him, hold on, and pray for help. That's what I did many times when I hit him and he was running over me. I know one time I grabbed his leg and held it until two or three of my teammates came to help me take him down.

Pro Football Hall Of Fame Induction

I think what excited me the most was the thousand cameras out there glaring at me. When you are there, you know that everybody in the world is looking at you. You had become one of the greatest players that ever played a game. You're in a fraternity with Jim Brown, Lenny Moore, and Paul Hornung. It's an elite group. The whole world's looking at you, your family's looking at you, even your fifth grade school teacher's looking at you. It's just a wonderful feeling knowing that you have accomplished something. It's just a great honor and probably the highlight of my life.

America's Team

We were America's team not only because we were winners and successful, but Gil Brandt and Tex Schramm did a great job of promoting the Cowboys. They promoted the cheerleaders. Their scouting program entailed going to all the colleges, becoming friends with the coaches, and giving them the cheerleader calendars, pins, and frequent visits. It wasn't by chance that we became America's team; it was by design.

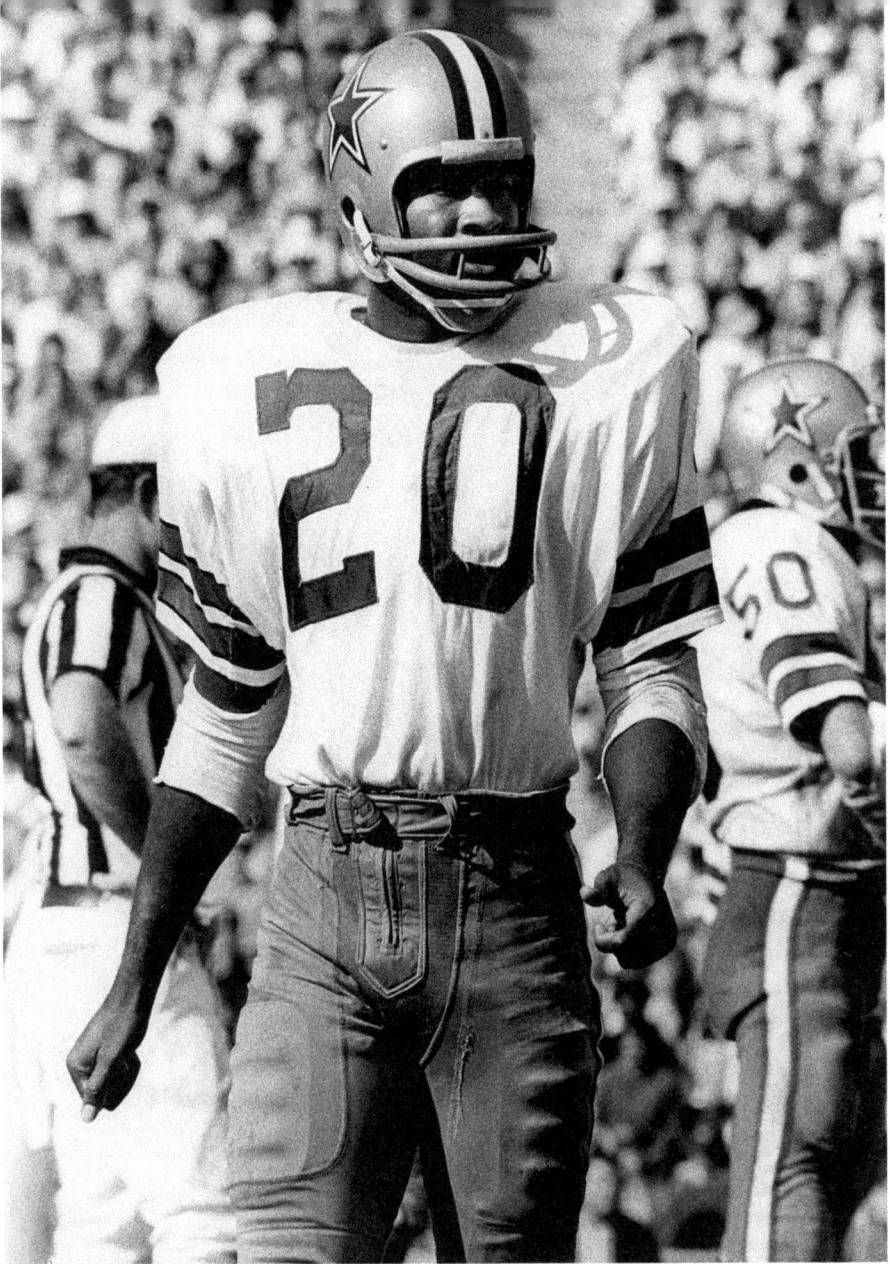

Photograph courtesy Associated Press

Chapter 20

Paul Krause

College:
Iowa

Career History
Washington Redskins (1964-1967)
Minnesota Vikings (1968-1979)

1998 Inductee Pro Football Hall of Fame

Playing Both Ways
We played both ways in my time. I think we were one of the last classes in the NCAA that played both ways. We played both ways in high school and both ways in college. All of a sudden when I went to Pro Football, there was only one way. I was a defensive back and that was easy because I didn't get tired or anything. It was a strange feel for me only to play on one side of the football.

College Choice
I'm from Flint, Michigan. It's 45 miles to East Lansing and it's 45 miles to Ann Arbor. I almost went to Ann Arbor and the University of Michigan, but I didn't even consider going to Michigan State. I don't know why, but I never had a desire to go to Michigan State.

Transition To NFL
I started as a wide receiver in college, and then I was a safety. I never did play cornerback. It really didn't matter to me because I had played both in college, so it wasn't a strange position. The Washington Redskins drafted me and told me I was their free safety, so I said, "Okay".

The first time I played in an exhibition game was against the Bears, and I intercepted a pass from Billy Wade. The first play I got into the game, I intercepted a pass. Then the first league game I ever played, I intercepted two passes. I acted like a wide receiver back there and it really didn't make any difference.

During the regular season I played against the Cleveland Browns. They had Paul Warfield and Frank Ryan. Frank Ryan threw to Paul Warfield twice and I picked both of them off.

Interceptions

I had seven games with an interception as a rookie and it was, I even hate to say I thought it, a pretty easy game. By the next year they stopped throwing in my direction. I think the second year I had six, which was still a great year. Then I went down to two I think, and they never threw anywhere near me.

I played one more year in Washington and the defensive coach didn't like the way I was playing I guess, and they traded me. I went to the Minnesota Vikings and right away I had, I don't know, eight, nine, or ten, something like that. It was a new life for me. I really wasn't interested in getting traded by the Redskins, but the backfield coach and I just didn't get along. So I accepted the trade and went to the Vikings. It was all history from there. In 10 out of the 12 years I played with the Vikings, we won the Central Division Championship and played in four Super Bowls. It was a good thing. I enjoyed my years with the Vikings. Even though we didn't win a Super Bowl, we played in four of them and that's more than a lot of people played in.

Washington Redskins

Off the Redskins we had a lot of guys go into the Hall of Fame. With the Redskins we just couldn't win, but we had some great players. My old roommate with the Redskins, Chris Hanburger, went into the Hall. So, both roommates went in to the Hall of Fame.

Bud Grant

Bud Grant was probably one of the nicest guys you'd ever meet. He was a great coach. If you didn't play the way he wanted you to play, you were gone. Everybody realized that he was a good coach. He had his own ways of doing things and if you didn't do his way, you were adios. After the records that we started to put together, everybody realized, this guy is good and he knows how to treat people. He's just a great guy and a great coach.

Favorite Teams To Play Against
There were teams that I liked to play against back then. I loved to play against the Bears, the Lions, and the Packers. They were in our division, we played them twice a year, and we knew each other real well, but I still liked playing against them. I probably had more interceptions against the Detroit football team than anybody else. It was always great to play against our Central Division rivals because we knew that we were in for tough games. We had tremendous respect for them.

Difference In Game Now
I think if I played right now I'd have twice as many interceptions because they throw it twice as much. They throw 50, 60 times a game sometimes. Plus, I don't think the quarterbacks are as good as the guys I played against.

When I played, the quarterbacks were calling their own plays. They knew the receivers. They knew the game itself. I personally do not think that the coaches that are calling the plays today are as good as the quarterbacks that we're calling them back in the '60s. Some of the guys that are calling the plays today have never played the game. They have not been in certain situations. All they do is go by the book, or history, or whatever. I don't know how they're calling them, but they've never played the game. How in the world do they know what would be the best way to attack the different players or different offenses? Then it gets into a whole different aspect of the game. I could spend a lot of time on that because I look at the tackling, I look at the blocking, and all of that. I just I don't think the players of today are being taught the way to block, tackle, run pass patterns, and everything. I don't want to get into all that, but it's a whole different game. It's not like it was in the '60s and '70s.

Watching Film

I used to watch a lot of film. I studied the quarterbacks and everything. I'm just going to come right out and say it; I had a God given ability. I watch coaches today and think, how in the world, if they never played, are they going to tell a guy how to play as a defensive back in certain situations?

It's pretty hard for them tell they guys what to do if they've never been out on the field against a guy who can run like Bob Hayes, Paul Warfield, or Randy Moss. They're just throwing paint on the wall and saying, "I hope you can do this. This is the way I want it done." If you've never been there, never been scored upon, or if you've never been run over by Jimmy Brown, then you don't know what it's like. Doggone it; I know what it's like. I've been there. A lot of the old defensive backs sit around at the Hall of Fame and we say, "Geez, I watch this or watch that I know what they're supposed to do and they don't do it."

Jim Brown

I think I made tackles on Jim Brown but you just hung on and yelled for help. He was the best running back I've ever seen in my life, or ever played against in my life. Right now I would say Adrian Peterson is the closest thing I've ever seen to Jimmy Brown.

Quarterbacks

I loved quarterbacks that threw the football. I just loved them because I had a great defensive line, and I had a better than average group of linebackers in front of me. If they were going to throw the football against us, or speaking of the Minnesota Vikings, they we're in a lot of trouble. Well, the Minnesota Vikings defensive line was probably the best group of guys for me to play behind. When we had the quarterbacks in throwing mode, they were playing right to our strength because they had about less than four seconds to throw the ball or they were sacked. It made the defensive backfield's job a lot easier.

I probably felt there was something that we had to prove all the time; that teams could not throw the ball on us. They could run the ball up and down the football field on us, but when they got inside the 20 they had a very, very tough time scoring against the Vikings.

As for the best quarterback, I wouldn't even single out any quarterback. I think Sonny Jurgensen was the best passer I ever played against. I mean pure passer. Then you come to Johnny Unitas, Bart Starr, and of course Jurgensen, Billy Wade, and all those guys. These guys were great quarterbacks. There weren't as many teams back then, so every team had a good quarterback. The thing I hated was when an offensive team started running the ball on us, and we couldn't stop the dang the run. That's what we hated because all of a sudden our defensive backs were making too many tackles.

Four Super Bowl Appearances

I think that we should have won a couple of those Super Bowls. I think we could have won the first one. I think we should have won the Oakland game. There was some reason why we couldn't win and I have no idea.

81 Interceptions

I was so happy to get 81 interceptions. I remember the first one, the one that I tied the record with, and the one I broke the record with. I caught a pass in front of Gene Washington, which was great. I'm going to say it was a great interception because it was a diving interception and I caught it right in front of him, knee-high. Then I got two against LA in LA to break the record. I remember those.

I don't really remember a whole lot of other ones. I remember getting one off Sonny Jurgensen and Johnny Unitas. I remember some of them, but, gee, I never really thought at the time I was playing, that I was going to get 81 interceptions. There's just no way. You don't go into the league thinking, "Oh, I'm going to break a record, or I'm going to go into the Hall of Fame, and all of that." Hey, that's a gift from God I think.

It just happened that Emlen Tunnell and I were both from Iowa. I talked with Emlen Tunnell quite a few times before he passed away. I rode on the airplane from Chicago to California with him. We talked a lot about football, a lot about defensive back play, and things like that. He was a great man, a great football player. You know something; he never said one thing about me getting close to his record or anything like that. It was just never mentioned.

I watch to see if somebody's trying to catch me, and I also think that the league would like somebody to break that record. I think they want a player who is playing or modern day player to break it. As of right now, I don't think anybody is really close. If it happens it's going to take somebody who's going to be in the Hall of Fame to do it because it's a record that I'm very proud of.

Minnesota Viking Paul Krause next to Head Coach Bud Grant
Photograph courtesy Associated Press

Chapter 21

Carl Eller

College:
Minnesota

Career History:
Minnesota Vikings (1964-1978)
Seattle Seahawks (1979)

2004 Inductee Pro Football Hall of Fame

Bobby Bell
Bobby was a great player and those were great University of Minnesota years. We go back and we're talking many years. I'm not even going to mention a number because it goes back to the days of the Great North Woods being discovered up here but those were great years. Bobby was a great teammate. They were National Champions one year and Big Ten Champions the next year. This year, our leader Sandy Stephens who was a pioneer quarterback, one of the first African American quarterbacks, and an All-American at quarterback, is going into the College Football Hall Of Fame. That's a big honor and we're all happy about that. Those were great teams. We never went to Michigan. Timing is everything. I was in the right place at the right time.

Minnesota Vikings Defense
Buddy Ryan was our coach part of the time. We had Jack Patera there too for a number of those years. They kind of combined there for a number of years but we started out with somebody totally different there. Again, it was the timing. We had great talent. We had Alan Page, Jim Marshall, and Gary Larsen. I just think that it was a combination. It was good chemistry. We all really cared and supported each other and just took great pride in being there. That was the kind of players we were and part of the team that we were part of.

Best Running Back Played Against

Well, it's very difficult. I played against some of the great ones, Jim Brown, Gale Sayers, O.J. Simpson, and Walter Payton. All of those guys are different. I won't say that he's my favorite, but I think that Gale Sayers was the biggest threat because he could score from anywhere on the field at any point. Any time he had the ball in his hands, he was liable to end up putting six points on the board. He was extremely quick for a defensive lineman to tackle. You watch these guys and they take a long time to get up to the line today and they can pick the holes. Gale Sayers would be at the line as soon as you made contact with the interior lineman and if you didn't stop him there he was gone.

Super Bowl Losses

Well, we were very close and very competitive. We played some great teams, one of the really great all-time teams in Kansas City, a team that was loaded. We played the Steelers team, which might have been the best Steelers team ever with Franco Harris, Lynn Swann, Terry Bradshaw, Joe Greene, and all of those guys. They just had a great, great, great team that was well balanced. That might have been one of the better teams. Then, we played Miami who was undefeated with Larry Csonka, Jim Kick, Bob Griese, and all those guys. We played great teams including the Oakland team. I thought that we were closer and had a real chance to beat Oakland. I think of the four teams that we played in the Super Bowl; we certainly had a chance to beat Oakland. I don't think that was our best Super Bowl team. Our best Super Bowl team was probably between the teams that played Pittsburgh and Miami in the Super Bowl.

Toughest Offensive Lineman

When I'm asked that question I generally refer to a guy, Bob Brown, who actually went into the Hall of Fame the same time as I did. Bob must have been put on this earth to just really be my nemesis. He was at Nebraska when I was at the University of Minnesota. We were actually the same age and in the same graduating class. I never could shake him and I could never get rid of him. When his teams showed up on our schedule I spent extra time in the locker room and the training room getting ready for him. He was great. The thing that was great about Bob was that he had a different philosophy. He wasn't just satisfied with protecting the quarterback, he wanted to annihilate the defensive end; so you had to be on guard all of the time.

Left to right Jim Marshall, Alan Page, Gary Larson, Carl Eller
Photograph courtesy Associated Press

Chapter 22

Floyd Little

College:
Syracuse

Career History:
1967-1969 AFL Denver Broncos
1970-1975 NFL Denver Broncos

2010 Inductee Pro Football Hall of Fame

College Choice
I had 47 scholarship offers. I was recruited by General
MacArthur in New York City with all of the famous Yankees,
Elston Howard, Roy Campanella, and some of the other great
players I got a chance to meet a great general in his room in New
York City at the Waldorf. He gave me an opportunity to get into
the Army and got me an appointment by Senator Humphries
before he became Vice President. He told me I would be the first
African-American general in the United States Army. That
means I would have been Colin Powell's boss, General Petraeus'
boss, and Norman Schwarzkopf's boss. I would have been a real
top level general during that time, if I had gone into the Army.

A guy named Ernie Davis, who won the Heisman trophy that
year, came to my house and sat with my sisters, my mom, and
me. We went out to dinner and I told him that I would go to
Syracuse, because I wanted to eat my steak and lobster, which
was getting cold. Three months later he died. I had given him my
word, and I don't have anything more valuable than that. When I
give my word, that is the only thing of value that I own. When
Ernie Davis passed away, I never even knew that he was sick. I
called the coach and told him I was coming to Syracuse because
I had given Ernie Davis my word. That is how I got to Syracuse.

Syracuse Football

I played with Jim Nance and Larry Csonka. I had two good fullbacks to play with. Jim Brown recruited Ernie Davis, and Ernie Davis recruited me. That is the trilogy. That is the three number 44s. Of course we had some other ones after us, like Rob Conrad, who played for the Miami Dolphins, who was number 44 here, as well as Michael Owens, Billy Owens' brother. We have had some other 44s after me, but Jim Brown, Ernie, and me are the real 44s.

They retired number 44 on Thanksgiving Day 2005. Since then, they have retired Csonka's number, as well as John Mackey's number. They could not retire theirs until they retired ours, so they retired number 44.

My Broncos number is retired, my high school number is retired, and my military number is retired. All of the numbers that I have ever worn have been retired.

Jim Brown

Jim Brown is an icon in the game. He was way before his time. He did some things as a player that nobody had done. That is the reason why his numbers are so high, playing in a 12-game schedule. It took players a long time to carry the ball twice as many times and play in almost twice as many games just to catch him. He is a great player, he's a good friend of mine, and he truly deserves to be a Hall of Famer. He's the best football player that has ever played. No question in my mind.

Nickname "The Franchise"

I saved the franchise. The Broncos were on the verge of being moved to Chicago or Birmingham, because they had never signed a number 1 draft pick. They drafted Dick Butkus and other future stars, but they went to the NFL, not the AFL. The NFL and AFL merged and the Broncos signed me. The Broncos decided to stay and built a new stadium, so I saved the franchise from moving to Chicago or Birmingham. That is how I got the name "The Franchise."

Pro Football Hall Of Fame Induction

Being a Hall of Famer with so many guys whom I've watched and admired over the years, and now I am one of them … I was just thrilled. And, going in with Emmitt Smith, Jerry Rice, John Randle, Rickey Jackson, Russ Grimm, and all of the other guys that went in with me … I think that's just fantastic. That was the highlight of my sports career.

I think a Sports Illustrated article really let people know who I am and where I have been. There are a lot more people today who recognize me since I am a Hall of Famer. I think there are a lot more people who recognize me because of the speech that I gave in Canton. They think that was the best speech ever. In fact, Walter Payton's mother said to me at a function, "I have never heard a greater speech in my life." I think the speech has helped me become more recognizable.

My son and I celebrate his life. He was injured in college and lost his leg and we celebrate his life every year. It took us about an hour, around the pool, for me to write it, he edited it, I re-wrote it, he edited it again, and we put it all together. We only had six to eight minutes to give a speech. I got to talk about my whole life as an athlete and a person, and I had eight minutes to do it. So we had to put in all of the things we needed to make it really effective.

My son went to USC. He was on campus and he went to the local store to get some lunchmeat and some bread, and two guys tried to rob him. They asked for $100 and all he had was $2. They said they needed $100 or they were going to shoot him. He said, "I guess you will have to shoot me." So they shot him at close range with a shotgun. On the way to the hospital, he flat-lined twice and they brought him back.

That is why it was so special for me to have him at my induction, celebrating the highest award in my life as an athlete. It was very special.

The thing about football is, when you are told as a child and a young adult, that you are not big enough, strong enough, smart enough, or fast enough, I think you build resentment in you that allows you to rise above. When you're given challenges all of your life, I think it helps you become a better person, because you know yourself that you are the only person who can say when you have had enough. Nobody can tap you out. You have to tap out yourself. No one can tell you what you can do.

Our problem is, too many of us allow someone else's opinion, or label of us, to become our reality. When people are told enough times that they can't, they start believing it. Me, I didn't believe it. I believed, let me fail me. Don't you fail me before I get an opportunity to fail. I want to be able to fail myself, and you are telling me I can't do stuff without me even trying. Not fair. I am not going to stand for it. I am not going to put up with it. I am going to try it and then I can actually say I couldn't do it, but let me say that. Don't say it for me."

Football has taught me a lot. Not believing what people think of you and you going out there and establishing who you are, what you are and rising to levels nobody thinks you can rise to. That is a part of what football has taught me about life. No one can tell me the level of success that I can reach. That is my call and I am not going to let you take that away from me.

Photograph courtesy Associated Press

Chapter 23

Dave Wilcox

College:
Oregon (& Boise JC)

Career History:
San Francisco 49ers (1964–1974)

2000 Inductee Pro Football Hall of Fame

College Choice
I went to Boise Junior College, which is now Boise State. Boise is about 75 miles from my hometown in Eastern Oregon. Then I went to the University of Oregon. I had an older brother who did exactly the same thing. Growing up in a small community, it was probably six gradual steps instead of leaping into the big city.

Len Casanova was a wonderful man. Actually there was a connection between him and my old coach at Boise Junior College, Lyle Smith. They served in the Navy together during World War II. I think my recruitment, part of whatever that was, included both Lyle and Len Casanova. Len was the most honorable and wonderful person.

There was a guy named Mel Renfro who played at Jefferson High in Portland. He went to Oregon. Even though we never played against each other in high school, I knew about him. He was the player of the state. It was sure wonderful to be able to go and play on the same team with Mel at the University of Oregon. When we played, you played everything. You ran down on kickoffs, did punt returns, played defense, and played offense. You weren't just a defensive guy or an offensive guy. The only guy that didn't play defense was the quarterback. That was probably good.

Oregon

I was a great tight end. I was a tight end in high school, at the junior college, and during my first year at Oregon. Right before spring practice during my junior year going into my senior year, the coaches asked me if I would move to play guard. We had a whole bunch of tight ends but we had no guards. I said I'd do that on offensive as long as I didn't have to do that on defense. I was a defensive end. I was a multi-talented position guy I guess.

In high school we probably threw the ball three or four times a game because we played a single wing. In junior college, I think we threw the ball maybe eight or nine times a game. Then when I got to Oregon, they threw it probably ten or fifteen times a game. About fourteen of those throws were to try to get the ball to Mel Renfro and the rest of us would get out of his way and leave him alone.

I never had one favorite moment. They were all favorite moments. Going to the University of Oregon there was no Pac-10 or Pac-8 or Pac anything; it was independent. My junior year, we opened with Texas in Austin. I don't know if it was the same year that we played Indiana. We played Ohio State, West Virginia, and Rice. We played all over the place, playing against all those teams.

I remember going to Ohio State and going out to warm up on the field. We had to go down to the corner of the end zone because Ohio State had so many players they took up the whole field. I think we got beat 17-14. They had a guy on their team named Paul Warfield.

I remember going back to West Virginia. We took two days to get there because it wasn't a direct flight. I don't remember the flight, but I do remember we were on a prop plane. I think we stopped a couple of times to get gas and that was good.

I remember going to Morgantown. We were getting ready to check into the hotel and we had a bunch of Hawaiian and a few black guys on our team. The hotel said that they had to come in through the kitchen. Len Casanova said, "No they won't. They'll come in through the front door." The guy said, "No they can't." We stayed somewhere else. The next day we beat West Virginia 46-2 with some of our players they wouldn't let walk into the hotel. We were in the middle of all that back in the '60s.

1963 Sun Bowl
We played SMU in the Sun Bowl. I was just talking about it with some of my old buddies. It just seems like it was yesterday. I think that two major colleges, SMU and Oregon were the first major colleges to play in the Sun Bowl. Before that teams like West Texas State, Texas Western, and New Mexico State were the schools that played in that. We did that and it was a wonderful experience.

Terry Baker
Terry Baker went to high school with Mel Renfro. He's a year older than Mel and me. He was a great athlete. I played against him our junior year in high school. He was a heck of a basketball player at Oregon State. I think they went into something similar to what the Final Four is now. He was a pitcher on the baseball team. Us in state guys followed him. He was the first Heisman Trophy winner out West.

I do know that he was such a great athlete. When people play Pro football, basketball, baseball, or something else, they have to have one skill that's pretty darn good. He was such a great athlete; he covered everything. Just because you're the Heisman Trophy winner in college, doesn't mean you're going to be a success in the Pros.

Draft
Len Casanova knew the owners of the 49ers. There was a guy named Franklin Mieuli who owned part of the 49ers. He graduated from the University of Oregon in the late '40s or early '50s. He talked to Len Casanova. Casanova had taught high school in Redwood City at Sequoia High School. The 49ers workout place was not in San Francisco, it was in Redwood City. Anyhow, that was the connection.

At that time, Houston drafted me in the AFL and then San Francisco in the NFL. Len Casanova told Mel Renfro and I to come see him when the draft was over. I went in the next day to see Len and he said, "You probably need to sign with San Francisco." I said, "You're my agent, so thank you." So that's what I did.

The draft was held in December 1963. That was the year we were getting ready to play Oregon State in our last game of the regular season. That's when John Kennedy was shot. They delayed all the games for a week. Mel cut his wrist sticking his arm through a window somehow or something happened. I don't remember the details, but there was a question about whether his arm would be ok. That's the reason he was taken in the second round.

Mel and I were at the Eugene Hotel for a while during that draft. A guy named Gil Brandt, who was the main connection to this area for the Cowboys, really wanted Mel. So, the Cowboys took Mel. I sure wish he came with me to San Francisco. He was a heck of a player.

Transition To NFL
In college we did everything. When I got to San Francisco they wanted me to be a defensive end, which would be a down lineman. I did that for about two days. Then they needed a linebacker and I did a little bit of that in training camp. When I played in the College All-Star Game in Chicago, I played as a linebacker. I'm not sure I knew what I was doing. Then I went from there.

Ed Pine, who was the linebacker ahead of me, got a bad line burn. They put the wrong chalk on the field at Kezar, and he got a burn. He was in pretty tough shape there for a while. His replacement, a guy named Bill Cooper, hurt his knee during the first game he played. Then all of a sudden, it's the second or third game of the season, and I've got to start. I went from there.

Gale Sayers
We played in San Francisco and Gale Sayers scored four touchdowns in Kezar Stadium. We played the Bears later in the year in Wrigley Field, in the mud and the rain. He scored six touchdowns. I remember somebody three or four years ago, talking about what a great running back he was because he scored 20 touchdowns in a

season. I started laughing. You've got to be kidding me. In two games against us, and we weren't very good, Gale Sayers scored ten touchdowns. I honestly think Gale Sayers was the best back we played against in the NFL.

A year or two later, we were playing in Wrigley Field and Gale ran a sweep. The guard was blocking for him. Our defensive back went and knocked the guard down and Gale was right behind him. The back hit Gale on the knee. I know the guy who did that and he felt awful. That's not something you try to do, hurt the guy. You might hit them and knock them down, but you didn't want to ruin their career. From then on it was tough for Gale. Up until that time he was a very special player.

Mike Ditka
Mike Ditka was one of the most tenacious guys to play against. You better be ready to play the whole game. He wasn't going to just play a few plays, that's for sure. Mike Ditka was the mentality of the Bears. You better take a lunch with you because you'd be there all day. It didn't make any difference if they were ahead or behind. You better pay attention to what was going on. You better focus on Mike Ditka.

Exhibition Game During Watts Riots
The exhibition game was always in the Coliseum. We stayed at the Sheridan West Hotel. You'd leave the hotel and go down to Vermont Street and that would take you to the Coliseum. Here we are on the bus at five o'clock in the evening going to the stadium for a seven o'clock game. We're driving down the middle of Watts with smoke coming out of the buildings. Guys with machine guns are on the buildings and I'm thinking, should we really be down here playing an exhibition game? I didn't know about that one.

Dick Nolan
Dick Nolan was a defense guy; I know that. He loved defense. That's what changed the makeup of the 49ers. When he became our Head Coach, it was so he could spend time with the defense. He let the offense guys go, but defense is where his level of specialty was.

When he was in Dallas, Tom Landry and Nolan put together the Dallas defense, which they called the "Flex" defense. It was a little bit different than what anybody else was doing. He brought that to San Francisco. Nolan was one of the most wonderful people. He brought a winning attitude to the 49ers.

Decision To Retire

I got clipped in an exhibition game in Miami prior to the 1970 season. I had torn cartilage in my knee, but I played the whole year. Oh God, that was awful. I missed one game. I couldn't take it. I had to rest. My knee would swell up all the time. After the season I had it operated on in Oregon. They fixed it up. You go in the morning; you're home in the afternoon, and playing again on Tuesday. I was in the hospital for a week for a cartilage operation. I played after that, it was really good for a couple years.

Then it bothered me once again and I had to go in and do again. In May, there was some stuff that started floating around and they had to operate. After that season I played a little better but it bothered me quite a bit. I went in to see the doctor; I was 32 I think, at the time. I talked to the doctors about my knee and stuff. Our team, the 49ers were going through some major changes. Brodie and a bunch of guys retired. I decided that I probably wanted to be able to walk around the rest of my life. The doctors showed me, this is what it looks like. This is what it should look like. This is probably what it will look like if you keep playing. It was a pretty easy choice.

I'd been a member of the team for almost 20 years. Your buddies and the camaraderie and all that, that's what you miss. That's what I missed.

Pro Football Hall of Fame Induction

I really hadn't thought too much about the Hall of Fame until the late '90s. My old coach Mike Giddings had been to the Hall of Fame induction. He called me and said, "You should be in the Hall of Fame." I said, "Well I guess. Whatever I did if it was good enough I think I should be there, if it wasn't then I shouldn't." I got the call in 2000. I'm very fortunate to be included with this group of people.

Bob St. Clair

When you went to training camp as a rookie back then, you'd have your first meal in the lunchroom. You'd all go sit in the corner somewhere away from the veterans. We didn't want to mess up things. We weren't sure what we were doing quite frankly.

After my rookie year, I anticipated this every year. Bob St. Clair would get a piece of raw liver and put it on his plate. He would come over and sit down right in the middle of the rookies and start eating it, letting blood run down his chin. The rookies would throw up and get up wondering what in the hell have I gotten into here with this Pro Football stuff?

Bob is one of the most wonderful guys. We'd have a lot of laughs about that. He did that on purpose. I know that.

A couple years ago in Canton, I'm sitting at this table with Franco Harris on one side and Bob St. Clair's on the other. They brought us our meal and Franco happened to look over. Bob had a raw steak with ice on top of it. Franco looked at the steak, and then he looked at me. I said, "Yes, he'll eat it." I thought Franco might lose his dinner right there. He'd never been around anything like that.

Bob is about 82 years old. That's probably the reason he's so healthy now.

San Francisco 49er Dave Wilcox stops Los Angeles Ram
Jim Bertelsen Photograph courtesy Associated Press

Chapter 24

Jan Stenerud

College:
Montana State

Career History:
Kansas City Chiefs (1967-1979)
Green Bay Packers (1980-1983)
Minnesota Vikings (1984-1985)

1991 Inductee Pro Football Hall of Fame

<u>College Choice</u>
Nowadays, you don't have ski jumping in the NCAA. In 1962 when I got to Montana State, between 45 and 50 schools in the United States had ski teams, and ski jumping was my specialty. I had to do two things, so I did cross-country skiing as well, but jumping is what I enjoyed.

I think they discontinued ski jumping in the NCAA in the early '70s. I heard some talk it might be coming back, but there aren't enough facilities.

I finished sixth in the junior nationals in ski jumping in Norway in 1962. A guy at Montana State who was already there on a ski scholarship, had a newspaper clipping of this, and he showed it to the ski coach. The next thing I know, I get a letter in the mail offering me a full ride ski scholarship. I thought it'd be a neat experience to come to the greatest place on earth. My plan was to go for one year and see how I liked it.

I also played soccer. That was my summer sport. I played on teams since I was eight years old, and I was a pretty decent soccer player. I would always take the corner kick and the free kick because I could kick the ball pretty hard. For some reason, that doesn't necessarily make you a great soccer player.

I didn't kick any kind of ball for two or three years at Montana State. As a skier, we ran the stadium steps every single day. One day, Dale Jackson who was a backup kicker on the football team and a safety, hurt his shoulder. So, I went down and kicked a few footballs for them. It lasted for my junior year.

I kicked with my toe like everybody else did in those days, and after a few attempts, I asked the coach, "Can you kick with the side of your foot like you take a corner kick in soccer?"

He said, "Yes, you can. There's a guy from the Buffalo Bills named Pete Gogolak who kicks with the side of his foot." Of course, I'd never seen him. I wasn't interested in football. But, I started kicking a few, and I did that once a week or so.

One day, the basketball coach, Roger Craft, was walking across the football field on the way to his office when he saw me. He took a second look and ran over to the football coach, Jim Sweeney. Sweeney later won 200 games at Fresno State, but he was the coach at Montana State at the time. Coach Sweeney finally took a look at me, and he made me try out for spring practice.

My senior year in college, they changed my scholarship from skiing to football. I did both sports my senior year. At the end of that year, the Kansas City Chiefs drafted me. It happened in the third round of what they called the AFL Red Shirt Draft.

After about 13 attempts, three of them being over 60 yards, I was drafted. That probably wouldn't happen these days.

Draft
I was drafted after the '65 season because that was my senior year. There were 25 guys drafted in the AFL Future Draft, or the Red Shirt Draft. We were on the quarter system at Montana State then, so I decided to keep seven credits. I didn't graduate the next spring, so I went to be on the football team in 1966. I graduated at Christmastime after that season. The NFL had a special draft of the 25 or so AFL Future Draft choices from the year before. Atlanta was the first one to have a pick of those 25 AFL Future Draft choices. I was the first one to be picked.

There was a choice to make between the Atlanta Falcons of the NFL and the Kansas City Chiefs of the AFL. Atlanta had been in the league for one year. People called the AFL the Mickey Mouse League. This was before Super Bowl I, when I had to decide. Bobby Beathard, who later became the GM for the Redskins and San Diego, was a scout in Kansas City. I really liked him. Tommy O'Boyle, the Head Talent Scout for Kansas City, and Hank Stram, were very convincing. I chose Kansas City and was a rookie there in 1967.

Super Bowl IV
The year before I joined them, the Chiefs played Super Bowl I against the Packers and lost 35-10, although it was 14-10 at halftime. The Packers won pretty convincingly again in Super Bowl II against the Raiders. Super Bowl III, is one of the most famous of all time. That's when the Jets of the AFL beat Baltimore 16-7. Our Super Bowl game, Super Bowl IV, was the last game played between the two leagues before the merger. The Vikings were 13- or 14-point underdogs, and we ended up winning 23-7. It was a huge deal for us.

I get asked, "Was the Super Bowl a big deal?" Forty-three years ago we thought it was. It's not like it is now, but still, at that time, it was becoming the biggest sporting event in America. We thought it was huge. It was a really big deal then, too.

During that season, our great quarterback, Lennie Dawson, was hurt in the first or second game. Our back up was Jacky Lee. He got hurt after a few series and our third string quarterback, Mike Livingston, came in. We won six games in a row with him as the quarterback.

The game has changed a little bit. It doesn't seem like you can win now if you only run the football. We mainly ran the ball and had a great defensive team. We won a lot of low-scoring games. Jerrel Wilson was a great, great punter for us, and I was known as a pretty good kicker in those days. We won six games without our number one or two quarterback.

The only thing I thought about the Super Bowl, was please, let us win. I don't care how I do personally, as long as we win. There's nothing worse than to lose the Super Bowl.

There was a guy on the sideline who was a friend of Hank Stram. This guy kept asking me if he had my warm-up jacket. It was a cold, blustery day in New Orleans. It's hard to believe, but I had mud cleats on for that game because the tarp had leaked in several places. This is the Super Bowl. It had rained the night before. Anyway, this guy on the sidelines kept telling me to get my warm-up jacket. Finally, I realized he was Pat O'Brien. I said, "You've got to wait until the game is over. Don't disturb me in case I have to go in and do something again."

Were You Isolated From Team

I've been asked that so many times. Of course, keep in mind that forty-six years ago, we only had one practice field. There was no other field to go and kick. Jerrel Wilson and I would kick the ball across the end zone, back and forth at the beginning of practice. Then we'd go over and watch practice, and hold the bags and help out anyway we could. We even filled in on the punt team if they needed somebody to run or whatever. I tried to get involved as much as I could, although obviously, I could not play football at a professional level.

They had such a veteran team in Kansas City. I was accepted really well, I felt at the time. I didn't have any problems at all. They talk about how nobody speaks to the kicker. The veterans in Kansas City, I think, appreciated my talent when I got there. They made me feel welcome and appreciated from day one, so I had a good feeling the whole time I was there.

Longest Game In NFL History Christmas 1971

At the time, I was bitterly, bitterly disappointed because I let the team down, and I still feel that way. If I had a decent day, we would have won that game.

The strange thing is, those thoughts do not get better over the years. I see a young kid now miss an important kick in a big game—playoff game, Super Bowl. He doesn't know it yet, but he's going to take that to the grave with him. It really stays with you. Although I kicked I don't know how many field goals and game-winning kicks, the one that sticks out is the one that you miss. That is the one that bothers me a lot. I did not realize at the time that it would stay with me my whole life. It says with you because you are accountable, professional, and you're supposed to make kicks like that.

Arrowhead Stadium

The first five years that I was in Kansas City, we kicked in the old Municipal Stadium. In Arrowhead, the wind comes in and goes in every direction. It's certainly not like indoors, by any means. What they have improved on now, it seems like they take better care of the turf versus 30 or 40 years ago. When you see film from way back, there's a lot of mud. There wasn't much grass on the field. Today they do a lot better job with that. As far as the wind is concerned, on a windy day, Arrowhead can be tricky.

Green Bay Packers

I had my best years probably, during my early years and my late years. In Green Bay, I kicked over 90% one year, and it was difficult. You had to adjust, because the footing was bad, it was windy and cold, and the balls were lying on the sidelines in bags for three hours. At the end of the game, the balls didn't go very far. Now they have warm up mats and you warm the ball up and you do certain things. It was difficult, but I had good luck up there. Of course, the kicking has become so much better. In my years at Green Bay, I think I kicked over 80% the four seasons I was there. I wasn't even as talented as I was 15 years earlier.

They started to get special teams coaches. The most important thing, we got reps, a few reps in during the week. They started breaking in the punter as a holder. We didn't have a snapper yet, but I got more reps. That was the big thing for me.

Jersey Number Choice With Packers

Tony Canadeo, a great running back with the Packers in the '30s and '40s, used to wear number 3, but it was retired. I had to pick another number, and that was number 10. It seemed to be an okay number. Not having number 3 didn't bother me. I just respected that the number was retired on Tony Canadeo. Now my number in Kansas City is retired.

Bart Starr was fired after an eight and eight season. The new coach, Forrest Gregg, traded me to Minnesota, and number three was available there. So, I had number three for the last two years of my career.

Favorite Stadium
There's no question, about it. If you kick indoors where it's 68 degrees with no wind and perfect footing, every indoor stadium is the best place to kick.

Centers
In the early days, the best center was usually the one who was the backup center in training camp. He would be the last cut before the season, and I'd get told about a new center four or five days before the first game. That happened so many times while I was in the league. For a while, I had Bobby Bell as a center, and Bobby Bell could do anything. He is a Hall of Fame linebacker, he won the Outland Trophy at Minnesota University, and he was a quarterback in high school in Shelby, North Carolina. He was a good snapper.

Lenny Dawson was a great holder. Keep in mind he didn't really practice it. I broke in Bucky Scribner, Ray Stachowicz, and Greg Coleman, who were all punters.

I just underhanded the ball to the punters, over and over again, so they could practice catching the ball, spinning it if they needed to, and putting it down. They became very good, but Lenny with very little practice, had great hands, and he did that extremely well.

Coaches
I just loved Hank Stram. He gave me a lot of confidence. He came to the practice field and was kneeling down, holding the ball for me. He did this a couple of times a week there for a month before training camp. He wanted to find out if he could see something that he could

help me with. He was just terrific, plus he was such an optimistic, positive person. I enjoyed him a lot.

Of course, I had a lot of good coaches. Bart Starr—there's no better person that Bart Starr. He was fired in Green Bay, but you don't fire a person like Bart Starr. He had a pretty good season and did a pretty good job coaching up there. We went to the playoffs in the strike-shortened season in 1982. We were eight and eight in '83. If he had one more year to get the defense shored up a little bit, I think he could have done really well.

I did not play for Forrest Gregg. He's the one that traded me to Minnesota. Les Steckel was there the first year, and Les was ridiculed a lot. They found a way to make fun out of him a lot, but Les was okay.

Bud Grant was the most amazing coach. He didn't tolerate mistakes. He didn't say much, but when he spoke up everybody listened, I guarantee you that. He was an outstanding coach as well. I was very fortunate I had all good coaches.

They're all pretty darn good at that level. I think the coaches are, frankly, fairly equal on that level, and so are the players. It seems that some are better than others, but most of them do the same things. Most teams do the same things, so the difference between a bad and a good coach and a bad and a good player in the league is not very much.

Avoiding Injury
I remember early on they would send a guy right after you, because we kicked from the 40-yard line in our first few years. I would kick the ball out of the end zone most of the time. There were some times that somebody would come right after you, but I could run pretty fast. I was pretty quick on my feet, so I avoided that.

I did get hurt one time in Cleveland when I broke my sternum. It was on the kickoff after a safety. Our punter was hurt, so we had to kick off on the 20-yard line, and somebody had to hold the ball. Emmitt Thomas held the ball for me and I think it was Greg

Pruitt who ran it back. Somehow I was able to hang on till they could tackle him at midfield. That was the only time I really got hurt. I never had a pulled muscle. I obviously had the flu, colds, and things like that from time to time, but I never missed a game, so I'm fortunate that way.

Pro Football Hall Of Fame Induction
When I got to Montana State, I said, "You mean, you can get a scholarship for kicking the football?" Then they were talking about the pros. You're kicking the ball further than the people that you see on television. They told me you could actually get paid for kicking the football. I thought that was amazing. Then I got into the league, and they said, "You can get a pension if you play for five years."

When I got nominated in 1991, it was two or three weeks before the Super Bowl and I had been out of the league for five years. I got a registered letter from the Hall of Fame, and it said, "You're one of the 15 finalists. Let us know where you're going to be at such-and-such time the day before the Super Bowl." As far as I knew, no kicker ever, or a person that couldn't do anything else but kick, had ever been a finalist, so I didn't know what to think of it.

I was surprised because that wasn't something that had really come up. I had heard television announcers saying during my 17th, 18th, and 19th years, future Hall of Famer. I thought, well, that's stretching it a little bit.

Anyway, I got in the first year. Nobody had been in that position before, so I didn't give it that much thought. I really didn't. It was a very exciting, very pleasant, surprise. I feel as lucky as anybody can be.

I know that Ray Guy has been a finalist many times. Let's face it, there aren't going to be too many kickers in the Hall of Fame. You can see that now. I could have guessed that, years ago. I guess I'm the only kicker in the Hall of Fame, but I thought that Morten Andersen would get in this year. When I got in, I had the most field goals in history of the league. I think I was All-Pro from various papers or whatever seven times. Morten has the same credentials, except he is also the leading scorer all time. I was the second leading scorer. I never caught George Blanda. The amount of Pro Bowls we made is similar. I know he is disappointed not getting in. I think he will get in. I think he deserves to get in.

You feel like you don't deserve to be there when you see all the names and all the people you read about. Other Hall of Famers will even tell you that they don't feel like they belong there. You feel very humble and very appreciative, but you wonder if it's really true.

I didn't go back for 10 years. I didn't really see the point in going but then they had a 10th reunion. It's almost like you go there to get applause. I enjoyed the 10th reunion very much. Now, they try to bring most people back every year. It's very special.

Looking back to 1991, when I was nominated, I thought a lot about my career and the people involved. My professional teammates, my teammates in college, and my coach in college, Jim Sweeney, all gave me the opportunity.

It's a fairy tale story in some ways, and it's funny how it works out at times. I'm very appreciative of the way it worked out for me.

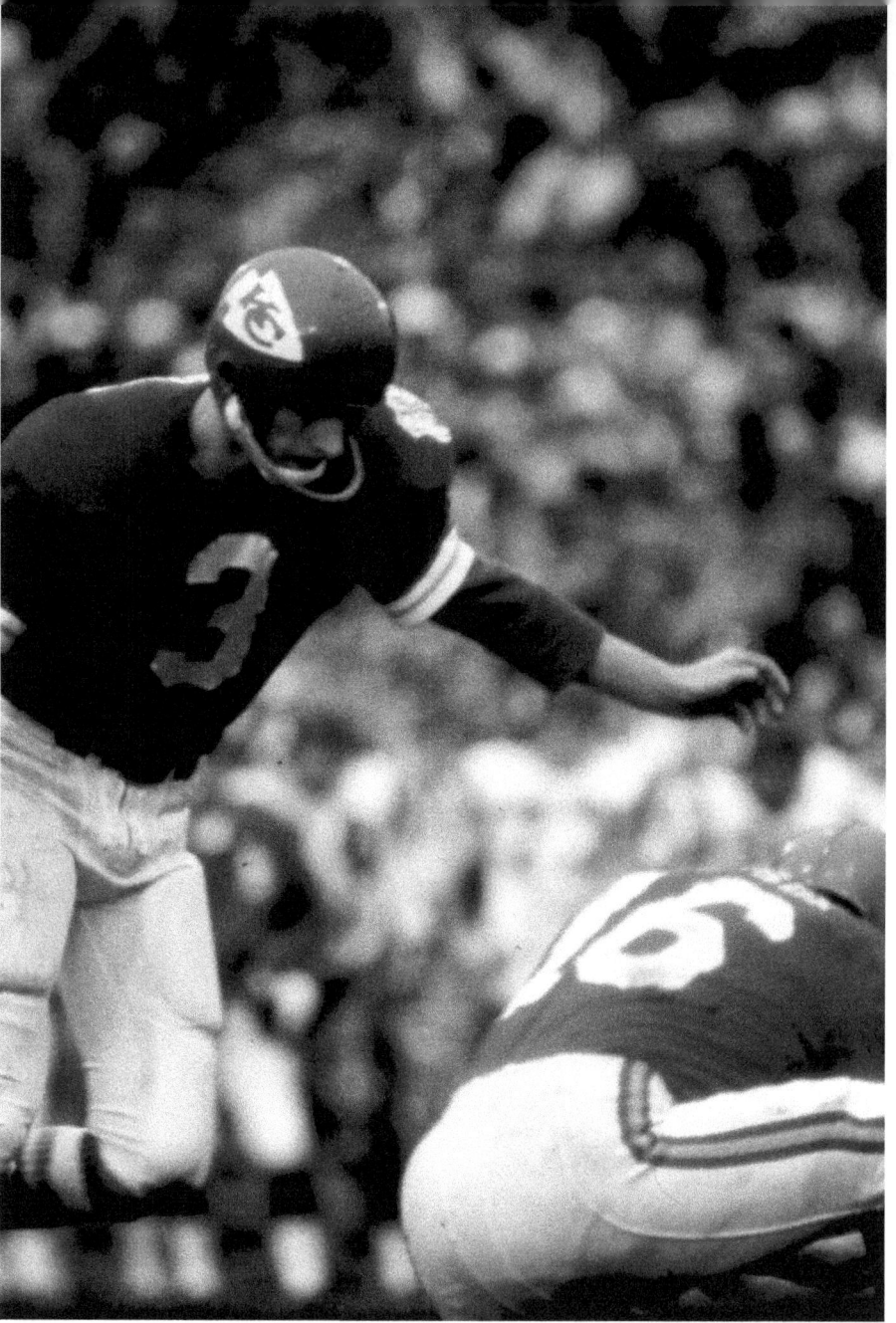

Photograph courtesy Associated Press

Chapter 25

Paul Warfield

College:
Ohio State

Career History:
Cleveland Browns (1964–1969)
Miami Dolphins (1970–1974)
Memphis Southmen WFL (1975)
Cleveland Browns (1976–1977)

1983 Inductee Pro Football Hall of Fame

College Choice
I was recruited on a national scale as a youngster coming out of Warren, Ohio. Coming out of high school, as far as I was concerned, Ohio State was what I was looking for. The Buckeyes had tremendous interest in me, but there were a number of other schools in the Big Ten that were vying for me, as well as other schools from around the country. I narrowed it down to two schools in Big Ten Conference, the University of Iowa and Ohio State.

The University of Michigan had a representative that talked to me via telephone, as did Michigan State. I probably had a little bit greater interest in Michigan State than the University of Michigan, because of Clarence Peaks, a former star player I saw on television. He immediately caught my eye on a Saturday afternoon ballgame that was nationally televised. It seemed like Michigan State was a school that generated a tremendous amount of excitement. Ohio State and Iowa were the two schools in the Big Ten that were of greatest interest to me.

<u>Style Of Football In Early '60s</u>

The style of football that was played in those years was a little bit different. Run-oriented offenses were very tight and compact with no wide receiver spread out. As a matter of fact, the position was called end, e-n-d, instead of wide receiver in those years. It was really part of the old, what one would call, smash-mouth football tradition.

There was no substitution in the era I played. It's really kind of interesting because colleges and universities during that period were more interested in the collegiate football program being a part of the educational process. I don't mean to demean colleges and universities today. It was a point of focus that there were limited substitution rules which meant that everyone played with the exception maybe of two players. Usually those players were the quarterback and maybe one other player when the ball exchanged hands. Everyone had to play both offense and defense. If you're an offensive player, you were automatically a defensive player at the same position pretty much. It was considered part of the educational experience. The biggest difference in college football in those days was you would find several different offensive philosophies within a conference or around the conferences.

Some teams played what they called T formation football where you had four backs in the backfield—quarterback, fullback, left, and right halfback. That was what was utilized at Ohio State. The University of Iowa had an offensive philosophy that was called the Wing-T. There would only be two backs in a line behind quarterback and another back called a wingback would be set off to a side right outside the in position, which would be the equivalent of a tight end position today. Then there was an option football running attack. You had all these varied styles of play. Today when one looks at college football, it resembles the professionals for the most part with the exception of maybe one or two adaptations. Everyone in college football is throwing the football as they do in the NFL. In those days, it was quite the opposite.

From the collegiate standpoint, it was not necessary that their game looked exactly like the professional game. They were more interested in the educational experience of learning how to really play football both offensively and defensively, learning how to tackle, learning how to block, and learning how to incorporate these. Collegiate football was considered to be a part of the educational experience. Today, it appears that collegiate football is a breeding ground, to an extent, for the National Football League.

In the years that I was in school from 1960 to 1964, athletic eligibility did not start for student athletes until their sophomore year. Freshmen athletes were ineligible to play their first year because major colleges and universities wanted youngsters to feel a level of confidence in transitioning from high school to college, and academics were placed ahead of that.

I was a defensive back and was considered to be a quarterback, as a matter of fact, when the Cleveland Browns first drafted me. They drafted me with the thought that I was going to be a quarterback instead of a wide receiver.

Position Change To Wide Receiver In NFL
Thankfully, after seeing me do a few things at the first minicamp as both a defensive back and a wide receiver, Coach Blanton Collier changed his mind and said, "We're going to make you a wide receiver instead of a defensive back." Originally, I was drafted as a quarterback.

Woody Hayes
Woody Hayes was one of the great football coaches in college. He was a man who was very, very insistent that Ohio State have teams that were so highly disciplined, that they would not make errors in any given situation. This would tend to allow players to operate at maximum efficiency and make few errors. He was a disciplinarian who demanded a lot of his players. All of us revered and respected him because we understood that he would do any and everything for his players and gave his great support as far as academics were concerned. We all revered the late Coach Hayes.

Draft

I hoped that I would be drafted as high as possible and close to the first round. It's kind of an interesting story because I came out during a period in which there were two separate leagues. The AFL was a rival of the NFL. The Buffalo Bills, of the American Football League, approached me the summer before I returned to Ohio State for my final year of playing football there and my final year in school. Their general manager had spoken to me and told me to complete my final season of football at Ohio State. He said the Buffalo Bills wanted to draft me in the first round, but were concerned because they understood that I was interested in the possibility of playing professional baseball. They were trying to ascertain as early as the summer of 1963, if I was going to play football professionally or baseball because they did not want to, as I was told, waste a first round draft choice on me.

Jim Brown

Jim Brown is the greatest running back who ever played in the National Football League. Yes, I had the experience of playing with Jim Brown for two seasons, my rookie year in 1964, and in 1965. Although I didn't play much my second year because of injury, I was still in all of the meetings and was in his presence certainly during the 1965 season. I was finally able to play late in the year. I played in the NFL championship game against the Green Bay Packers that year.

Rookie Year With Cleveland Browns

I was very fortunate to lead them in receptions my rookie year. I played on the other side of another receiver by the name of Gary Collins. I've said this time and time again, and I'll say it here and now, in my mind, he is the best red zone receiver that I have ever seen. He was phenomenal inside the 20-yard line, a phenomenal receiver and a big receiver. He was one of the first big receivers at 6'4", and 225. Inside the red zone area, he was just unbelievable in terms of his capacity to score. He beat some of the top defensive backs time and time again, including guys who are in the Pro Football Hall of Fame. That combined with playing with pro football's greatest runner, Jim Brown, it was a great opportunity for me coming in to find some area of success. When you have that kind of supporting cast, people don't pay a great deal of attention to the newly arrived player.

Additionally, I want to add that once the Cleveland Browns made the decision that I was going to be a pass receiver, they really did a wonderful thing for me. They asked Ray Renfro, a former player of theirs who had just retired, to come in and be my private tutor. During four weeks of training camp, he worked solely with me on a daily basis. I benefited from Ray Renfro's instructions because he shared his twelve years of experience with me. We walked through them step-by-step. He taught me pattern execution.

As a first year player, I executed like an experienced veteran because of the expertise passed on to me. It helped me out immensely. My transition was smooth thanks to the coach, the Browns staff, working with veteran passer Frank, and my coming in and playing with other talented players. Frank Ryan understood the offense philosophy of the Browns.

Cleveland Browns Offense
I played with a team that emphasized running the football for the most part. When you have Jim Brown in the backfield, you're not going to be throwing the ball all over the lot. With the kind of ability that he had, he's going to be the main emphasis of the offensive strategy and rightfully so. After Jim Brown's departure, Leroy Kelly, who was drafted along with me, became one of the top backs in pro football along with Gale Sayers. The emphasis was still on running the football. After being traded down to the Miami Dolphins, I was playing with a team that emphasized the run even more. As Napoleon said, "Ability is of little account without opportunity."

Trade To Miami Dolphins
The trade to the Miami Dolphins was a nice surprise. I was in my sixth year in the NFL and things were going well. It was something that was unexpected. When I received a telephone call from the owner, Art Modell, informing me that the team had made the decision to trade me for the Miami Dolphins' number one pick which was the third pick overall in the 1970 draft, I was

206

disappointed. I was leaving an organization that was a perennial title contender and now Super Bowl contender. The Super Bowl was just in its third year. The Browns were eliminated in 1968 and 1969, by teams that represented the NFL in the Super Bowl. One team was the Baltimore Colts and the other was the Minnesota Vikings. Had we won those ballgames, we would have been in the Super Bowl. I was leaving an established title contending team to go to an expansion team out of the old American Football League. That team had never won more than five games in any season in its four years of existence.

First of all, I didn't want to be traded because I'm a native of Ohio. I grew up in a small town about 50 miles east of Cleveland. The Cleveland Browns were the team that I supported as a youngster. In my wildest dreams, I never thought I'd be with them, but if I was going to play pro football, that's the team I wanted to be with. It was one of pro football's elite teams. Even though they were a run-oriented team for the most part, I relished my role in which I could make a contribution here and there. I loved every facet of playing with the Browns. It just so happened that I got traded. Players didn't decide where they were going to play in those days. You couldn't demand to be traded to a team. Perhaps I could dream or wish that, but I had no control over that. Things worked out well in Miami for me. As I've always said about that trade, I didn't necessarily want to go, and I didn't know it was coming, but in the end, it turned out very well. Things changed overnight in Miami with Don Shula's emphasis, his input, and the willingness of those young players to want to be better. We went on to have as great a success as anybody has ever had in a few short years.

Don Shula
Don Shula came along 10 days after I was traded. I think it was a surprise when he resigned his position. It was his decision. As the story goes, he was approached by the Miami Dolphins, and given permission by Baltimore to talk to Miami. He subsequently signed a contract to coach the Dolphins.

Once he came onboard, I began to feel a little better. I knew of his excellence in the National Football League. Don Shula got the Baltimore Colts to the 1969 Super Bowl against the Jets.

Unfortunately, it didn't work out when they were upset by the Jets and Joe Namath.

Look at it from this perspective. He was going to a team that had never won more than five games in any of the four years that they had been in existence. They were an expansion team out of the old America Football League. Expansion teams were usually put together with castoffs or players who were considered to be on the downside of their careers from existing teams. The America Football League was not on par with the National Football League at that point. There were a couple of teams that you might say were, but basically as a league, it was considered to be slightly inferior to the National Football League. The makeup of the team, except for a few individuals, was basically players who weren't considered to be on par with the stronger league the National Football League. Don was coming into a situation in which, yes, there was a nucleus to build a winner, but the entire thing had to be built. There was no tradition of winning.

Sports Illustrated would do their yearly analysis of pro football teams just before the teams went to training camp. It's 1969, and I'm reading about all of the National Football League teams that I'm familiar with. Since I knew the leagues were going to merge the following year, I looked at the section on the AFL. I'm thumbing through to see what I can read about the AFL, and I come across, ironically, the Miami Dolphins. The headline of that section said, "The Worst Team In Pro Football." I didn't want to read that. I read about the Chiefs, Raiders, and Chargers who were good. Little did I know that seven to nine months later, I would be on "The Worst Team In Pro Football." Don Shula was taking on an enormous challenge going down there.

Monte Clark
Monte Clark, who was on Don Shula's staff, did a tremendous job. Monte Clark was my teammate in Cleveland in 1969. He retired and was looking for a coaching job. Don Shula brings in Monte Clark, who was highly recommended by Blanton Collier, a great coach who coached Monte and me in Cleveland. Monte Clark transformed Jim Langer, Bob Kuechenberg, and Wayne

Moore. He also helped develop Larry Little and Norm Evans. He made them one of the finest offensive lines in pro football.

Football Philosophy

I sincerely believe this: football is a team game, and the objective is to have monumental success and win. In Miami, we had a tremendous amount of success in a very short period of time. We had that because of the willingness of players who wanted to be better and the coming of a great young coach who fulfilled his destiny there. It was an organization that won with a philosophical concept which was a run-oriented, time-consuming, offensive attack that took tremendous amounts of time off the clock and with a defense that proved itself over and over again to be one of the best defenses during those championship years. It was a team effort, and we all benefited from it. We were all a part of the championship play whether you were the high guy on the totem pole or the low guy on the totem pole. In that short period of time, we accomplished something that no other team in the history of the game has done up until now, which is to go through an entire season undefeated, untied, and won a championship. Team play is what I learned from scholastic football to intercollegiate football and certainly in professional football. Play for great teams with great coaches and you win as a team. Individual accomplishments are something that you can be proud of, but basically the real thing you want to do is win championships and that's the most important thing.

Key To Success As Wide Receiver

Whether you're talking about today's game or yesterday's game, I think the ability of pass receivers to create separation for themselves from the individual who is defending them at breaking point, is in essence one asset that pass receivers must have. You can do it with quickness, explosiveness, speed, or if you're fortunate, you have all of those traits, or you can do it with a combination of things. The ability to separate at the instant when the ball is in the air, to create space between the receiver and the defender, is the pure essence of pass pattern running. From a philosophical standpoint, you can do it with technique. There are a number of techniques that I learned from the late Ray Renfro, but again, I must hone in on the fact that the ability to execute your pattern, to create space against the defender, is the key to getting open.

Toughest Cornerback

Early in my career, there was a little defender named Brady Keys, who played for the Pittsburgh Steelers. I thought he did a pretty good job on me. He created some problems for me whenever we played the Steelers. Later in my career, defenders began to get bigger and taller.

Mel Blount of the Steelers was 6'4". That's four inches taller than me. He had a long wingspan in terms of arm length, the ability, and the speed to run with me. Rarely, in the early years that I played, would you find a defender who had the height, the foot quickness, or the flexible hips that Mel Blount had. The same was true of Mike Haynes, who I faced in my final year or two. He was just coming in as a young cornerback and was approximately the same size as Mel Blount. He had the ability to turn, rotate his hips, and run with speed. They made it a little difficult, but at that point, I was trending down and going out of the league. Fortunately, I didn't have to face them on a game-by-game basis when I was in my prime.

Running Style

The uniqueness of my running style was that it appeared I was not exerting a lot of effort, but I was. It probably helped me deceive my defenders who were trying to determine exactly how fast I was going. It appeared to them that I was not running as fast as I was. It was more of a long gliding stride instead of quick acceleration. It was part of my style and deceptiveness, and it came naturally for me.

1972 Miami Dolphins Perfect Season

A few years ago, the Patriots almost had a perfect season. There were just one or two plays in the Giants game that kept them from equaling the mark. First of all, a lot has been made of when the mark will be broken. Teams play two more games now. The feat itself is undefeated, and so we were undefeated. You're going to have to say that the new team is the new and latest undefeated team, but they really don't break that mark. It was a wonderful season as I recall. The season happened primarily because, as I saw it, we were not trying to accomplish perfection.

It's something that I never thought would happen as far as I was concerned. My objective in playing football was to play Sunday-in and Sunday-out to the very best of my ability, to have a great experience in doing so, and help my team win football games.

I grew up as a youngster in Northeast Ohio watching Otto Graham and Marion Motley, who played alongside him, in the Cleveland backfield. The two of them are in the Pro Football Hall of Fame. You think of other great players like Jim Brown, who I've had the honor of playing with, or Johnny Unitas who played and was so brilliant.

I watched the 1958 Championship Game between the Giants & Colts in which the two-minute offense was invented. The events of that game were mindboggling. It was the first time sudden death was ever played. Maybe it's not akin to the first time that man walked on the moon, but it had never happened before because football games ended in a tie during that period. It's taken for granted today, but to see the mastery of Johnny Unitas in that game was unbelievable.

Then there was the million-dollar backfield with the San Francisco 49ers, Y. A. Tittle, Joe Perry, Hugh McElhenny, and John Henry Johnson. They were great, great players.

I never thought what I accomplished in pro football would lead me to be in that special place with the greatest players who have ever played. I was overwhelmed. When you are inducted, certain things come to mind. You think about how it happened, and take into consideration your support system. The people who helped you get a spot in the Pro Football Hall of Fame are your family, your coaches, and great teammates that you played with through the years. I think most of us want to acknowledge the great, great respect we have for those who helped us achieve our success and get there.

Years ago, I had the privilege of being with Brooks Robinson, the great third baseman for the Baltimore Orioles who is in the Baseball Hall Of Fame. We happened to have a conversation about the hall of fame. He agreed with me, saying that he just tried to be the best player he could be every time he stepped on a baseball field. We just try to play up to our expectations and our ability. We are overwhelmed. I think about the individuals who said I belong there with the greats who have played this game. I also remember the gentlemen who preceded me in the National Football League. I certainly was a great, great fan of those guys. I've had opportunities to be with Chuck Bednarik, who's a veteran of World War II and was a hero during the war. It's always an honor to be in his presence not only because of what he accomplished in the NFL, but also because of his service to the country during World War II. That was a period when there were a lot greater things at stake in terms of the freedoms of individuals and our nation along with its allies. I was just born right around that time. Things could have been vastly different if the United States and its allies had not been successful.

Hugh McElhenny was as fine as a runner as this league has ever seen. I remember him and his electrifying running skill when he was with the San Francisco 49ers. I was just a youngster. I had the pleasure of meeting him.

I had the pleasure of meeting Don Hutson at a past Hall of Fame session. In my opinion, he is certainly at the top of the list when you start talking about great receivers of an era. The things that he was able to accomplish in his era—it's just incredible.

Richard Nixon Calling Don Shula Before Super Bowl VI With A Play For Paul Warfield
President Nixon contacted Coach Shula and asked him call a quick slant pass to me. I've been a Democrat all of my life and he was a Republican president. It certainly makes one feel special when the President of the United States takes notice of what you do and sends a special note to your coach saying that you gotta do this.

Football Philosophy
I see a lot of things that are happening today. You know, I am an old school guy who obviously comes from another era. I just believe that you respect your opponents. You respect them for their toughness, for what they've accomplished, and you give

212

them the ultimate respect when you're playing on the field. I wanted to beat them as bad as the next guy and my whole focus and concentration was on doing that. I just don't think you do it on the sidelines with all this verbiage about what you're going to do and so forth. After all, you know you're talking about football and it is a team-oriented sport. I may personally feel that I am capable of doing a whole lot of things, but I've got to have people to help me accomplish those things. If you're playing an individual sport like tennis, golf, or something like that and you want to engage in a lot of verbiage, then you can back that up yourself. You can't account for the rest of your teammates. But, I believe in respect and competitiveness, and that's a part of all sports.

Photograph courtesy Associated Press

Chapter 26

Fred Biletnikoff

College:
Florida State

Career History:

As Player:
Oakland Raiders (1965–1978)
Montreal Alouettes (CFL) (1980)

As Coach:
Montreal Alouettes (1980)
Orange Glen High School (1982)
Palomar College (1983)
Diablo Valley College (1984)
Oakland Invaders (1985)
Arizona Wranglers (1986)
Calgary Stampeders (1987–88)
L.A./Oakland Raiders (1989–2006)

1988 Inductee Pro Football Hall of Fame

College Choice

Joe Paterno always told me he missed out on me. Ken Meyer, who was coaching at Florida State at that time, was from Erie, Pennsylvania. He had an aunt and uncle that lived in Erie, Pennsylvania. One of the coaches on my high school team, Ray Dombrowski was a good friend with Ken. Ray recommended me to Ken. Ken came out and watched me workout and that's how I went to Florida State.

Bobby Bowden

I always tell Bobby Bowden, he would never have become famous if he weren't my receiver coach. Bill Peterson was our Head Coach. We had a pretty good coaching staff at that time with a lot of pass-oriented type of guys in terms of philosophy. Those guys were used to throwing the football. They built up a pretty good core of guys to bring down there to play and do what they wanted to do as far as passing.

Bill was a good friend of Sid Gillman. Bill spent a lot of time in San Diego at training camp with Sid to get the passing game that he wanted. That's kind of how everything fell into place there.

Florida State
My first two years at Florida State, if you were a receiver away from the call, you lined up like a tight end. We ran a tight formation with one wide receiver split out wide and the other wide receiver lined up tight all the time. Those were pretty interesting camps that I had to go through because I had to do all the blocking drills, along with the wide receiver drills. I got beat up pretty good. It made me a lot tougher, though.

Draft
When I made the move from Erie down to Tallahassee, at that time, it was a big move for somebody to go that far away to school. At the end of my four years at Florida State, I was drafted by Detroit and the Raiders. I really hadn't made up my mind that I was going out to Oakland to play for Al Davis. It was a really hard decision for me. I wanted to get away from the cold and snow and go out to California, which I had the opportunity to do. I just figured I'd take a shot and sign with Oakland and go out there. The AFL was going to throw the ball a lot, which was right down my alley. My last two years at Florida State we threw the ball quite a bit. That's the thing that really put it over the top for me as far as signing with the Raiders, and of course, Al Davis's influence, too. That's basically how I made up my mind. There wasn't any hesitation on my part.

Al Davis just gave you a contract and the money was already on there. He had already signed it so he just expected you to put your name on it.

At that time Joe Namath had gotten a big contract. Harry Schuh, who was drafted ahead of me in the first round by the Raiders, also made pretty good money.

I got a decent contract at that time. It was a good enough contract that when I got to camp, all the veterans on the Raiders were mad at Harry Schuh and me because we were making so much money. We still had to go get our offseason jobs. It wasn't that much but we went through that period of time, even in 1965, where we were making a lot of money. It really made a lot of veterans mad.

There was no negotiation. At that time, everybody was given a two- or three-year contract guaranteeing the first two years and the bonus money that ran for each year of the contract. In my third year, I had bonus money but no contract. It worked out well for me.

Oakland Raiders Quarterbacks
I started with Tom Flores, Cotton Davidson, and Dick Wood who would later play for the Jets, as the quarterbacks. Cotton actually played on the Baltimore Colts with Johnny Unitas and Raymond Berry for a brief period of time. Flores was the starter. In later seasons, Al Davis brought in Daryle Lamonica, George Blanda, and Ken Stabler.

I had a chance to play with all four of them. Obviously Lamonica, Blanda, and Stabler were the main guys I played with. I played with Flores for a couple of years. All four of those guys could really throw the football, along with Cotton Davidson and Dick Wood.

With Flores, I was just a young kid and I didn't really help him out. It was hit and miss with me when Tom threw me the ball. Everything turned around for me when they brought Lamonica in and we were throwing the ball more down the field, along with Blanda. Blanda had come from Houston, where they threw the ball 40 to 50 times a game. I had a good rapport with Lamonica, Blanda, and Kenny because we spent a lot of time on the field throwing passes, running routes, and that type of thing.

The quarterbacks were used to seeing what all the receivers did because everybody worked together. You weren't just working with Lamonica; you were working with Blanda too. Later on when Kenny came and Lamonica left, it was Blanda and Kenny. You spent so much time working with those guys on the field in practice, training camp, and during the season that the quarterbacks knew how all the receivers ran routes and what they did. It was a comfortable situation with all of the quarterbacks that I played with.

Adjusting To NFL

When I was a rookie in my very first preseason game I was playing behind Art Powell and Bo Roberson at that time, two outstanding receivers. In the preseason, I wasn't doing very well and was dropping balls. Al Davis probably wondered why he drafted me. I struggled during my first year. Then he traded Bo Roberson away allowing me to be the starter across from Art Powell. The following season, I torn my knee up, so that wasn't very good as far as Al was concerned.

When Al let Claude Gibson go that opened up number 25 for me, so I was able to get my college number. Previously Dick Romanski, our equipment guy, gave me the number 14 and it was probably the worst jinx number I've ever had in my life. When I got the number 25 everything started going better for me.

Super Bowl XI

Super Bowl XI, for me, was something that we had been, to use the term "knocking on the door," every year. In previous years we were losing close championship games where we had an opportunity to get to Super Bowls.

It was almost like we were jinxed. Something always happened, like in Pittsburgh or wherever it may be, that just prevented us from getting to the Super Bowl. When we finally got there, we were a well-seasoned team. We were all veterans at the time. A lot of us were basically at the end or toward the end of our careers. The whole group that we had at that time grew together for a good period of time. We had a lot of veterans that had a lot of experience.

We were always a pretty confident team as far as knowing what we could do with the players that we had because we had a tremendous amount of great players on the offense, defense, and special teams. It was an unbelievable roster that we had at that time.

Super Bowl XI was played in Pasadena and we had over 100,000 spectators. We beat Minnesota. It was pretty awesome. It was really good.

I had a lot of sentiment after we beat Minnesota. I thought about all those guys that I played with when I was young who were playing football in the AFL. I thought about the guys who didn't have the opportunity to go to and win a Super Bowl.

That crossed my mind a lot because I had a lot of close ties with those guys. They brought me up with very good guidance as far as being able to play tough, being a tough guy out there, having a good work ethic, seeing what those guys did and how they worked, and what it took to be a professional football player. We had a lot of veterans on the team when I was a young kid first coming to the Raiders.

Jack Tatum & George Atkinson
I figured I'd have it easy the rest of my career if I could deal with Jack Tatum, George Atkinson, and Willie Brown in practice. We went through a lot of live practices and got hit by those guys. We were able to avoid them at times too. That whole group of guys was a big plus for us. Those guys have always been looked at as the best defensive backs that played in professional football.

Turning Point In NFL Career
After I came back from an injury early in my career, things started to fall into place. I learned that this is a game where if you get hurt and can't make it back on the field, you weren't going to play. You had to have that type of attitude.

After the injury, I really understood that basically football was a business now, not like the football that I had played as a kid in my backyard in Erie, Pennsylvania. I enjoyed playing it there but now I was in a business that if I wanted to survive, I really had to go at it, work at it, and be professional at it.

It was probably in my third year with the Raiders that I finally started coming around as a receiver. I felt that I could compete with the guys we had on our team at the receiver position and against the guys we were going to play to against.

John Madden
John Madden was pretty active, a great coach, and a great motivator. The one great thing about John is that he knew each player individually. He knew how to handle them individually. Even though he had a whole slew of players that he had to handle, he knew everything about the players on his team. He handled you accordingly. If you needed to be reprimanded about something he did it.

There were times when he was not easy on you because he wanted to make sure you were competing. John was really unique in being able to handle that many guys in that manner and really, really understand what he had as a team and what he had to do as a head coach.

John was a tough guy to play for but he was a fair guy to play for. You went out there, practiced hard, played hard in games, and spent time working on whatever position you were playing. John appreciated that. John had the greatest appreciation for the work every individual on the team did as far as the position they were playing. John was a terrific guy to play for.

Toughest Defensive Backs
Herb Adderley was tough because we didn't play against him very often, and he was a really aggressive guy. Jimmy Johnson over at San Francisco was a very good player because he was tall and rangy. During that time, there were basically no rules. Those guys came up and played bump and run on you.

You were getting hit all the time. It was a physical game and you had to learn how to be physical. You also had to learn how to handle the different styles of the guys that you were playing against because they were all different sizes, had different speeds, and had different quickness levels. You had to understand whom you were playing against.

Jimmy Marsalis was a tough guy in Kansas City. Bobby Howard was a good player down in San Diego. There were a lot of good players in the league that you played against when they played bump and run. It was just a physical game. You just had to learn that you just couldn't let somebody get out there and dominate you. You just had to keep fighting.

Al Davis
Willie Brown and I were both fortunate because we spent our entire coaching careers with the Raiders. It was fortunate for us because we didn't have to move all over getting jobs with other teams, like a lot of coaches did. Al Davis had a philosophy about how he liked his receivers to play. I knew what he wanted and what needed to be done with the receivers.

Al had a philosophy about defensive backs, how they should play, and Willie was the example, like I was the example with the receivers. Al wanted to keep that consistency because defensive backs and wide receivers were a big priority on our team. He wanted consistency so he kept Willie and I as coaches, fortunately for us, all of those years.

Pro Football Hall Of Fame Induction
You really didn't know how you got there and what the procedure was for getting in. The writers in your area were basically the ones that promoted you to the rest of the committee to be inducted into the Hall of Fame. You had to depend on the writers in your area promoting you. When that happened with me, I was like, "Oh, wow!"

When you finally go there for the ceremony, it's a whole different perspective, a whole different outlook, and a whole different feeling than when you first found out you're going into the Hall of Fame. When you're actually there with all of the guys already in the Hall of Fame, guys who played for Cleveland, the Eagles, and Pittsburgh years ago when I was a kid, and have the chance to be around them in person and be in the Hall of Fame with them, it seemed unbelievable.

It's not a very big group but that's the great thing about it, being part of a small, unique group of guys. I've always felt that the recognition you get from being in the Hall of Fame is not enough. After being in the Hall of Fame for a number of years and getting to see a lot of the things going on, being in the Hall of Fame isn't recognized enough for what that group means to professional football.

Tommy McDonald

I followed Tommy McDonald of the Eagles. He was my guy. Tommy McDonald still doesn't believe me. I told him, "When I went to Florida State, I got number 25 because you were my hero. I loved watching you play. That's why I got number 25." He didn't believe me. He still hasn't sent me a signed jersey either.

Chuck Bednarik

I'll tell you why Chuck Bednarik was my all-time guy. I call him an all-time guy; I'm one of them now, because those guys have a history of toughness when they played in the league years ago. They played during a time when it was physical and tough. You were getting hit and all type of stuff but man, those guys played tough. That was a rough and tumble group of guys. They were tough.

Favorite Play

We played Miami in a playoff game in Oakland. I had one catch down in the corner of the end zone, right by the goal line, against Tim Foley. To me, that was a pretty good catch. I don't say that too often about myself, but when I see that video every once in a while or see a picture of it, that's a hell of a catch.

Football Philosophy

When you have to pay bills and child support you find ways to get down the field pretty quick. Deception is a word everybody else uses. I've always thought, hey, I'm fighting for my life out here. I better get going right now. There were times you look at yourself on film and see yourself moving a little faster than you think you could move and I think it's just the fact of you having that competitor's spirit. Every athlete has a gift; some of us just don't have all the gifts. At times we're able do something exciting or something good, and we can definitely be proud of ourselves. Playing football all those years, there were times when I looked at film, and I thought, "Oh, I'm not that slow." Other times I looked at myself and said,

"Oh, you are slow." It juggled back and forth quite a bit during my career.

Fred Biletnikoff, left, and quarterback Ken Stabler
Photograph courtesy Associated Press

Chapter 27

Gale Sayers

College:
Kansas

Career History:
Chicago Bears (1965–1971)

1977 Inductee Pro Football Hall of Fame

College Choice

In my senior year at Omaha Central High School, my football coach wanted me to go to the University of Iowa. He graduated from the University of Iowa and came back to Omaha Central High as a high school coach. I believed in everything he said. If he said go to Iowa, I was going.

I went on a three-day visit to the University of Iowa. Jerry Burns was the coach at that time. He was looking for a kid named Henry Carr who was a world-class sprinter. The only bad thing about that was he didn't have the grades to get into the University of Iowa.

I was there for three days and Jerry Burns didn't see me one time because he was after Henry Carr. So I thought, there isn't any way I'm going here if Jerry can't at least take time and say how are you doing and shake my hand. If he would have just shook my hand, I was going there. It was automatic since my high school coach told me to go there.

I went to the University of Kansas and talked to the coach, Jack Mitchell, who I liked. He was a great coach and he told me, "Gale, I want you to see a man in Kansas City." So we drove down to Kansas City and saw a man named Ray Evans. He was a good football coach, and was an All-American. He said, "Gale, if you get your degree, I can promise you that we can get you a job after you get your degree."

No other person ever said anything about me getting a degree. I got my degree and didn't have to go to see Ray anymore because I was playing football. That really made me like the University of Kansas, because they were concerned about me after football, not just playing it for them.

Dick Butkus

The first time I ever met Dick Butkus we were both at an All-American game in New York. We talked about the Bears, and I told him, "I think I'm going to sign with the Chicago Bears." He said, "Well, Buffalo is looking at me out of the AFL. I'm going to take little bit more time and see what they've got to offer. Finally he came to the Bears.

I had never heard of Dick Butkus in my life. He had gone to the University of Illinois, but after a half an hour I knew why the Bears drafted him. He was a killer. He was hitting me as hard in scrimmage as anybody had in a game. He came to play the game. I came to play the game too. It didn't make any difference whether he hit me hard or not; I was still going to go get him. He was a great, great football player in the NFL.

Brian Piccolo

Brian always had a joke. He just was a guy who laughed all the time and a good football player. When he came out of Wake Forest, people thought that he wasn't big enough or fast enough and the Bears took a chance on him. He became one hell of a football player. He was fun guy to be around. After about two and a half years, he came down with a cough, and he went in to see what was going on and they found he had cancer. It was just one of those things that happened. It's too bad because he was a good football player.

The movie was 100% accurate. Joy Piccolo and I spent about two months with James Caan and Billy Dee Williams going over mannerisms of Brian and me and they did an outstanding job. Jack Warden was in the movie too. It was a great time doing it. Before they put it on TV they had all the players, their wives, and coaches' wives come to Halas Hall and watch the movie. We saw the movie before anybody else saw the movie. There wasn't a dry eye in the house.

The players enjoyed Billy Dee and the other film people coming out to training camp to film the movie. They did a real good job.

Billy Dee was a nice guy. I really liked him. The only bad thing was we had to put a lot of padding around Billy Dee to make him look bigger, because he weighed about 145 pounds. He was a small individual. He did a nice job.

Barry Sanders
I think Barry Sanders was the only person who could run like me. He had the moves, like I had the moves, and he did all that playing for the Detroit Lions. Now he's in the Hall of Fame. He was a great, great football player. He had a chance to break the rushing record but he decided to quit. He wasn't injured. I asked him several times, "Barry, why are you quitting?" He said, "I don't want to play football anymore." He wasn't concerned about the records or anything. If he played two more years, he would have set all kinds of records.

NFL Career
When I played the game, I ran back punt returns, kickoff returns, and played running back. Many times when we'd go out there for the start of the first quarter after I had run back a kickoff return for maybe 30 yards or so, I'd come back into the huddle and carry the ball for the first four plays. I had to be in shape. No question about it. I had to be in shape. I did it in high school and I did it in college. It didn't bother me if I was going to run a punt return back or a kickoff back at the beginning of the game. I knew I had to be in shape and I got myself in shape.

I think Jim Brown's the best. O.J. Simpson is in that category too, among the best. Me playing in only 68 games, I'm happy to be a part of the top 10.

Jim Brown's Advice
I did not have a TV growing up. Very seldom did I watch the

pros play on TV. I had a chance to meet Jim Brown one time when I was a senior at Kansas and he said, "Gale, I heard you are a pretty good football player. Make sure when you come to training camp, you come in shape. That's where you are going to make the team, in training camp. You're not going to make it playing exhibition games. They want to see what you do in training camp blocking, catching balls, and things like that."

I took that advice and it probably made me a better football player.

College All-Star Game
I got injured playing in the College All-Star Game. Otto Graham was the coach of the college all-stars at that time and I told him I hurt my knee. He said, "I don't think you hurt your knee. I'm going to sit you out and I'm not going to let you play in this ballgame because I don't think you hurt your knee." I said, "Okay, fine."

After the ballgame, I got in my car and drove down to Wesleyan, Indiana, and I went in to talk to Coach Halas. Coach Halas said, "Gale, I know you had some problems with Coach Graham. I'm going to judge you by what you do today at the game and that's it. I'm not even going to talk to you about what happened to you at the All-Star game. I'm going to just judge you by what you do on the field."

Rookie Year
We had some decent running backs, but none of them were as quick as I was, as fast as I was; couldn't catch the ball like I could catch it, and couldn't make moves like I could. I knew that if George Halas gave me a shot, I would be a starting running back. I knew it. I felt it. I could see in practice there's no way these people can beat me running and things like that.

George Halas would always go out onto the field before the game. He would come back into the locker room, and name the names of who was going to play. The third ballgame of the season up in Green Bay, he calls out the names of the tackles and guards and I was the last one to be called. "Sayers, you are going to start today." I was nervous but it worked out okay. They beat us but I scored on a

65-yard touchdown run and caught a couple of passes. When Green Bay came back to Chicago, we beat them.

Photograph courtesy Associated Press

Chapter 28

Tom Mack

College:
Michigan

Career History
Los Angeles Rams (1966-1978)

1999 Inductee Pro Football Hall of Fame

Michigan
In the early '60s we went from last place to winning the Big Ten and going to the Rose Bowl during my junior year. We won the Rose Bowl beating Oregon State.

Back in my day, we had a very strong and consistent running game. Although I played tackle, I was probably as fast as any lineman around there. Over the years, Michigan seemed to be able to recruit good linemen who were big but also very agile, and I would attribute most of that to the running game. Certainly Bo Schembechler, after Bump Elliott, had a very strong running game too.

Bump Elliott
Probably one of the classiest people both on and off the field I have ever run into. He was really a true gentleman, as was his brother, who ended up being the director of the Pro Football Hall of Fame in later years. The two of them had played at Michigan in the late '40s on championship teams. They were just really, really classy people.

College Choice
I guess it's sufficed to say that I wasn't exactly a star high school athlete. Interestingly enough, probably my best sport was

swimming, not football. I had a chance to go to a number of schools on a swimming scholarship.

My swim coach had been to Michigan a lot and he got hold of some local alumni recruiters. He really helped sell Michigan on the idea that I was going to mature later in life rather than earlier in life. Between the time I went to college and I ended up getting out of school, I gained about 50 pounds of real good weight and I still had all the speed. So, they were right about me maturing late so to speak.

Rose Bowl

At that time when you grew up in the Midwest the family kind of sat around on New Year's Day and there were three or four games you watched. The biggest of them all was the Rose Bowl. I can remember watching Minnesota, Wisconsin, and different teams. When I got to play in the Rose Bowl it turned out to be a bigger deal than I probably realized.

Maybe the most interesting thing is I met a girl on a blind date in Pasadena while we were there. Forty-seven years later she is still my wife. So it was pretty eventful.

She was a young lady who had gone to Cal, was transferring to UCLA, and was putting herself through junior college at Pasadena City College at that time. I honestly met her on a blind date.

Draft

The last year there were two leagues in the AFL and NFL was 1966. They actually competed vigorously against each other. In fact, Miami, which was a new team in the AFL, actually went to my parents' house and tried to convince them to get me to sign with the AFL instead of the NFL.

I had a bunch of people following me around trying to get me to go with them. It was pretty obvious that I was going to get drafted fairly high.

The Los Angeles Rams, partly because of the fact that I had this girlfriend in California, turned out to be the perfect team for me. It was coincidental that the Rams were in last placed in the NFL at that point, so they had the first pick. I was obviously pretty lucky to be in that position. I think the most interesting thing was I was not an All-American. I made the second team, All-American. That was as close as I got to any kind of notoriety, so it really was a big surprise when people heard my name. They were all looking around "Who the hell is he?"

That year Mike Garrett won the Heisman Trophy, the first in a long line of USC backs who have won the Heisman. I have a headline in an old scrapbook. It says Rams draft Mike Garrett and in the second round, a guy named Mack and then it goes "Who" with a question mark. That's an interesting article because nobody knows who the hell I am and it says he better turn out to be good. So, I am glad it turned out both for them and for me.

First Training Camp
It was fairly brutal. Coincidentally, George Allen became the Head Coach after I got drafted but before training camp. He publicly made it clear that he wasn't going to put up with a lot of rookies and he went out and started acquiring veterans. Bill George, a linebacker for the Chicago Bears and Coach Allen talked to him into coming to the Rams. It was just absolutely fascinating. He had all kinds of old players. At the beginning of the year, even though we had probably 10 or 12 guys who had been draft choices and all of us had gotten some kind of guaranteed money, only four of us started the season on the actual roster. By the end of the season I was the only rookie who was actually still on the team and playing.

Well, timing is everything. You've got to be in the right place at the right time. It was interesting because a group of Rams offensive linemen kind of begrudgingly adopted me about a third of the way through the season. I ended up playing with three of those guys for another nine years or so. We became a pretty close group of guys, the four of us.

Fearsome Foursome
Rosey Grier was the guy I practiced against on a daily basis, so that was interesting by itself. Deacon Jones would be on the

other side with Merlin Olsen. Lamar Lundy was the defensive end next to Rosey Grier, who played tackle. That was the original fearsome foursome. That kind of got supplemented over the next few years.

Rosey retired after he tore his Achilles tendon and Roger Brown played for a couple of years. Then Coach Allen started to move people around and it changed the complexion a little bit. The whole time I played, we had very, very good defensive lines.

Head Slap

Nobody tells you exactly how to protect yourself against the head slap. I got slapped more than a few times. When I asked the coach how to protect myself, he told me to put my arm up with my hand high at kind of an angle. He said, "When Deacon tries to slap you, it will slip up over the top of your helmet." So, I tried that. In practice one day, I put my right hand up and sure enough Deacon did not slap me on that side, he slapped on the other side of the head. So I tried putting both hands up and then he used a whip maneuver and came up underneath my arm and took me up into the air and we ran in and jumped on the quarterback. That didn't work very well. Over the years you find out that the best way to prevent a head slap, when it was legal, was to let the guy slap you in the head and while he is slapping you in the head, he is wide open to a hell of a punch in the ribs if you know what you are doing. So you just punched him in the rib as hard as you can and pretty soon he will stop slapping you in the head.

George Allen

George Allen really did serve us well in terms of going out and get a veteran player that could help us. He picked up Maxie Baughan, Myron Pottios from the Steelers, Richie Petitbon from the Bears, Irv Cross from Philadelphia, and got Jack Pardee to come out of retirement. He was an amazing guy. What he did was find veteran players who were playing on bad teams but were still intense people. He would get them to come to the Rams, employ them in our mix, and develop good teams. He is an interesting guy. He was hard to work for because he was primarily interested in defense.

He really did not care what the offense did as long as we did not turn over the ball, which sounds kind of silly. The offense had two jobs, one was to hang on to the ball and not turn it over and the second was that we were supposed to use forty minutes out of the clock in any game playing keep-away from the other team. The reason being that if they didn't have the ball, they couldn't score. As long as we had the ball, whether we scored or not, we were keeping it away from them. He would depend on one or two big plays. Either we would get an interception or we get a touchdown after we worked our way down the field. He was an interesting guy.

One of the George's grandkids is named after Deacon Jones. George was very good with Deacon and Deacon responded by becoming not just a good player, but a great player. Deacon was very much a key leader on the team and that was extremely important. Without George I don't think Deacon ever would have been the great player that he ended up becoming.

Defensive Lineman
To be a good defensive lineman, you have to believe in yourself and Deacon Jones certainly believed in himself. I played against great defensive tackles. Of course, our own Merlin Olsen was a great defensive tackle. I played against people like Bob Lilly and Alan Page, guys who in my mind were the greatest players that I experienced. I always felt it was harder to become a great player on the inside than on the outside.

We were playing the Bears in Chicago and the tackle next to me was having a good game against Doug Atkins. Doug was kind of taking it easy, not really coming all that hard. We ran a play that was supposed to look a little bit like a sweep but it was more of a cross block thing and I came up under Atkins and I cut him and knocked him down. He said a few nasty things to me and called me some names and rookie and blah, blah, blah. So I told him where I thought he ought to go. I walked right to the huddle and the offensive tackle jumps all over me and says, "What the hell are you doing? I am having a good game because that guy is kind of asleep. I want you to go up down next play. After the play, apologize to him." I said, "You've got to be kidding." He said, "No. If we wake that guy up, you know we've got a problem.

I've got a problem, you've got a problem; we've all got a problem." So after the next play, I went over, and said, "I am sorry Mr. Atkins, I didn't mean to cut you." He said, "That's okay kid." He kind of went back to being a sleeping giant again. I just kept away from him and the tackle had a good game the whole game.

I saw him when he was down in New Orleans playing at the end of his career. He was still a fearsome competitor when he wanted to be. He was just really an intimidating player.

Biggest Rivals
You would think the San Francisco 49ers would have been our biggest rivals. We played them, including exhibition games, 38 times and lost about six games. Interestingly, we just seemed to have a whammy on them; we really dominated them.

I played in four championship games and we lost them all. We lost two to the Cowboys and two the Vikings. It was bitter frustration and disappointment but they were great teams.

Favorite Moment In NFL
Well, it is hard to say, probably when we beat the Cowboys in key games and the playoffs. When I played the Cowboys and the Vikings I always had my hands full because I was playing either Bob Lilly or Randy White or I was playing Alan Page. All three of those guys are in the Hall of Fame with me and they were great defensive tackles. Any game we beat one of those teams was the kind of game you remembered.

Pro Football Hall Of Fame Induction
I felt a little overwhelmed by the fact that I was inducted. Back in the day, announcers didn't talk much about offensive linemen at all. You listen to announcers now and they are picking kids in their second and third year in the league and say that guy is a sure Hall of Famer. As a lineman, you've got to be good enough and consistent enough for a long enough period of time. You have to be the

dominant player at that particular position for about a decade, and have people remember all that to get in the hall.

I was a finalist to get into Hall of Fame 11 times and I did not get in. After a while I got to the point where I became a little bit cynical about it. When I got nominated, as far as I was concerned, that was as good as the first time.

Career
It helps to be on good teams and it helps to play with other good players. You have to keep from getting hurt. I ended up playing every game for 13 years. It is not that I am tough. I'm probably more of a monumental tribute to stupidity, because you play hurt a lot but I was able to do it.

I played against Dick Butkus in college and then I played against him when he was with the Bears. Dick was a tough guy. I don't think he ever missed a game.

We might have lost one game to the Bears in 1966, and didn't lose again to the Bears until we were trying to play Joe Namath as our quarterback. Joe could not physically play anymore. His legs were no longer good and his arm wasn't any good that year. He was pretty well done. We kept changing quarterbacks, and honestly that probably hurt us more than helped us.

Los Angeles Ram Tom Mack blocks Dallas Cowboy Bob Lilly
Photograph courtesy Associated Press

Chapter 29

Claude Humphrey

College:
Tennessee State

Career History:
Atlanta Falcons (1968–1974, 1976–1978)
Philadelphia Eagles (1979–1981)

2014 Inductee Pro Football Hall of Fame

College Choice
I visited quite a few schools before deciding where I was going to college. I narrowed it down to Tennessee State and a little school up in Kentucky called Moreland. Tennessee State appeared to be the best deal for me. Everybody has things that they like. I visited Grambling, Texas Southern, Jackson State, and a few other schools in the Southwest. I liked Tennessee State because it was close to my hometown. That was really a factor for me in choosing a university.

Southern schools shied away from the black athletes. I had one school tell me they would enroll me, but a couple of teams in their conference probably wouldn't allow me to play against them. I was told that, so going to the bigger southern schools was eliminated at that point.

Eddie Robinson
Eddie Robinson almost had me, had he not brought me in to visit there. It had nothing to do with the school. Not that being from Memphis made me a real city person, but I wasn't quite as country as you needed to be to be able to live in Grambling. Grambling's a small place. You had to go so far to do anything other than the activities on the campus. If he had not done that, he may have had a better chance to get me.

Tennessee State was the best decision that I could have ever made for my education.

College

My Head Coach at Tennessee State was John Merritt. The assistants were Joe Gilliam, Alvin Colman, J. C. Coffee, Shannon Little, and Samuel Whitman.

We played San Diego State my senior year. Of course, they beat us, but we beat them physically. We beat them down. I think they scored on a punt return, and something else. They were one of the four losses that I had in my four years at Tennessee State.

At that time I had no interest in playing professional football. I was just there to try to get an education and just play football.

Joe Gilliam

I really didn't realize how great a player he was. He was such a great athlete. I learned that by taking stunts and tumbling from him. He could do stuff that some of us seventeen and eighteen-year-olds couldn't do. He was a great athlete.

Being Drafted By Atlanta Falcons

John Merritt was my coach and agent. He was pretty well informed. That was the one thing about him; he knew what was going on. Maybe a month before the draft, I knew that the Falcons, if they had a chance, were going to take me.

The Falcons were drafting second, but third overall, because that year Minnesota had a bonus pick and picked Ron Yary. Cincinnati picked Bob Johnson, a center from Tennessee. Then it was the Falcons' choice and they picked me.

First Training Camp

It was a killer! It was a rude awakening to professional football. At Tennessee State we practiced really hard. We practiced three times a day. We had two regular practices, and a special team practice, so we were practicing three times a day. I guess, because I was so relaxed practicing at Tennessee State, it went pretty good there.

When I went to the Falcons in Johnson City, Tennessee, it was so hot it was ridiculous. They made no allowances for the heat. We could have practiced earlier in the morning, or later in the afternoon. We went out there in the hot part of the day to practice, and we beat each other down. It was tough. It was nothing like college. Even though in college we practiced three times a day and we were only practicing two times a day in Johnson City, Johnson City was hot.

Norm Van Brocklin

I had Norm Van Brocklin as Head Coach in the College All-Star game. He was tough, but he seemed like a nice guy. Coaches have to be disciplinarians. He disciplined us pretty well at the College All-Star Game. Three games into the season; they fired Norb Hecker and brought Norm Van Brocklin in as Head Coach. Wow! What a difference with Norm. Norm Van Brocklin worked us like crazy. Not only did he work us physically, he worked us mentally, too. It was tough.

He expected everybody to play as well as he did, and better. It didn't take him long to tell you that. He got right down to it. Norm didn't beat around the bush. If there was something that needed to be said, he said it. He disregarded your feelings. You were a professional, and you were going to be treated that way.

Everybody got treated the same, which is really one of the good things about him. When he got on me, he got on everybody else the same way. That's one of the things that I respected most about him. He was pretty tough on us.

College All-Star Game

I was up against the great Forrest Gregg. Forrest gave me a lesson in how to play in the NFL. I thought I was ready. I was up there, practicing, working against Ron Yary, John Williams, and those guys. I thought I was pretty good. I found out that I had a lot to learn and a short time to learn it in. Forrest Gregg gave me a lesson in how to be kept away from the quarterback.

242

Toughest Offensive Lineman Faced

I caught Forrest Gregg at the end of his professional career, so I can't quite rate him up there with some guys like Bob Brown, Ron Yary, and Rayfield Wright. The time that I faced Forrest Gregg, even though I knew his greatness, I didn't get a chance to experience it, because he was at the end of his career. I understand he was a terror when he was younger.

Early Years With Falcons

Don't remind me of the '60s. We got a little bit better in the '70s when we started to get some good players, like George Kunz and Steve Bartkowski. Prior to that, we weren't very good. Teams knew it, and they took advantage of it.

Larry Csonka

It was a Monday night game and Larry Csonka just ran right up my chest. He used his shoulder and used that form of his. I wasn't ready for him the way you normally get ready for a running back. He showed me that you have to be ready all the time. It never happened again. That was real abuse, having to tackle him. He was a great fullback. He played great for a long time.

Career

I enjoyed the whole game. There was no part of it that I enjoyed more than others. At that time, a sack was just a tackle. Nobody really counted sacks. The most fun was batting balls. I felt like that was one of my strong suits. I got a chance to bat down a whole lot of balls. I probably batted down more balls than some of the defensive backs did for a season, until they stopped throwing my way. They used to try to throw a lot of quick outs on me my rookie year, and I got a chance to bat down a lot of balls.

I was happy about the hurries that I got. It wasn't roughing the quarterback like it is now. We got a chance to tee off on the quarterback. Those were good things that I remember.

Philadelphia Eagles

When I went to the Eagles, I played for Marion Campbell, whom I played for in Atlanta. We became real good friends. When I got to the Eagles, I was playing the same defense that I played in Atlanta.

The only thing is, the offense was better, so it made me play better. I wasn't getting beat up. I wasn't out on the field all the time. In Atlanta we spent most of the time, defensively, out on the field, because our offense didn't do very much.

The offense was very good with Wilbert Montgomery, Harold Carmichael, Ron Jaworski, and Jerry Sisemore. When you'd come off the field, you wouldn't be as tired. When you'd go back in, you could play harder, because the game had progressed so much. I enjoyed playing with a good offensive team.

Super Bowl
It was kind of a lowlight for me. Nothing seemed to go right for me for that game. During the season we had played the Oakland Raiders, and we had beat them. I had three sacks in the game. When we got to the Super Bowl, I didn't get a chance to start. I was standing over on the sideline, getting angry about not getting in the game. When I finally did get in there and roughed the quarterback, they threw a flag. It was just a disaster for me. The Raiders beat us. It wasn't a good week.

I was really pissed, because the referee threw the flag at me, instead of throwing it on the ground. I got offended. I guess he was pissed, too, because he threw the flag right at me. I picked it up and threw it at him. If I had the chance to do it all over again, I wouldn't do it. At the moment, it was the way things were. It was the passion of the game, and the way the game was going. Jim Plunkett had completed a pass to Ken King down the sideline. Ken King was still running. All that stuff just created a furnace inside me. Then he threw the flag at me. That was just too much.

Reason For Having To Wait 28 Years To Get Into Hall Of Fame
I had to wait probably because of my win-loss record with the Falcons. Also probably from the misinterpretation of the reason I left the Falcons. I think that may have had something to do with it. We didn't win a lot of games. I wasn't on a winning team. We didn't go to the Super Bowl. You notice that most of the guys that go into the Hall of Fame are guys who played in the Super Bowl three, four times, like that.

Not to say it, but there seem like there are some rules and regulations that govern you getting into the Hall of Fame. My career just didn't meet that criteria based on the years that I spent in Atlanta and Philadelphia. I think that probably had a lot to do with it. The Philadelphia years may have helped more than the years that I spent in Atlanta, because we were winning.

The good thing about waiting is, it makes it so much better. I don't know what I would have done if I had gotten in my first year of eligibility. I might have been beside myself. It gave me a chance to gain some validity and respect for the game.

Decision To Retire

I wanted to give up after a while. It was tough. It was tough, because it wasn't like the Atlanta Falcons are today under Arthur Blank and Thomas Dimitroff. Those guys really work to put a good program on the field. I don't think they did that back in the day. They were more satisfied that we were filling the stadium every Sunday rather than the caliber of players that they were putting out on the field.

Pro Football Hall Of Fame Induction

In the past, when you were a finalist for the Pro Football Hall of Fame, you had to stay by the phone and wait for the phone call. They would tell you, "If you don't get the phone call, you didn't make it." You had to wait to see who made it on the TV. That was a couple of hours after. You were waiting all that time for the phone call. The phone call never comes. Then, all of a sudden, on TV you see the guys who made it, and your name isn't up there.

This time they did it a little different. They brought all seventeen finalists for the Hall of Fame to New York and put us up at a hotel. They told us that they would call our room. I'm in the room with my daughter, Claudia. I turned to Claudia after twenty minutes, and I said, "Looks like we're in trouble." After twenty-five minutes, I said, "Well, you might as well call everybody and tell them that we didn't make it." Just as I got that out of my mouth, the phone rang, and they said, "Congratulations, you're a member of the Pro Football Hall of Fame." I almost passed out. The blood rushed to my head, and everything. It was amazing! I sat there waiting since I was a first round draft choice for the Atlanta Falcons.

My wife was my biggest supporter, and, of course, my biggest PR person. All those years I was up for the Hall of Fame she worked diligently trying to do what she could to get me in. We really didn't know what it was that she was supposed to be doing. She tried to get in touch with the voters. She wrote letters, and she had people write letters. She just worked. When I didn't make it, we cried together about it. To make it now, and not have her here to enjoy, is kind of bittersweet. But life goes on.

You know what? I felt her presence. We were in the orientation meeting after the voting. I was just sitting there, and I was thinking about her. All of a sudden, I just felt good. I think she's proud of the fact that I finally got in.

Atlanta Falcon Claude Humphrey puts pressure on Los Angeles Ram
Pat Haden Photograph courtesy Associated Press

Chapter 30

Ken Houston

College:
Prairie View A&M

Career History
Houston Oilers (1967–1972)
Washington Redskins (1973–1980)

1986 Inductee Pro Football Hall of Fame

Transition From Small College To NFL

At that time, it was prior to integration, so all the guys had to go to Grambling, Southern, Texas Southern and schools like that. We called it the Black SWAC, the Black Southwest Athletic Conference. We knew we could play. We always wanted to play other schools. As a matter of fact, Texas A&M was down the street from us, Texas up in Austin, and we tried to get games with those schools, but for a lot of reasons it didn't happen. I had the mindset when I got to pro ball that I was as good as anybody in America. Most of the guys had that mindset. We just knew that we could play.

Once we got to camp, it was just talent against talent. I think that the first Oilers team that I played on probably had 15 to 17 guys from small colleges. Then when you played Kansas City, they may have had 20. I think if there was only one league that would have existed at that time, a lot of college guys would not have gotten the chance to play pro ball.

I look at the guys who were on my college team. I played with Otis Taylor, Jim Kearney, Seth Cartwright, Bivian Lee, Alvin Reed, and all those guys. As a matter of fact, Charley Taylor came to Prairie View and he couldn't make the team, so he went to Arizona State. He became a number one receiver. At Prairie View, they had so much talent I ended up playing offensive center. I played safety in the pros. Alvin Reed was a defensive end in college and ended up playing tight end in the pros. They had so many players, you just had to go there and find a spot that was open.

Practice In AFL
Practice back then was a little different. We scrimmaged once a week, which was extreme considering we were playing on Sundays. If you can go into a game with a partial injury, you can't play at your full capabilities. During that time, you worked with pads three days a week and one of those days would be a scrimmage.

Becoming A Returner
It was a little bit different back then. I didn't start off being a kick returner. As a matter of fact, we were having a practice in the dome at that time, preparing to play the Chicago Bears. Both teams were working out at the dome and I ran back a punt because I loved to do it. The Chicago coach mentioned to our coach, "He'd make a good return person," and he actually put me back on punts probably two weeks later. I didn't do it full-time because I was a full-time player on defense. You were more exposed to injuries, which is why the coach didn't do it.

I did run back kicks also. My son and I were sitting there watching TV and it came on that he had broken my record of touchdown returns. It was like 35 years the record was there, and mine was an interception return that set the record. I had nine touchdowns by interceptions, I had one punt return touchdown and I had two fumble returns for a touchdown. My son looked at me and said, "Don't worry, Dad, I'm going to break his record. Tell Devin he's got somebody on his trail."

Favorite Quarterback To Compete Against
I really enjoyed Joe Namath, for two reasons. First of all he was a great quarterback. He always brought notoriety with him. You knew that he was going to throw the ball. The Jets probably threw the ball more back then than anyone else, so you were going to have a chance at least to get an interception or make a big play.

We played Kansas City. They had the moving pocket with Len Dawson and they had John Hadl out in San Diego. My favorite people to play against were the people who threw the ball the most.

Daryle Lamonica

As a matter of fact, we gave Daryle Lamonica his nickname, the Mad Bomber. We played the Raiders and they beat us like 50-something in one of the championship games. He got the name the Mad Bomber after that.

Houston Oilers vs. Oakland Raiders Rivalry

Something about the Raiders made them everybody's rival. They were the tough guys. Warren Wells and Willie Brown of the Raiders were from the Southwest Conference where I played in college, so we had a conference thing going on there too. A lot of guys had played in that same conference in college, especially with Houston and the Raiders, so it was a carryover from college.

Toughest Receivers

If you could cover Otis Taylor, you could cover anybody. A name that really struck fear in my heart was Lance Alworth. This guy was very quiet, not a violent receiver, but he could run and jump. He did it very quietly, until he had the respect of all the players. You had guys like Fred Biletnikoff with the Raiders, who was really, really good. He had all the moves. You had Paul Warfield. You have all these Hall of Fame guys who I played against back then, and you know how good they were because they ended up in the Hall of Fame. You could go to any team and find a great receiver. One receiver who is not mentioned much but gave me fits was the tight end for Cincinnati, Bob Trumpy. He was a long guy who ran out in the middle of the field, had good speed, and was a good tight end.

Trade To Washington Redskins

Being traded to the Washington Redskins was frightening for me, because I was an AFL player my entire career up until that point, and I knew how the NFL teams felt about the AFL. They thought we were just a junk league. For them to lose that amount of players for me, and for me to go up there again having to prove myself was really, really interesting. The Redskins had two good safeties, Roosevelt Taylor and Brig Owens, when I got there. They were starters.

I remember being there about three or four weeks and I wasn't starting. I started to question myself. As fate would have it, Roosevelt Taylor broke his arm. They moved Brig Owens over to free safety and moved me to strong safety. About a week later when the season started, I had an opportunity to tackle Walt Garrison on the one-yard line. Thank God I did that, because it changed the whole existence of me as a Redskin. That was just almost instant feedback, and from that point on, I had a tremendous career there.

George Allen was coach, and it was a great time to play for the Redskins. We were called the "Over The Hill Gang." Washington really, really supported that team. It was a good time to be in football period, especially with the Redskins or the Cowboys. They were two of the major teams back then.

The Redskins had an owner back then by the name of Edward Bennett Williams, who was a famous trial lawyer in the Washington area. You had George Allen, Billy Kilmer, Sonny Jurgensen, and Charley Taylor. A lot of those guys ended up being in the Hall of Fame. That was just a good time to play football.

Photograph courtesy Associated Press

Chapter 31

Bob Griese

College:
Purdue

Career History:
Miami Dolphins (1967–1980)

1990 Inductee Pro Football Hall of Fame

College Choice
I was not a highly recruited athlete coming out of high school. I was probably a better baseball and basketball player than I was a football player. I went to a new Catholic high school when I was a freshman, and the program wasn't really developed. The coach wasn't that knowledgeable. We didn't throw the ball a lot. The only reason I was the quarterback on the team was because he knew that I was a pretty good baseball pitcher, had a strong arm, and had thrown some no-hitters. He figured that would be a good guy to have at quarterback.

The head coach was a defensive lineman in college and didn't know a lot about throwing the football. We had three passes; one to the right called Rex, one to the left called Lavender, and one over the middle called Milton.

I was not highly recruited by colleges for football. I could have gone to a couple places for basketball. I also had an opportunity to sign with the Baltimore Orioles as a baseball pitcher. I wanted to go to Purdue to get an education.

Purdue
Bob DeMoss was my offensive coordinator at Purdue and Jack Mollenkopf was the head coach. They kind of straightened me out by showing me how to throw the ball. One of the highlights

while I was at school was when we went to the Rose Bowl my senior year. It was the first time that Purdue had ever gone to the Rose Bowl, and we beat Southern California in the game. I give Bob DeMoss a lot of credit for showing me how to throw the football properly.

Purdue had quite a few quarterbacks who were very successful and it's basically because of Bob DeMoss being the coach. The system, the way they threw the ball around, and the good coaching that they got were because of Coach DeMoss. We've had some good quarterbacks at Purdue.

Miami Dolphins
We knew we weren't going to get very far until Coach Don Shula came. I got there in '67, the second year of the Dolphins franchise. Coach Shula came in 1970, which was the fourth year. I think in '69 we were like 3-10 and 1. We only played 14 games back then.

In 1970, we completely turned around and were 10 and 4. The next year we were in the playoffs then we were in three Super Bowls in a row. We won the last two. One of those Super Bowls was during the undefeated season, which nobody had done before or after. I would say Shula made a big impact. The first four years of Coach Shula we were in the Super Bowl three times.

Monte Clark
Monte Clark was pretty good. Monte had just gotten out of the league after playing himself. The main thing that he did aside from coaching these guys up real well was that he brought in guys who weren't drafted. Jim Langer, our center, was a practice squad player with the Cleveland Browns. Monte knew about him and he brought Jim Langer in as a free agent. Jim Langer ended up playing for 10 or 12 years and is now in the Hall of Fame. He also brought in Bob Kuechenberg who was also a free agent and played 14 or 15 years. He brought in Wayne Moore from San Francisco. Then Larry Little was brought in. Four of those five guys on the offensive line were free agents. Most of them Monte Clark knew about. We had a really good offensive line.

Paul Warfield

Today's game is a passing game. Back then it was not that much of a passing game; it was more of a running game. The other thing is the rules have changed. Now you can jam a guy. Within five yards of the line of scrimmage you can jam a wide receiver. Then you can't touch him down the field. Back in the day when Warfield was playing you could throw a cross body block on the receiver coming off the line of scrimmage. You could hit him if he was down 15, 20 yards down field as long as he was in front of the defensive back. The defensive back could jam him and knock him off his feet as long as the ball wasn't in the play.

The rules back when Warfield played were a heck of a lot different than when Jerry Rice played and the guys today are playing under. If Jerry Rice played back when Warfield played, he wouldn't have caught nearly as many balls as he caught during his career. I guarantee you.

Favorite Moment In NFL

I'd have to say winning Super Bowls. The first one we lost to Dallas in New Orleans. The second one we were 16 and 0 and ready to go undefeated. We played in the Super Bowl against the Washington Redskins and we were the underdogs. Here we were 16 and 0 and hadn't lost a game. We were the underdogs and we beat them. If Garo Yepremian made a field goal at the end of the game we would have beat them 17 to nothing. Garo kicks the ball and gets it blocked and they run it back for a touchdown. We won the game only 14 to 7.

The following year we go back and validate that win by winning the Super Bowl again. This time, we won against the Minnesota Vikings.

The highlights of my career: in college it was winning the Rose Bowl and in the Pros it was winning two Super Bowls.

Pro Football Hall of Fame Induction

I never expected that I was going to be inducted into the Pro Football Hall of Fame. The last couple years of my career I wore glasses when I played. I had a vision problem. When I retired, they put my glasses in the Hall of Fame because no quarterback had ever worn glasses while he played.

My son Brian, he must have been a teenager at the time, looked at me one time and said, "That's as close as you'll ever come to being in the Hall of Fame; your glasses being in there."

In 1990 when I was inducted into the Hall of Fame my kids were there in the front row and Brian was right there. The first thing I said was, "This is the Hall of Fame, huh?" I looked down at Brian and I said, "In your face Brian." We like to kid each other back and forth. I think that was the best one that I've ever got on him.

Photograph courtesy Associated Press

Chapter 32

Alan Page

College:
Notre Dame

Career History:
Minnesota Vikings (1967-1978)
Chicago Bears (1978-1981)

1988 Inductee Pro Football Hall of Fame

College Choice
At the time I had a choice of a number of schools. Notre Dame just seemed to be the one that provided the greatest opportunity beyond the football field.

It was a transition for any young person. You are leaving home for the first time and going off to a place where you really don't know anybody, but I managed to make that transition. In retrospect I think it was a very good decision.

Ara Parseghian
Ara Parseghian was great coach. He was very driven, very determined, very much focused on doing things, and putting things in place that would allow a team to be successful.

1966 National Championship Game
My approach to the game, whether it was a national championship game or just another game, was pretty much the same. The goal was to go out and perform as well as I could and hopefully come away successful.

1966 Notre Dame vs. Michigan State 10-10 Tie
I was tired, beat up, and just worn out. It was a tough, hard-fought game. I had a feeling of exhaustion, and was more or less glad that it was over.

You go out, you play, and you do the best you can. You hope you do all those things to give you the best chance to win. The fact is, that day we didn't win. As it turns out, we didn't lose either.

There was a lot of tension and a lot of pressure, but from my perspective I approached it as just another game. There was a lot of attention, both local and national. If you're going to be good at what you do, if you're going to be successful, you have to approach, at least for me, each game as though it was the important one. It couldn't possibly be any more important than the situation you were in the week before. The week we played Michigan State, was the important one. To me, it was no more important than the team we played the week before. You can't do anything about past games and you can't do anything about future games, but you can do something about the game you are currently playing. That was always the critical game for me.

Draft
I was excited about the opportunity to play professional football. It was a chance to continue doing something that I enjoyed, and I was going to get paid for it. I was happy to be drafted. It didn't really matter in what place.

Transition to Professional Football
It was learning to play with new people, learning variations in the game, and in my case, learning a new position. I was a defensive end at Notre Dame. When I got to Minnesota, they had Jim Marshall and Carl Eller as defensive ends. Quite frankly, both of them were exceptional. It wasn't likely that I was going to be as good as either one of them. Somebody saw something in me and switched me to defensive tackle. Once I started down that road, it all came pretty naturally.

Bud Grant
Stoic, as he has been projected to be, but also very focused on creating the team atmosphere that allowed the players to minimize their mistakes and increase their chances of success.

MVP of the NFL

It was pretty exciting. It's not something that happens to you every day, and certainly not something that I had anticipated or would have ever thought would happen. I was pretty pleased.

Buddy Ryan

Buddy was always very feisty. He was a great coach. He understood the game both offensively and defensively. Again, he was one of those people who put you in the position that allowed you to be successful. I loved working with Buddy. If I had to pick my favorite coach, it was probably Buddy Ryan. He was a coach who had high expectations of his players. He expected you to not waste time and energy on things that weren't particularly relevant to getting the job done.

Purple People Eaters

We were a group and had a lot of fun playing and working together. As names go, you don't have much control over it and so "Purple People Eaters" was what we got named. I loved being a part of not only great and talented football players, but also a group of good people.

Four Super Bowl Losses

It was about the game in front of you. You go out and try to win. You do everything you can, whether it's the Super Bowl or a game like the 1966 game against Michigan State, or a preseason game. The object is to go out, play well, and do the best that you can. Did I like losing those games? No. I didn't like losing any game. It was hard; it wasn't particularly that much harder than losing any of the other games that I played in. Over the years, while the teams that I was on fared better than they statistically should have, the ones that we did lose I wasn't particularly amused.

The fact is nobody wins all the time. Some people never seem to be able to be successful. For me, the journey was more important than the destination. It is how you did, what you did along the way, which was important in terms of playing. As for the rest of it, it was just a game.

Being an NFL Player Representative

Football back in the '50s, '60s, '70s, and even before that, players didn't have many rights in terms of where they played and the other terms and conditions of their employment. I got involved in the Players Association early on to try to improve those terms and conditions. While our success was modest while I was playing, I think it paved the way for the working relationship, a very good working relationship that players and owners have today.

His Perpendicular Pinky

I had multiple dislocations that ended up with the ligaments on the inside of the finger being destroyed and the ligaments on the outside of the finger pulling the finger out. It's been this way for quite a few years. The first time I injured it was in the middle of a game. I don't even remember what game. It was early on in my career with the Vikings. Jim Marshall, who played next to me, found me holding my finger as the other team was coming up to run the next play. He grabbed it, put it back into place, and away we went.

Going from the Minnesota Vikings to the Chicago Bears

It came to a point in my career where I had probably been playing in Minnesota too long. Going to the Bears reunited me with Jim Finks, Neil Armstrong, and Buddy Ryan. The people of Chicago welcomed me and welcomed my family. It turned out to be a really positive experience. My wife, my children, and I had a great time in Chicago. Those were the good days.

Being From Canton, Ohio

In Northeastern Ohio, particularly Canton, Massillon, Alliance, and Warren, football is very, very important. It's a part of those communities in ways that you don't find in many places. There's a little of that same thing in Northwestern Pennsylvania. Football is just very important and that draws out the best talent in those communities. There has been a lot of good talent.

Pro Football Hall Of Fame Induction

First of all, it was hot. It's always hot in Canton; it's hot and humid. It was kind of neat to be recognized and appreciated by the people in your hometown, people who knew you when. That was nice. It was obviously exciting and fun to be recognized for my football. It gave me the opportunity, on a larger platform, to talk about some of the things that I think are important, particularly the importance of education.

Minnesota Viking Alan Page gets double teamed by Oakland Raider
Jim Otto (00) and George Buehler (64)
Photograph courtesy Associated Press

Chapter 33

Willie Lanier

College:
Morgan State

Career History:
AFL Kansas City Chiefs (1967-1969)
NFL Kansas City Chiefs (1970-1977)

1986 Inductee Pro Football Hall of Fame

College Choice

A lot of historically black colleges were recruiting me at that time. The traditionally major white colleges in the South were not recruiting African-Americans at all. Some of the schools to the north and west would recruit, but more at the skilled positions, running back and receiver. Very few were recruiting linebackers, especially inside linebackers at that time. I had interest from some of the other historically black colleges in the Virginia and Maryland area, and decided that I was going to go to Virginia State initially. I felt it was too close to Richmond and too close to the Deep South, not as though Maryland was a great distance away, but being a little bit further north was something I thought was important. I reached out to the coach and that's how I ended up going to school there.

It wasn't as though I was this very well known, great high school football player. My skills were developing and starting to present themselves, but my size didn't start to flower until I finished my senior year of high school and was getting ready to go to college. It wasn't as if I was this very well known recruit across the country.

Morgan State

Morgan State had a very good team at that time. They were constantly winning in one of the bowl games. Leroy Kelly attended Morgan and was there my first year. They had a number of players who would go to the pros—Raymond Chester with the Raiders, Mark Washington with the Cowboys, George Nock with the Jets, and John Fuqua with the Giants. There were a number of fellows whose skills happened to be showing. I ended up playing in three bowl games in the four years I was there. They had a 34-game winning streak. Morgan State had a lot going for it, and its notoriety was pronounced.

Draft

I think the reality was that the position of middle linebacker was not being manned by African-Americans, so it wasn't one that teams in the old, quote, National Football League, were interested in. The position had not been played full time by someone who was African-American. The American Football League had become a haven of opportunity for players from historically black colleges.

First Training Camp

When I was drafted as a middle linebacker, Jim Lynch was the other second-round draft choice, and he was also drafted for the position. They were looking to replace Sherrill Headrick, who was a veteran middle linebacker. He was aging and didn't have a big physical stature.

That first year we were both competing to be in the middle. We were both drafted as middle linebackers, which we played in college, and the competition was going to be playing for that position. That's just the way it turned out. The team was not viewing us for any position other than that one. I ended up being injured the last four games of my rookie year. I think Jim was playing but not starting at that time. He ended up stepping into the starting lineup as the middle linebacker the last few games of our rookie year.

We did the competition again the next year, going at it as far as who was going to be the starter at middle linebacker. I was acknowledged as the starter and they shifted Jim to the outside.

Being The First Black Starting Middle Linebacker

Games kept coming too fast, and performance was required. I had a whole lot of work to do. I knew the significance of being the first black starting middle linebacker, but playing in football is performance based. You're trying to win games, you're trying to have others look to you for leadership, and so you're trying to show that you can play. It was just good that it worked out in Kansas City.

I think the Kansas City Chiefs team coming off of having lost to Green Bay in the Super Bowl, were interested in winning. Whichever one of us could help them win quickest was the one that they were going to probably react to. Jim and I became great friends. I was in Kansas City only a week ago, and we had lunch together. We've known each other for years and are very close. He was a realist in that I was a more physical player than he was, so the odds of that position being awarded to him was probably not going to be in his favor.

Realization I Could Play In The NFL

It wasn't anything about getting to Kansas City and really playing the game with all of the players. I was 6'1", 245 pounds, quick, and had upper body strength. The Washington Redskins recruited one of my college classmates. He went to the Redskins for a visit and I went with them. They weren't recruiting me; they were recruiting him. After we left the field, in the bowels of the stadium, I ended up meeting Sam Huff. I saw Sam and shook his hand, but he didn't realize who I was. I was a college student. He was this well-known middle linebacker in pro football. As I shook Sam's hand and I told him a story, I looked at his height. He was a little taller than me. I looked at his build. He was not as broad in the shoulders as me and didn't appear as physical as I felt I was. I had this very clear view—and this is a positive about Sam and not a negative in any way—if he could play, and now I'm standing in front of a guy who's a middle linebacker in the National Football League, there should not be any reason why I can't play.

I had some scouts saying they thought I might be too short and all these different kind of comments. I said wait a minute, I'm looking at a guy who is very well known, a starting middle linebacker, a pro football player. That was sort of a marker for me in terms of confidence and then having the opportunity.

Hank Stram
Hank Stram was very innovative and very competitive as you can see on NFL Films. He was one who had a reach of excellence that was important to him. He always strived for trying to create an environment that you could excel in and hopefully show the talents that God had gifted you.

Super Bowl IV
Super Bowl IV was like any other game, because the game was one week after the Championship Game. All of the games had run one week after another. There was no gap of two weeks from the Championship Game to the Super Bowl like there is now. It was another game that occurred in a round robin elimination at the end of the season. We had played the Jets in New York one week, went out to Oakland the next week and played them in the championship, and the following week we were in New Orleans for the Super Bowl.

This thing had a very fast East Coast, West Coast, and Gulf Coast run in that you found yourself constantly in preparation for the next game that had to be played in a string. The whole idea was to be the last one standing. It moved very quickly, but I think with it moving quickly it didn't give you a chance to focus on it being more than what it was.

The reality was that the two teams that were there at that moment were the Kansas City Chiefs and the Minnesota Vikings. For many of us who were not there for the first Super Bowl they lost, it didn't really mean anything that they lost. We didn't feel it when we went there. We weren't a part of it. The players who had come after that season were all in their moment and their opportunity to play out whatever the reality would be that day, as it had been all season. It was of the opportunity at the moment.

Speech To Teammates Before Goal Line Stand Against New York Jets In Divisional Playoff Game

There was an interference penalty on Emmitt Thomas of our team in the end zone so the Jets had first and goal at the one-yard line. I told the team in the huddle, "It becomes one of opportunity and action and being accountable." I was trying to get the guys to lift their heads, not feel it being a concession, and trying to get them to perform at a little bit higher level. In doing that I realized very quickly that words without action don't mean anything. My thought was that the Jets were going to have to go on a shorter count because of the risk of being offside in motion is a 500% penalty. They go from the one to the five. If I'm offside they only go to the half-yard line, so that's 50%. The odds are completely in my favor, even if I'm offside.

I decided that on whatever play, if they didn't go on the first count he had to go on the second. All I would do is turn sideways and step in between the guard and the center and try to disrupt, and that's what happened. After that occurred everyone else was more livid and viewed the opportunity as being more clear. Then everybody really came to life. We were able to stop them and that made a difference in the game.

Nicknames

Jerry Mays started calling me "Contact" the first year I came to Kansas City because I was improperly tackling people. I'll say it like that. I was tackling with the crown of my head and trying to crush people. After that, about the next year, I was nicknamed "Honey Bear" because I was wrapping people up. I put that "Contact" thing to rest because I wouldn't have survived three years in the league if I continued to try to play like that.

Pro Football Hall Of Fame Induction

I didn't play each game, each season with a long-term view of the Pro Football Hall of Fame. I was near-term in trying to win the game, trying to win a division title, and trying to win or get to the playoffs. If I was fortunate, I played well enough to get to the Pro Bowl. The Hall of Fame was not something that ever entered my mind during the time I was playing. I was not playing for that, I was playing for all these other purposes. The call came during my third year of eligibility. It's an overwhelming, "Thank you, God," because I had been granted the opportunity to play long enough … because you need longevity, with a quality team that had some success and very few injuries. It's a very special moment and one that you never forget because of the clarity of it.

Trade To Baltimore Colts

Retiring was my decision because toward end of my career, I had moved to the East Coast and started working for a tobacco company. I was trying to leave the game two years before the trade to the Colts. I was between the thought of whether I would play or not play. My heart was not in it, so I decided not to go forward and play for the Colts. Again, it had nothing to do with Kansas City.

Favorite Moment In Career

The one I think of, which had nothing to do with winning the game but was the essence of the game, was when the Chiefs opened Arrowhead Stadium in 1972. The Baltimore Colts played in the first preseason game at Arrowhead Stadium. I knew the Colts players because some of them lived in Baltimore. Some of them would come by Morgan State to talk to us about our expectations if we were going to make it to the pros. Sometimes they would just come by to watch games. I knew many of them, like Tony Lorick, Willie Richardson, Jim Parker, Tom Matte, and Johnny Unitas. We all knew them.

In that preseason game there was a swing pass from Unitas to Tom Matte, over the middle. Matte came over the middle, reached up for the ball, and I hit him with a tremendous tackle in his ribs. I knew him and was not trying to hurt him. I'm trying to make a great play, which I thought I did. He hit the ground on his back, I'm on top of him, and he says, "I caught the ball." I'm saying, "No, you didn't, because I felt I hit him with this great tackle." Then he shows me the ball and you can hear me laughing.

The game is one that should be played for the joy of the game. It has nothing to do with anger. It has nothing to do with harm. It has to do with the quality and the joy of the contest. If individuals play it that way, they come away from it with a different view and I think a different approach to the way the game should be played.

271

I enjoyed the game most of the time. As long as I stayed away from coaches who had a different view and ideas. Unfortunately, that would create conflicts at times. I'm saying the game should be played for joy and not anger, but you have a lot of people who don't quite grasp that. Think of how this all conflicts.

There's more to life even when the game is played, when the game is over, it's always a game. I heard Urban Meyer, a new coach at Ohio State, made a comment last year that he liked his players to be angry when they played. I thought, "That's an odd view of the game. My view is somewhat different."

Kansas City Chief Willie Lanier leaps on top off Baltimore Colt Don McCauley after McCauley fumble Photograph courtesy Associated Press

Chapter 34

Rayfield Wright

College:
Fort Valley State

Career History:
Dallas Cowboys (1967–1980)

2006 Inductee Pro Football Hall of Fame

College Choice

I went to Fort Valley for the simple reason that I had a cousin who was captain of the football team. I couldn't make the high school football team, but I went to Fort Valley on a basketball scholarship. When I left high school I wanted to play basketball so bad because I didn't make the high school football team. I was a pretty good basketball player at the time. Loyola in Chicago also wanted me to come and play basketball for them but we didn't have the financial resources for me to go there, nor any other school. Fort Valley was a state school, and I got a pretty good scholarship and that's why I went to Fort Valley.

There were a couple of schools out of Atlanta that wanted me but I chose Fort Valley because they had a new coach, Stan Lomax. Coach Lomax, my college coach, was the gentleman who introduced me at the Hall of Fame.

Not Making High School Football Team

I'm from a tall family. I have a brother who's 7 feet tall, my dad was 7 feet, and I was 6'7". We just played basketball. When I went out for football, I didn't make the team because I was a tall, lanky guy. My high school coach thought I would get hurt playing football, so I started playing basketball. I was 6'7", and I only weighed 200 lbs. when I left high school.

Turning Down Loyola Chicago
We didn't have the financial resources because it was just my mother and grandmother raising four kids. If you think about the south back in the '60s, you can understand what I'm talking about.

Playing Football When On Basketball Scholarship
Back in those days you went to college on what was called an athletic scholarship, instead of just a football scholarship or just a basketball scholarship. It meant that I had to play two sports. That's when I started playing football. I chose football because I wanted to play football and I wanted to play wide receiver because I was a pretty fast guy, I thought, running a 4.8 forty.

The first position I played in football was free safety. I played defensive end, tight end, and I was a punter. When basketball season started I started playing basketball.

NFL Draft
I didn't want to play professional football. I wanted to play basketball. The Cincinnati Royals wanted me to play basketball for them. I decided that I couldn't because it was my junior year in college. When I received my scholarship, I had made a commitment in high school with a guy who was in the Air Force. I told him that I wouldn't drop out of school until I received my college degree. Since I made that commitment, I did not go to, or even try out for the Royals.

Then my senior year, the Dallas Cowboys drafted me. The Cowboys were only six years old at that time. I had a football scholarship and training camp started in July. I had a basketball offer with the Royals and practice started in August. I had two opportunities, one in football and one in basketball. I told my mother and grandmother that I had two opportunities. I didn't know what God really wanted me to do, so since football camp started first, I went to the Cowboys training camp. I ended up making the football team with the Cowboys. Back in those days, we had 137 rookies in training camp. That was when they were just signing free agents. I ended up making the team as a tight end. Coach Landry had a system and he knew that his system would work if he could find the right athletes to play in his system. It didn't matter whether you played football, basketball, ran track, or whatever. He was looking for athletes. He didn't build his system around a player. He built his system around athletes. That's what really made him very successful and made the team very successful.

When Roger Staubach joined the team in 1969 after having to serve four years in the service, Coach Landry called me in his office and said, "Rayfield I'm going to move you to offensive tackle." I thought he was crazy because I had never played offensive tackle before in my life. Ralph Neely was playing right tackle at the time. He had an ankle injury and couldn't play, so Coach Landry told me that I was starting. That was about halfway during the season, so I had to come in and start playing a position that I had never played before.

The first player that I had a chance to block in the National Football League, God bless him, was David Deacon Jones. That was my first start. I was blocking the Secretary of Defense, the most feared defensive lineman that ever played in the National Football League. My first start was against Deacon Jones.

I never will forget the first play of the ball game. I got down in my stance and I was looking at Deacon squarely in his eyes. He was kicking his back leg like a bull. When a bull starts kicking his leg you know what's going to happen. He's coming. There isn't anything you can do about it. He's going to come and that's exactly what Mr. Jones did. When Staubach made the call, the ball was going to be snapped on two when he said hut and then between the different huts from a quarterback's call, there's a little pause in that call. I hear a statement because an offensive lineman is dedicated to hear only one voice and that's your quarterback voice because he can call a number or color. We call it an audible and he could change the original play that was called in the huddle. I'm listening and in between that first and second hut, in this pause I hear a voice and the voice wasn't Roger's voice, it was Deacon Jones' voice. He asked me a question, which really blew me away because he asked me if my mother knew that I was out on the field. When Staubach called the second play, I was still in my stance and everybody was running their assignment out. He came across that line of scrimmage and hit me with that head slap and knocked me all the way on my back. I rolled over, looked to the sideline to see if Coach Landry was going to take me out of the game, and he turned his back on me. By that time Deacon Jones reached his big arms down to help me up off my back and said, "Hey rookie, welcome to the NFL." I wasn't a rookie; I'm in my third year. He called me rookie, but I was a rookie as far playing offensive tackle. I ended up getting the game ball and I was MVP of the game because Mr. Jones never touched Roger again. That's what started my career at offensive tackle. I played offensive tackle for 10 years.

Playing Offensive Line
The offensive line, as I look at it, is like an engine in an automobile. If you take that engine out of the automobile, no matter how beautiful the car looks, the car is not going anywhere. You put that engine in the automobile then it is going to move. Well, the offensive line is like that. If you don't have an engine, or your engine isn't running properly, then your offense is not going anywhere. You must have everything that the engine needs for the offensive line to move. We were one unit and all of the guys on the offensive line worked with each other. We had a great offensive line coach, Jim Myers, who really taught us how to play that position, based on our athletic ability.

The center is like a quarterback. Your center calls signals like a quarterback. The center calls the blocking assignments for the offensive line based on the defense scheme. The offensive lineman may have a certain blocking assignment, but if the center calls a signal then we know that we going to have to block a different way then the play normally is called.

Turning Down Opportunity To Play In NBA With Cincinnati
I would have been teammates with Oscar Robertson and Jerry Lucas. I was the first professional athlete to come out of Griffin, Georgia and the first one to end up playing professional football. It

was a tough decision to make because I wanted to play basketball, but at the same time I had two opportunities. When you receive an opportunity you just don't let it go when it's something that you want to do. I wanted to play professional sports because I knew I had the ability to do so. I just didn't know that the Dallas Cowboys were going to draft me.

Living In Dallas After Being Drafted

I was drafted right after John F. Kennedy was assassinated in Dallas. I'm saying to myself, do I really want to go to Dallas? Things really hadn't straightened out and in some areas, even today, things have not straightened out as far as color is concerned. I decided that I would just go to Dallas. It was an interesting situation. I didn't get a chance to really have a roommate and I can't answer the question why not. Maybe it was because segregation was still out there and our rooms had roommates of the same race. If there was an extra roommate that would cause black and white to be together, then back in those days, they would get two rooms. One player would have his own room and the other player would have his own room.

Bob Lilly & Randy White

Bob Lilly was still playing. Bob was the first player who was ever drafted by the Cowboys in 1960. He came out of Texas Christian University, and was a tremendous athlete. He had a lot of quickness and he moved pretty fast on that defensive line. Of course, Randy White came from Maryland. He came in as a linebacker. Randy made the adjustment to the defensive line because he was an athlete. He was just as quick as Lilly. That's what Coach Landry was looking for in his defense. We had Jethro Pugh, a tremendous defensive tackle on the other side of Bob Lilly, also on the side of Randy White. Jethro put a lot of pressure on the quarterback himself. I don't think that Jethro has gotten the credit that he deserves because no one really talks about him that much. Jethro was a great player.

Playing In Five Super Bowls

In 1970, we played in our first Super Bowl and that was the most important one. I played 13 years and we were in the playoffs 12 of those 13 years that I played. Prior to going to the Super Bowls, we were named as the team that couldn't win the big game.

The first Super Bowl that we had was against the Baltimore Colts. I was blocking Bubba Smith in that game. He was a big, tall, strong guy. I held my own against him, but we lost the game by a field goal that was kicked by O'Brien. That's the game they said that Mel Renfro tipped the ball and John Mackey caught the ball and ran it in for a touchdown. After seeing the film, Mel Renfro didn't touch the ball. O'Brien kicked a field goal and the Colts won that game.

The next year we beat Miami 24-3 for our first Super Bowl win. We picked Coach Landry up and put him on our shoulders and carried him off the field. The Super Bowl was something that we really strived to get to because we knew we could win it. That was a great game for us.

Cowboys Running Backs Blocked For

We had a series of great running backs. I thought Walt Garrison was one of the top fullbacks in the league. Then Robert Newhouse came in as a fullback and the halfbacks were Calvin Hill and Duane Thomas. Calvin and Duane both were excellent running backs. They had their own different styles of running.

Duane Thomas was like a glider. He was fast as well. Calvin was a more powerful running back and he liked to jump a lot over his blocks. That made those two guys a little different. I loved blocking for Duane Thomas because he set up your blocks really well, but he wasn't a straight runner.

Tony Dorsett came in after Duane was traded and Calvin was playing in Washington. Dorsett came in from the University of Pittsburgh. Tony was a power runner even though he wasn't as big as Calvin was and a little bit smaller than Duane. He had the quickness and he could read the plays and the blocks. One of the things that made him a great running back was that he knew the plays and could make adjustments based on the blocking of the offensive line.

Star Defensive Lineman Played Against
We start out with Deacon Jones, Bubba Smith, Carl Eller, Claude Humphrey, Jack Youngblood, and L.C. Greenwood. Each of those guys was awesome. All the guys that I blocked against are in the Pro Football Hall of Fame, except L.C. Greenwood and Bubba Smith.

Dallas Cowboys Being Named America's Team
We didn't give ourselves that name. The fans and the media had a lot to do with it. Since we had become successful in the game, they started calling us America's team. It was because we had a lot of fans in different stadiums or cities that we played in around the country. Everyone knew our names, even the offensive linemen's names, in the different cities in which we played. I think that was one of the main reasons why the team became America's team. It wasn't because it was something that we did or said.

More Popular Cowboys Or Cowgirls
As far as the players were concerned we were. I took my youngest son to a game and I wanted him to take pictures of some of the players. When the game was over and I got the films developed, the only things on the film were cheerleaders. I thought he was taking pictures of his favorite players. He had his priorities in the right place, but we didn't because we couldn't focus on any cheerleaders. We couldn't even focus on the fans because we had to pay attention and keep our focus on the plays that were called.

Hail Mary Pass
Drew Pearson caught the Hail Mary pass from Roger Staubach and went in for a score. I was blocking the Vikings' Carl Eller on that particular play and one of the reporters came up and asked me if I saw the play. I said, "No, I didn't see it." He said, "Well you were on the field." I said, "Well I know I was on the field, but I was doing my job. If I had not been doing my job, I would

have seen the play. You do your job and watch everything from the game when we watch game films."

Pro Football Hall of Fame Induction
Well it's very difficult to remain composed because when I was inducted in 2006, my mother was there. My brothers, sister, my niece, and nephews were there. My mother had never flown on a plane before and she didn't fly to Canton. I rented a private bus to take my family to the Hall of Fame because my mother would not fly, period. The nervousness I had of looking at my mom and remembering everything that she had done in raising me, brought a lot of tears to my eyes. At certain times it was a little bit tough to maintain my composure, but the rest of the fans that were in the audience were cheering all of the players that were inducted. That kind of warms your heart a lot. It meant a lot to me because we played, not just as a team, but for the fans too.

The Pro Football Hall of Fame selects the best players who played the game, as well as the best players who helped their team win ballgames. Those are two major factors that really bring a player out for a vote in the Hall of Fame. Even though I knew I was a great football player, I had no idea that I would be a Hall of Famer. I felt overwhelmed to be amongst the greatest players that had ever played the game. We have a little under 300 players in the Hall. I was number 245 placed in the Hall of Fame.

I was overwhelmed. It was exciting. I was just honored and happy to be a part of the Hall of Fame and to be a Hall of Famer who played for the Cowboys, because we didn't have many at that time.

Players Patterned Himself After
You look at a lot of players and you kind of pattern yourself after some of them. Since it was hard for me to make the adjustment to tackle, I went to my offensive line coach and got films of the best offensive tackles that played the game up to that point. St. Louis had two guys, Ernie McMillan and Bob Reynolds, and Green Bay had a guy named Forrest Gregg. Those were players I looked at on film. I tried to pattern myself after those players and I couldn't do it. Bob

Lilly and those guys would pick me up and throw me around and I got tired of that. I stayed up all night watching films and one day it came to me. I'm thinking, "Well, what are you trying to do Rayfield? Well I'm trying to keep guys from the quarterback, so I'm pass blocking, right? The way that you do that is something that I had while playing basketball, quick feet. I had to stay in front of the player. I used my quickness that I had developed playing basketball.

Uniform Number 70
I was given number 70 by the coaches and the equipment manager because no one had number 70 at that time. I think it was a great number because seven is a good number and it's Biblical. I thought 70 was a good number because it's a number that really stood out among other numbers, like 67 or 52, on the offensive line. It was a great number and I loved it.

Tom Landry
He was awesome. He was one of the greatest coaches that ever coached the game. The thing is that Coach Landry was a player in New York prior to being hired as Head Coach here in Dallas, so he understood and knew players. We became one team. We all respected each other and played together as a unit. He was a coach who really respected the players and a coach who taught us more than just football. He taught us about life itself. He taught us how to deal with people and respect those who are teaching you. A lot of players don't do that. A lot of players feel like they are the ones that are most important and they can forget about everybody else who's on the team. No one player wins a ball game. Coach Landry said, "We win as a team, we lose as a team." One thing he said to me when I first started playing tackle was, "Rayfield, I'm going to tell you something." I said, "What's that Coach?" He said, "Remember that the player you're playing against is a professional just like you." So you respect not only your teammates, you respect your opponents because they are professionals just like you.

Physical Effects Of Playing Football

Fans are just there to watch the game. They don't really know what a player goes through mentally to prepare himself to play a game. There are a lot of hits. I looked it up one day. Players average 60 plays a game offensively. We have 16 games a season. You take 60 plays a game, multiplied by the 16 games played a year, times the 13 years that I played, and I came pretty close to sustaining 3,000 hits. Every time that ball snaps, you're going to hit somebody or someone's going to hit you. That's a lot of hits.

Change In Game

We didn't have all the protection or the equipment the players have today and we couldn't block like players block today. You couldn't reach out and grab a guy and hold him. That was a penalty. That was a 15-yard penalty for us, but today the offensive line, they can just reach out and grab a guy and then it becomes a wrestling match, to me. You don't see the quickness in players today like you did back in my day. The thing that gets to me is that a lot of teams and coaches look for guys that are 300 pounds and run a 4.6, 40-yard dash. That doesn't really impress me because an offensive lineman moves about 10 yards a play. My point is how quick can you get from point A to point B being 10 yards? I don't see any offensive lineman running 40 yards. If they did, they'd be on the sideline sucking up oxygen. The 4.6s, 4.7s, and even 4.5s, that doesn't mean much to me because offensive linemen don't get a chance to run 40 yards. The game is about quickness.

Decision To Retire

You get a feeling and knowledge that based on what you have gone through for so many years the body is only prepared and developed to take a certain amount of hits. Every time you hit someone and they hit you upside your head everyone says, "The man got his bell rung." That could develop into a concussion because it knocks him out or things like that.

When I retired, I thought my body had gone through enough. Once you feel that you can't compete like you should, then you know it's time to get out of the game. You don't just hang around the game just to make money.

Injuries
Don Meredith used to get his nose broken every game. You look at situations like that and there were times when Roger really got his bell rung. Sometimes when your head hits the ground, the ground is not soft. When I played the game we played on regular grass, which I loved playing on instead of Astroturf. Under the Astroturf it's almost like a bed, you got a cushion under the bed. You sleep on that cushion on the bed for a long time and that cushion kind of shrinks, it kind of goes down. Astroturf, to me does the same thing. Under the Astroturf, below the padding is cement. It's a very difficult thing for me to even continue playing on it even though I did.

First Coach My Mom
She was my toughest coach. She used to tell me things like, "Son I know you want to be successful, but you can't become successful by yourself. It take's other people around you to become successful." I don't know anyone who has been successful just by himself. Whether you're the owner of a team, the head coach, or the general manager, you have to have the right people around you.

Financial Help From Others While In School
There was a guy when I graduated from high school and went to Fort Valley for college. A man came to my high school coach and said that he wanted to help a student who didn't have the financial resources but was trying to get an education. My high school principal selected me. This gentleman sent me $50 a month until I graduated from college. I told my principal, "Mr. Daniels, I can't pay him back until I graduate and get a job." He said, "Well, he doesn't want to be paid back." I said, "Well what does he want?" He said, "If you ever got in a position to help another student to do it." That's why I started my foundation. The other thing is that I never knew the gentleman's name. I never cast an eye on him. I knew nothing about him, or anything of that nature. He didn't put it in the newspaper or go on TV to talk about what he had done. That's what I do with my foundation. We try to generate funds to help kids go to college whether they are athletes or not. Very few of them are athletes. We've had several kids who we sent to college, graduate.

284

Career Perspective

When you go into the National Football League or any other professional sport, you don't go there for the All Pro honors, Pro Bowl honors, or Hall of Fame honors. I never looked for those. I just wanted to perform and do my job to help the team win ball games. That's what players did. We didn't make the kind of money that these guys are making today. Most of the players, had to have second jobs to sustain their families and those who they loved and were trying to help. It's an interesting life that we lived.

Dallas Cowboy Rayfield Wright carries Coach Tom Landry off the field Photograph courtesy Associated Press

Chapter 35

Lem Barney

College:
Jackson State

Career History
Detroit Lions (1967-1977)

1992 Inductee Pro Football Hall of Fame

College Choice
I had offers from most of the Southwestern Athletic Conference schools, which included Texas Southern, Prairie View, Grambling, Southern University, and Alcorn State University. None of the bigger schools offered me a scholarship. It wasn't that wide open at the time. I think it was because of guys like Walter Payton and me that the Big Ten schools and other universities started looking down on that coastal area for great ballplayers. In addition to me, Jackson State had Walter Payton, his brother Eddie; Willie Richardson, who later played with the Baltimore Colts; Gloster Richardson, who later played for Kansas City; and Thomas Richardson, who was my roommate at Jackson State and played with the Boston Patriots. A lot of players at the small African-American high schools weren't getting offers at that time, but their eyes were open later on, particularly after Walter came out of a small school in Mississippi.

Eddie Robinson
Eddie Robinson was a great guy. As I look back on my college career at Jackson State, the only school we didn't have a winning record against was Grambling. Grambling beat us four years in a row, twice down in Grambling and then twice at Jackson State. Eddie Robinson was just a phenomenal head coach and a great

communicator. He was a father figure. In fact, a lot of people don't know the ins and outs about Eddie. Eddie was a guy who was a one-man show at Grambling. He would tape ankles, do curfew checks every night, make sure the guys were eating right, and going to class. He was just a tremendous guy and he had a great friend over at Alabama, Papa Bear Bryant. It was just amazing, particularly because of the racial tension, which was high in the early '60s. Eddie and the late great Bear Bryant were dynamic friends. They worked together at camps during the off-season. He was just a tremendously great coach.

Eddie Robinson had to give a lot of his ballplayers away to a lot of the Texas colleges like Texas Southern University, Prairie View, and some other smaller schools since he didn't have enough room on the team. Eddie was just a dynamic recruiter. Guys from Detroit and across the country wanted to play at Grambling.

Jackson State
I went to Jackson State as a quarterback. A lot of people never knew that. John Merritt from Tennessee State recruited me during my senior year and said, "Boy, you're going to have a chance to play." He had a great quarterback by the name of Roy Curry, who ended up playing for the Chicago Bears. They didn't give Roy an opportunity to play quarterback in the NFL. They put him on at wide receiver. He was a big quarterback about 6'4" and weighed about 225. He threw a ball to Willie Richardson, who would have been a Hall of Famer if he'd had the opportunity to play in Miami like he did at Jackson State. Willie Richardson was one of the Richardson brothers. There were three of them that ended up playing at Jackson State.

We had Leslie Duncan, who played with the San Diego Chargers, Verlon Biggs, who played with the New York Jets, and Frank Molden, who played with the Pittsburgh Steelers and with Philadelphia. We just had a bevy of great guys. There was just an abundant amount of talent at those African-American schools in the '60s.

Draft
When I was drafted, I said to my college coach, "Wow, I'm going to Detroit." My college coach said, "Just continue to do the things that you were doing to get you there. Keep doing what you've been doing and you'll be fine."

Joe Schmidt
I played my first seven years under the great Joe Schmidt with Detroit. Ironically, as I look at my career, I ended up playing under five head coaches in 11 years. I played my first seven years with the great Hall of Famer and middle linebacker, Joe Schmidt, as my coach. Then, I played for Don McCafferty, whose nickname was Easy Rider. He came from the Baltimore Colts where he was the coach. Don was a great coach. He died the second year in Detroit during training camp. Then Rick Forzano from Navy, who coached the great Roger Staubauch at Navy, took over. After Forzano, it was Tommy Hudspeth and then Monte Clark, who played for Cleveland.

I had five head coaches in the span of 11 years, but had a great time with all the coaches. I always respected the coaches.

Key To Success
Training was the key to my success from middle school, through high school, college, and through the league. My sophomore year in college, I found out that I was going to be a defensive back and not quarterback, so I started running backward for training. I would run down to the beach and I'd run a mile and a half forward and then I'd run two and a half miles backward in the sand. People thought I was crazy. For a long time I thought I was crazy as well.

You find that great sprinters, like Bob Hayes and Dave Sime, practice getting out of the blocks as low as they can, as fast as they can for 15 to 20 yards, then they'll start rising up. To become a good defensive back, I started training running backward in the sand. It was tough. A lot of good athletes could never buy into that theory, but it was my key to being a successful defensive back.

I played in high school, college, and then in the league for 11 years. It was always a joy because you had to learn and teach and train those muscles going backward. As a defensive back, I do realize you're employing yourself in a backpedaling position for over 93% to 95% of the time. You would stop and come forward to help make a tackle, but most of your activity is moving backward, so the more you can train and adapter your muscles to moving backward, the better you'll be. I did that for my entire career.

Jim David

Jimmy David, "The Hatchet", as they called him, was just a tremendously great teacher. He was a great defensive back and he was a great coach. He should be in the Hall of Fame. He went to six Pro Bowls. He should be in the hall with his former teammates who are already in the Hall of Fame.

He wasn't one of those coaches like you see today. Most guys today that are defensive coordinators or defensive back coaches get hired because the head coach was a friend of theirs in college, cronies in college, or something of that nature. Even though Coach Schmidt and Jimmy played together, Coach Schmidt new that Jimmy David could coach because he played the game with that same type of intensity.

I had a couple of people who I thought about being my presenter for my Hall Of Fame Induction. I chose Jimmy David because of the training, confidence, and courage that Jimmy gave me to play that game. It was just unbelievable. We had a relationship that will never end. I still call his wife and speak with her from time to time and his kids. Jimmy was just a tremendously great asset for me and to me as a Detroit Lion Pro Football Hall of Famer. He was just so great. Joe Schmidt, who played the game, could coach the game. Jimmy, who played the game, could coach the game. It was almost like the Lord had Angels on me from my middle school years all through my professional years and I will always be appreciative of that.

Playing Philosophy

My high school coach told me if I wanted to play defensive back, quarterback, or wide receiver, I could do it and do it with a bit of ease.

I discovered nothing was easy about it. It was always a dire, hard, work effort. I was never a guy who would loaf during practice or during training. You see a lot of guys who kick it around during the course of practice. They'll do the same thing in a game. Your body just adapts to what you do for it. So I always played with intensity. In fact, I remember Coach Joe Schmidt telling me on offensive days, "Lem, let the guys catch the ball. This is offensive practice." I'd say, "Coach, if you want them to catch it, you need to put somebody else over here. I'm not letting them catch it." He said, "You're right about it, Lem. If you slow up in practice, your body will take the initiative to slow up during the course of the game."

It was always, right full rudder, full speed ahead for me, and Jimmy David agreed with it. He would sit down and tell me, "They call me the hatchet because I was whacking in practice."

I really enjoyed practice. I was a gentleman who really enjoyed the practice sessions. The particular reason for that is because my training before going into practice was always there.

One of the things that I loved was being able to study film. We really didn't have film in college. We didn't have the means for it. We would see film but they wouldn't break it down like in the pros. We watched everything the opposition did. If we were playing the Chicago Bears, I would have the opportunity to get the last five games the Bears played on film. How you break down film is a tedious job. It's hard work. A player is going to do the same thing in the game against me that he did in a previous game. So, learning how to break down film was a great asset for me. The late, great Jimmy David taught me how to do it; he trained me. He was a great guy.

Marvin Gaye

Mel Farr and I sang on the *What's Going On* album with Marvin Gaye. I think Mel and I might be the only two NFL stars to have a gold record. Marvin was one of my favorites singers when I was in high school. He had to be everybody's favorite. When I found out I was being drafted by the Detroit Lions, I said, "Motown!" The first thing that came to my mind was Motown. Motown was at its pinnacle in the mid '60s with Marvin Gaye, The Temptations, The Miracles, The Four Tops, and The Supremes.

When I was in training camp, I said I wanted to go by and meet Marvin Gaye. One day after practice I found out where he played golf, which was a public golf course named Palmer Park. After the morning practice, I missed lunch and I drove to Palmer Park to look for Marvin Gaye. Everybody said, "No, he's not out here now, but he doesn't live that far." They told me where he lived, and I drove around. I go over, and I see a big brown Brougham Cadillac. That was the marker for me. He drove a big brown Brougham Cadillac. I pulled into the driveway, went up, rang the bell, and I stepped back. The bell had a chime to it, a little musical chime. About 25 seconds later, I was getting ready to hit it again, and the door opened. Who stood in the door? Marvin Gaye.

He said, "Yeah man, what's going on? I said, "Look Marvin, my name is Lem Barney with the Detroit Lions. I just wanted to come by and tell you what a great musician I think you are." He said, "Who'd you say you were?" I said, "Lem Barney." He said, "Not the guy that played with the Detroit Lions?" I said, "Yes sir." He said, "Man, you're too small to be that guy!" I said, "Do you want to see my driver's license?" He said, "No man, come on in, man, I was having lunch."

I go in, and he is in the kitchen having lunch. I said, "No, I'm okay. I'm going to go back to the training camp and have lunch before the second practice. Well, I just wanted to come by and just meet you and tell you how much I appreciate your singing and everything, man." We started kibitzing and I looked at my watch, and I said, "Oh, man, I got about 30 minutes before I have to be on the field, man." It was about 25 miles from where he was to training camp. I was driving, and I mean I was driving like Mario Andretti. I was just hoping the cops wouldn't find me and they didn't. I got back to training camp. I had just enough time to put on my uniform, and nobody knew it because I would've gotten fined for it. I didn't get my ankles taped that day for the second practice because I was a little late, and everybody was gone, but it started a dynamic relationship between Marvin and me.

I told Mel Farr about it, and he said, "Oh man, that's wonderful, man. We have to go back by and see him again." We started visiting Marvin after that. We were getting tickets for him and Smokey Robinson at Tiger Stadium for the Lions games. The players had a special place they would go eat after a home game at Tiger Stadium, and Marvin and Smokey started coming by. Everybody quite naturally was going to love these guys. They would eat with us and have fun. They'd take the piano over. They would do sing-a-longs. Not the sing-a-long with Mitch, but a sing-a-long with Marvin and Smokey, and the bond began from there. They were just wonderful guys. I still stay in contact with Smokey. He's just a great guy.

We'd always go by the studio and listen to Marvin record. One day, he took Mel and me to the studio and sat us in the music room with him. He said, "Lem, you take this part. Mel, now you take this part." The next time you are listening to "What's Going On", you can hear a voice that comes on and says, "Say brother, what's happening?" I said, "Yeah brother, like solid, right on! Wee-doodle-dwee, wee-oodle-dwee, ooh, ooh, mother, mother." As a result, it ended up being a gold record. Berry Gordy, the big guy for Motown, gave us gold records for singing background with Marvin on "What's Going On." It's been a joy. Marvin was a great guy.

I would pay Motown to have a gold record, man. There were no residuals coming, but it was a just a joy to sing with a guy who you fell in love with and became great friends with; and what a dynamic guy he was. A lot of people didn't really know the ins and outs about Marvin. He would give you the coat off of his back, and wouldn't ask you for a receipt or a dollar for it. He just had a compassionate, loving heart. He always wanted to be an athlete. He just didn't have it.

I got Marvin a shot with the Detroit Lions as a walk-on. He went on The Shirley Eder show, The Jack Parr Show, and a lot of shows in the Detroit area on radio and TV. He kept saying, "I'm going to be a Detroit Lion." Coach Joe Schmidt said, "What's this about your man Marvin saying he's going to be a Detroit Lion? Doesn't he know he has to train with us?"

I said, "Coach, I keep telling him that he can't just, you know, walk on. Even if he is a walk-on, he has to get permission from the team." Coach Schmidt set up a meeting where Marvin would come and talk with him. He knew Marvin would be over at the restaurant where all the coaches, players, and the wives would be Sunday night after a game at Tiger Stadium. Coach Schmidt said, "Marvin, do you have any film from when you played in high school?" Marvin sort of held his head down and said, "Well coach, I never played in high school." He said, "That's okay. What about college? Do you have any film on you from when you played in college?" He held his head down again and said, "Coach, I never played in college." Coach said, "Well Marvin, what makes you think you can walk on as a professional without having played in high school?" He said, "Coach, I just believe in my heart. That first time I touched a pass, I score a touchdown, you know, every time I try, I just believe that in my heart." Coach said, "Marvin, I love your attitude and everything, but let me think about that. I'll get back with Lem, and I'll let you know." Coach called me back that evening and said, "Man, I would, but this guy would go out there and get his leg broke or something, and I couldn't live with myself if he did. Let me think about it and I'll get back with you."

Coach had a three-day workout in shorts and a helmet in Flint, and he invited Marvin to come out and practice. Marvin tried out at running back, tight end, and wide receiver. He had the heart for it, but he didn't have the skills or the talent for it, but he was appreciative that coach gave him an opportunity to work out with the guys.

I think the entire squad, the organization, the town, and the state were pretty much balled out after Chuck Hughes died on the field. A lot of people thought Dick Butkus had hit Chuck Hughes. We were playing the Chicago Bears at Tiger Stadium. A lot of people don't know the ins and outs of this. A week before playing the Bears, we were playing the New England Patriots in Foxboro. Chuck ran a few patterns, came back, and sat on the bench. He had a PVC, a premature ventricular contraction that just shook his heart so bad, it knocked him off the bench backward about 5 yards. When he came back from New England, he started going to the hospital with his doctors. They were checking him out every day, two and three times a day, and thought he had, what looked like, a PVC. They saw no scars or anything, and they thought he was okay.

The next week, we are playing the Chicago Bears at Tiger Stadium. Chuck came in on a 1st and ten down and ran a pass route, and the ball wasn't thrown to him. As he was coming back to the huddle, he gets another pass call, and he runs another route, and the ball wasn't thrown to him. On his way back, as he is passing the Chicago Bears' huddle to get back where the Lions were huddling, he fell between where the ball was and where the Detroit Lions were huddling. He started foaming at the mouth. It was just a horrible site. Butkus started waving because during those years at Tiger Stadium, both the teams were on the same side of the field. Butkus was waving for some of his physicians to come by. People thought Butkus was taunting Chuck because they thought he'd slipped and hurt himself. When the doctors got out there, they saw how his color had changed, and they rushed him off the field and to the hospital. He made his transition to death before they even took him off the field. It was that strong of a PVC this time.

The whole team flew down to Austin, Texas, where Joe Schmidt had the funeral for him. I always had great respect for Dick Butkus, but I fell in love with him when he called the Lions and asked if he could go down on the flight with us to the funeral. I have always admired Dick for that. I have a great relationship with him.

Paper Lion
I love George Plimpton and Alan Alda. My first role as an actor was in *The Paper Lion*, which was written by George Plimpton, a great writer. George always wanted to get a shot at playing professional ball. George was a tall guy and wanted to play wide receiver. In fact, he got the Lions and coach Joe Schmidt to give him an opportunity to play in a pre-season game at University of Michigan. From that, he wrote the book, *The Paper Lion*, about a writer trying out with the Lions, which became a best seller.

Then they made a movie about the book and cast a big guy from *Mash*, Alan Alda, to play the role of George Plimpton. It was just so much fun doing the movie. We filmed it down in Florida at a Boca Raton private boarding school. It turned out being a great film. Mike Weger and I did a lot of singing in the movie. The movie detailed what a rookie has to end up doing during the course of indoctrination as a professional ball player during their rookie year. It was a lot of fun.

The Black Six
The guy who did the Linda Lovelace movie, *Deep Throat*, contacted Carl Eller from the Vikings, Joe Greene from the Steelers, Willie Lanier from the Chiefs, Mercury Morris from the Dolphins, Gene Washington from the 49ers, and me, about doing a motorcycle movie called *The Black Six*. In the movie we were all Vietnam War Veterans, and while we were in Vietnam, the six of us had a pact that if we survived the Vietnam War, we would come back to the states and buy motorcycles and just ride all across the country, enjoying life. Our motto was, "We will show love and peace; no hassle." That was our motto, but everywhere we went, we ended up running into dangerous troubles across the country.

Dick "Night Train" Lane
The Train. What a great guy. May his soul rest in peace. Train helped to scout me during my junior and senior years down at Jackson State. I thought it was an honor to have him to come down.

As modernized as the game is now with all the defenses, he still has an all-time league-leading record as a rookie with 14 interceptions. They were only playing 12 league games at the time; it's four more games now. He played the left side, and he was left-handed. When a sweep would occur, the cornerback's responsibility is to come up and go on the outside shoulder of the pulling lineman to turn everything back in for the pursuit, to make the tackle. Train, for whatever reason, the coach couldn't figure it out either, would not turn it in. He would go inside and turn it out. Night Train was left-handed, and Night Train would hit you with that meat hook. He would hit you around the neck. It was like a clothesline tackle around your neck. A guy running the ball would think he was outside of Night Train's grasp. When they woke him up, the official would be over him, and he would say, "What happened?" The official would said, "The Train got you, baby, the Train got you."

Interceptions

I could almost describe all of them. I still remember them fondly. The first one was so special. Maybe because of the fact that I had great admiration for Bart Starr, and I still do. Bart and I became very good friends. Again, I had a tremendous respect for Bart because I wanted to be a Bart Starr. Bart was a quarterback at Alabama and ended up going to the Packers. I watched Bart's techniques and fundamentals of the game in passing. He had a great mind as well. After being drafted by the Lions, I found out that I was in the Central Division and I was going to be playing against this guy a couple of times a year.

We go up to Green Bay. They are the defending Super Bowl champions. Coach Vince Lombardi, as well as Bart, used to always test and pick on rookies. The second offensive play of the game, it's 2nd and 7 and Bart takes a 3-step drop. He tries to throw a quick out to All-Pro Boyd Dowler. As Bart sees me closing, he is in the motion to throw it, so he throws the ball like a good fastball pitcher to a good fastball hitter. He throws it low and away. I dive in front of the receiver about 3-1/2-yards, I stretch out, intercept the ball, and do a fall with a shoulder roll. I get up, and I run it into the end zone about 22 yards for a touchdown. As I slam the ball when I get into the end zone, I watched the ball go skyward. I put my hands on my hips, and I said, "Lord, this is going to be easy." First play in the league, first pass, second play of the game, lines up 7 nothing.

Pro Football Hall Of Fame Induction

I'm still feeling that feeling. It's one of the greatest feelings. I'll always remember it, because it's a feeling like you never had before. I don't think playing in four or five Super Bowls would've have given me that type of feeling. First of all, it was something that was totally unexpected. The first year I was on the finalist list, I didn't think I was going to have a chance to go in. Then the next year, I was on the finalist list again. It happened that second time around, and it was news across the country.

Al Davis from the Raiders, John Mackey from the Baltimore Colts, and number 44 from the Washington Redskins, John Riggins, and I were inducted. It was just so unbelievable because, again, coming out of Jackson State, Mississippi, playing with the Lions, I'm thinking that you had to be a two-time Super Bowl MVP and things of that nature to get in. I guess the second time around it was good enough for the writers and the voters. It was just one of those things that I was so appreciative of. I got Jimmy David, my professional football coach, who had signed me, as my presenter at the hall. I had coaches from high school, coaches from college, friends, and teammates, that I could have asked, but it was Jimmy David that I had asked to do it.

The day of the parade, before the enshrinement, I was asking my driver, "Has anybody ever sang at the Hall of Fame enshrinement?" He said, "Oh yeah, they sing the national anthem and things like that." I said, "Oh, no, no. My daughter's going to do that." I said, "What about any of the enshrinees? Have they ever sung before?" He said, "Enshrinees? No enshrinee has ever sung before. Why? Are you thinking about singing?" I said, "Well, if I can muster up to it, yeah. I'm thinking about it." He said, "What are you going to sing?" I said, "No, I can't tell you that now. I'm just going to let everybody know if I sing."

When Jimmy enshrined me and made his last remarks about me, he said, "Lem Barney, if there was ever a greater defensive back than him that played in the National League, I've yet to see it. Here he is, Lem Barney." Everybody started applauding. I walk up and I give a little sigh and I look out and I sang, "For once in a lifetime, a man knows the moment. One wonderful moment when fate takes his hand and this is my moment." It was the greatest moment of my life in football, so I had to sing about it or shout about it or I was going to cry, one of the three or four. I ended up singing. It came off good. I didn't get any music offers or anything of that nature, but it was something I really wanted to do.

Toughest Receiver To Cover

It could've been a fat lady in front of me and I was going to respect her because if she was in front of me, she had the abilities and the talents to beat me. There were some small receivers that had speed and could run smooth patterns, like Paul Warfield, for instance. Charlie Taylor had speed, quickness, and moves. You have guys like Cliff Branch and Bob Hayes who had great speed. Paul Warfield and Isaac Curtis would run good routes and had great speed. Otis Taylor had great speed and was a fine route runner.

Detroit Lion Lem Barney grabs Larry Brown of the Washington Redskin by the leg to bring him down Photograph courtesy Associated Press

Chapter 36

Larry Little

College:
Bethune-Cookman

Career History:
San Diego Chargers (1967–1968)
Miami Dolphins (1969–1980)

1993 Inductee Pro Football Hall of Fame

College Choice

When I came out of high school, it was during the time of segregation so I didn't have a chance to go to a major college. I only had two scholarships coming out of high school, Bethune-Cookman and Saint Augustine College in Raleigh, North Carolina. All of my good friends, classmates, and teammates were going to Saint Augustine, so I decided to stay closer to home and went to Bethune-Cookman in Daytona Beach. Ironically, my senior year, Saint Augustine dropped football. So, I made a big choice that was very important to where I am today.

Draft

Before the draft I got a call from Houston and the Rams, who told me they were going to draft me. In the dormitory where I was living, my room was right next to the telephone booth. I wouldn't let anybody use the phone all day since I was expecting a phone call. I stood by the phone. I couldn't eat or sleep. I was waiting on a phone call that never came. The next day I got a call from the Baltimore coach who said they wanted to sign me as a free agent. I asked him how much bonus money I was going to get, and he told me they weren't giving any bonuses to free agents.

So then I got a call from a guy in Daytona Beach by the name of Bud Asher who was scouting for the Chargers at the time. He said they'd give me $750 for a bonus and I jumped at it. The next day, Joe Thomas of the Miami Dolphins called me and said "Larry how'd you like to play at home in Miami?" I said, "Well I would've loved to come to Miami to play but I'm going to sign with San Diego." He asked, "How much money did they give you? I asked him, "How much bonus money are you going to give me?" He told me, "$500." I told him "San Diego gave me $750 so I'm going to San Diego."

Trade To Miami Dolphins

Joe Thomas made a trade for me to come to Miami for my high school teammate, Mack Lamb. Sid Gillman who was my coach in San Diego at the time called it a nothing-for-nothing deal. I don't know if two high school teammates had been ever traded for each other.

Well I really didn't want to play for Miami because they were an expansion team. San Diego wasn't winning championships, but we were winning. We had a lot of talent in San Diego, guys like Lance Alworth, John Hadl, the quarterback, and Paul Lowe, a great running back. I played for one year under George Wilson in Miami. Then they fired George and brought in Don Shula in 1970.

Position Change With Dolphins

Early in my college career, you had to play both ways. It was not until my senior year that I had the choice to play offense or defense. I was accustomed to playing both offense and defense, so it didn't matter what side of the ball I played with the Dolphins. The only thing I wanted was an opportunity to prove myself.

When I got to Miami, Sid Gillman had all the guys in shorts and shoulder pads. I ran a 4.9 forty in pads.

I picked up the San Diego Union newspaper and read that Sid Gillman brought a lot of free agents to training camp before the drafted rookies got to camp, and maybe one or two free agents stick around when the drafted rookies got to training camp. I felt kind of insulted and that upset me because I thought I would have a chance to compete with all the rookies not just the free agent rookies.

So what happened was, I made it through that first week. I was glad it happened that way because I was able to be a week up on the rookies who were coming in. The first four games I was on the taxi squad. After the fourth game I was activated to the regular roster.

I wasn't worried that they had me on special teams. I was a pretty good special teams guy because of my size and speed. They had me at fullback for two days before I moved to guard. They said I could be the next Jim Nance, but I thought they moved me there because they were getting ready to cut me. Then I was told they wanted to try me out on the offensive side of the ball, and I guess you could say the rest is history.

Don Shula
You could tell it would be a whole different atmosphere with Don Shula than it was with George Wilson. On a hot summer day during our two-a-day practices, George Wilson would tell us, "Oh it's too damn hot to practice. Go jump in the pool." No way Don Shula would ever do that. We'd practice through any kind of heat and we'd practice very, very hard. We were probably the hardest practicing team in football. I don't think anybody worked as hard as we did.

Dolphins Offensive Line
One thing we did have was a lot of pride on the offensive line. We liked to call ourselves the best in the business. We always took that attitude on the field with us. We knew we could play the game.

Chicken Little
We were training in Escondido, California and the first night out we were going to the city of San Diego, to a fried chicken place owned by a former Pittsburgh Steeler. I ate a whole chicken, drank a fifth of Ripple wine, and I got the name "Chicken Little."

It followed me all the way down to Miami. I'm still called "Chicken" by a lot of my teammates. I do love the bird though.

Playing Weight
When Don Shula first met me at his press conference when he became the head coach, I was leaning towards 285 pounds in weight. That's what I played at my first in Miami for George Wilson. So I went up to Coach Shula and said, "Coach my name is Larry Little and I'm one of your guards." The first thing he asked me was, "How much do you weigh?" I said, "Oh, 285." He said, "All right. That's all right," and walked off just like that. When I got the letter to report to training camp, the report said, "I want your weight to be 265 pounds." I hadn't been that small in I don't know how long. I knew it was something I had to do and it made me a better football player. I realized that. When I played, it made me faster and more agile. So he knew what was best for me and I accepted it.

Paul Warfield
Paul Warfield was the consummate trophy. Paul did what he could to help the football team win and you couldn't have had a better teammate than him. Paul was also a great down field blocker. He was great for our team.

Marv Fleming
We got veteran leadership from people like Paul Warfield and Marv Fleming when he came to Miami. They had been on winning teams. To this day I still say Marv Fleming was the best blocking tight end to ever play the game. Marv made my job very easy of pulling for sweeps because I knew he would cave and run down and I could get to the corner much easier. He was a great teammate.

Super Bowl VI
Super Bowl VI was an awesome experience. Just two years before that, we were 3-10-1. Two years later we were in the Super Bowl. It was an experience. A lot of things needed to happen for us to be there. We were happy to be there, we were expecting to win but we were just beaten by a better football team I guess, the Dallas Cowboys.

Bob Griese

Bob Griese was another unselfish player. Bob called his own plays. We had a great wide receiver in Paul Warfield, but Paul knew our offense was based on the offensive line and our running backs. He knew that if we did our jobs, which we did very well, we'd be in a position to win football games. Keep the other team from getting the football.

1972 Miami Dolphins Undefeated Season

When we lost to Dallas in the Super Bowl, our main goal was to make sure to get back to the Super Bowl and win it. That was our whole attitude in training camp. We saw the film of the Dallas game and Coach Shula stood up in front of the team and said, "You see how you feel now and how you felt then. You don't want to have that feeling again, so we've got to go back to the Super Bowl to win the Super Bowl." That was our attitude, to go back and win it. We weren't talking about going undefeated, it just kept happening. We played a lot of close games that year too but we always found a way to win.

Toughest Defensive Lineman

It was probably Joe Greene. We had some great battles against each other. Joe intimidated a lot of offensive line guards. The strongest guy to play the game was Curley Culp. All around Joe was quick, strong, and nasty. He whipped my ass up.

Mercury Morris

When Mercury Morris came to Miami, I saw this guy walking and running his mouth. He was wearing red pants with the buckle in the back. I was like, who's this guy? We didn't get along when we first met because he was from the North and I was from the South, and he probably had more sense than me. Now we are best friends forever. He's a talker.

Photograph courtesy Associated Press

Chapter 37

Elvin Bethea

College:
North Carolina A&T

Career History:
Houston Oilers (1968-1983)

2003 Inductee Pro Football Hall of Fame

College Choice
North Carolina A&T was not my choice; my mother made that choice for me. At that time, I had probably about 18-20 scholarships and I really wanted to go to Villanova. My mother went to school with a gentleman who was a football coach at North Carolina A&T, and that was the end of it. I didn't have a say-so in it.

I'm glad I went. I went to a small college and they say if you can make it a small black college, you can make it anywhere in the world. That is the motto.

It was quite a culture shock. I went from a high school, which was very integrated and multicultural to a college, which was predominantly black. It was an adjustment but I enjoyed it. One thing that really shocked me was that the facilities were worse than I had in high school. I adjusted and everything worked out for me. I always tell people that if I had to do it again I would do it the same way.

Houston Oilers Training Camp
I left North Carolina and went southwest. We're talking about real culture shock. My first stop over was in Kerrville,

Texas. I would highly recommend doing that for anyone from up north. You'll learn a lot about cactuses.

It was a little west from the middle of nowhere. It was about 80 miles west of San Antonio. Nothing was there. You didn't have a Walmart or Kmart or any real restaurants to go to. It was just a little country. Our training camp location was at a Shriner Institute. It was just a boarding school, and the best facilities at that time were your sleeping quarters. Everything else was back in the 1940s I think.

This was Bud Adams' choice. It was cheap and it was an institute that was small and private. The sleeping facilities were in dormitories but as far as the practice facilities, it was second to none and I mean none. There was no air conditioning unit in the gym. The only thing that was green in that whole area was the football field. Seriously. The temperature at 2 or 3 o'clock in the afternoon was always at least 95-100 degrees, and that's the way we trained.

We trained there and that's what you were there to do. We had six to seven weeks before going to training camp and there was nothing to do. Zero. All you did was drank beer on the weekends. You had a scrimmage on Saturday morning and were off from Saturday afternoon until Sunday and then back to work on Monday. Being there was strictly for training and it was good. It got you away from your family and other obstacles that might tend to bend your ear the wrong way.

We didn't have a winning season because of the type of players they had chosen. Quite a few guys made it by leaving there and going to other teams. Everybody enjoyed it for what little money they were making. We were there for six weeks and we were making $50 a preseason game, before taxes. After taxes you got $46.24.

Adjustment To Professional Football
When you get to the pros you think that you're the hottest stuff showing up, but after you get there, you find a lot of players are above and beyond your talent level and everybody is good at that point. There are people who can help the team and hope to make the team. In my case, I had a lot of competition back then and I just wanted to make the team. As far as the money, I earned $15,000 my

first year. All I wanted to do was just have that emblem and logo on my helmet, jacket, or where ever. That's what it was.

You came in with 100 players and only 40 of them were going to stay. For me, I was lucky enough to stay. I worked my tail off because I wanted to be a Houston Oiler. I had no idea what the hell I was doing, but I enjoyed football. Sixteen later I was still there.

Stats

After I realized that there were stats, I would build on my previous year. Every year I wanted to have one or two more than the last year, such as tackles. So, that was my goal. I was always trying to reach a higher goal and set those numbers for myself, but this happened later in my career. When I first started out, all I wanted to do was play. There were no goals except making the Pro Bowl. That was the incentive. I really tried to make. I never thought that I would be in the Pro Bowl for eight years. The incentive if you made the Pro Bowl was you got $1,500 extra. So, that was the incentive. It wasn't like it is now. If you go to the Pro Bowl, the winning and losing teams each get seven figure paydays. We would kill each other for the extra $250 or whatever it was the winning players got. I was just glad to be there.

Experts estimate I had 105 sacks, I still don't agree with it. The NFL didn't keep any records of sacks when I played. I still think I would have been close to the record of 200 sacks that Bruce Smith has. Who knows, life goes on.

When I got chosen for the Hall of Fame, the guy who really helped me was Mark Adams. He kept every stat on me from the day I started. I never followed stats. I just went out and played the game. After I saw the stats, I was impressed with myself. I said, "Boy, I must have been really good."

Earl Campbell

In 1978 when Earl Campbell came, we would have the second team go against the first team in training camp. The offensive first team would go against the second team defense. The first team defense would go against the second team offense. We really never met up in practice. Bum wanted to make sure that nobody got hurt. Bum wanted to make sure that he took care of his players and Bum was a player's coach.

Bum Phillips

Bum Phillips took good care of us. Bum was a player's coach. He understood every player. That was amazing. I sat there and watched him for years. He knew each player on that team; what button to push as far as getting him motivated. That was a crazy thing because we had players who were from other teams. We were basically misfitting characters. We picked up anybody and everybody who was on the trading block.

The thing is, Bum knew how to push each players button to get them motivated. He is the type of guy who would pull you to the side and say, "Hey, you either get in line or get out of line because I will trade you." You knew right from the start where he was coming from. He was trying to build a team by having them build themselves. It was the greatest thing. If we had a problem with one guy, he would keep pestering him and ask us to take care of the problem. We'd take care of our own house. That was the greatest thing about him. He would let you play the game and make sure that you were fit and that you were prepared. After every game there was a party that he would set up for us. It was a great time for me, especially in the later years.

Bum Phillips Use Of Earl Campbell

Bum would run Earl right, Earl left, Earl up the middle. I think Earl Campbell wanted to run the ball. He was the man. I think that he proved he was the man. That's football. If you have something that's going for you, a play or a player that's bringing you your wins, you go with it. It's sad that Earl only played maybe seven years. I think it was, but now he can barely walk, but that was football. You play the best. I'm sure that Earl didn't want to be sitting on the bench at any time. You go out there, not knowing the effects of playing until after you leave the game. Earl could have backed off if he wanted to, but that was Earl and that's the way Bum saw these things. He knew every button for each guy—what to push and how hard to push it.

Pro Football Hall Of Fame Induction

It got to a point, I think in my 17th or 18th year after retiring, people would say, "Oh, you're going; you're going to the Hall." I would say, "If I haven't gone by now, I'm not worried and not concerned about it." The craziest thing, the day I got the call, I was working for Anheuser Busch and I was heading to a meeting in St. Louis. A guy called and said, "You're in the Hall of Fame. Your name was called." I said, "You know what, until someone calls me and tells me I won't believe it." There was a time that I never thought it would happen to me. It never dawned on me. I thought that my memories were enough. I played on a very bad team. The Pro Bowls I went to helped me get in. How many winning seasons did the teams that I played on have? I didn't expect it. I didn't even follow the Hall of Fame, honestly. I'm just a simple person. It's a very humbling feeling to say that and every time I look at my jacket or look at a picture of myself in the Hall, I'm saying this is it. I've told people that one vote could've gone the wrong way for me and it could've been another 20 years. I'm very happy that I'm there and I wear the jacket very proudly. I go back every year. They have a parade that's better than the Macy's parade, with over 250,000 people every year. Each and every year that I've gone there, we have a parade on Saturday. It's about two hours long and it's just amazing how people come out to see us and just to wave at us. There's one thing they always say is thank you for coming back. That's what really makes me feel that I've accomplished all my goals and I'm finally getting a little accolade for what I did.

There was one kid standing on the side my second year in the Hall. He had a cut off of cardboard and written on it was, "You coming back to Canton, priceless." That sold me. I will be there every year.

Houston Oiler Elvin Bethea puts the pressure on Dallas Cowboy
Roger Staubach Photograph courtesy Associated Press

Chapter 38

Curley Culp

College:
Arizona State

Career History:
Kansas City Chiefs (1968-1974)
Houston Oilers (1974-1980)
Detroit Lions (1980-1981)

2013 Inductee Pro Football Hall of Fame

College Choice
I had an opportunity to go to UCLA on a wrestling scholarship.
The only catch was that if you made the team you would have a
scholarship. I won the state championship a couple of years in a
row at Yuma High School. At Arizona State, it gave me an
opportunity to do two things: one, to play football and second, to
wrestle which was really dear to me at that time.

I enjoyed wrestling and football in my hometown, Yuma,
Arizona. We had some decent years, but I think my wrestling
success was probably overshadowed by my football endeavors.

Frank Kush was the Head Coach at that time. A gentleman by
the name of Jack Stovall at Arizona State pursued me heavily
through the support of my high school coach at the time, Frank
Thomas.

Frank Kush
Frank Kush was a super coach. He brought in a lot of individuals
and gave them opportunities in pro football and to get an
education at Arizona State University. I think his style of

coaching probably wouldn't fit in college today, but he had great success at Arizona State University. He got things done and was a winning coach.

There were a lot of good athletes at Arizona State University, like Charlie Taylor, Mike Haynes, Randall McDaniel, and me. Reggie Jackson started out at football and didn't play much, and then he switched over to play baseball.

Name Curley
I have a twin sister and her name is Shirley. She was born about 15 minutes before me. My sister Lucille told me that she came up with the rhyme between Shirley and Curley.

I had to live with that. A lot of people think that Curley is a nickname. A lot of people have Curley as a nickname, but that's my given name. No middle name just Curley.

Reggie Jackson
Reggie Jackson was a running back. I had an opportunity to block for him as an offensive guard when I was at Arizona State during my freshmen year.

I think there was a situation at Arizona State University where Reggie had to go through the hamburger drill. I think the hamburger drill was what made up his mind which sport he wanted to pursue at the time.

College Wrestling
My junior year I won the Gregorian Award. That was quite an accomplishment. I had a Head Coach by the name of Ted Bredehoft for wrestling. I must say that I was in the best shape I had ever been in my life going into the nationals.

In the first round, I wrestled this gentleman from Lehigh and I beat him 15-5. I took the rest of my opponents to the mat and pinned them all.

In the championship round, I pinned a guy from Adams State in 51 seconds. It was really a great feat for me to be a part of the team. I think that's the first time Arizona State University ranked so highly in the nationals, so it was a big deal. I think it was probably more pure strength than anything. Although we had a weight program at Arizona State, it wasn't really extensive. It wasn't the kind of weight training that they have now in colleges and universities.

I won the nationals during my senior year. Since in my junior year, I had an opportunity to compete for the Olympics. In fact, I made the Olympic squad. I was the number two heavyweight in the country at that time. Larry Kristoff was number one and I was number two.

I went to the trials, I believe in Lincoln, Nebraska. They said you needed to win two out of the three matches. You had the opportunity to pick which way you wanted to wrestle, freestyle or Greco.

Freestyle wrestling is where you use your legs and your upper body. That was my choice. The powers that be wanted me to go with Greco. I wrestled this guy in the first round and I thought I pinned him. A couple of judges said he was pinned and I relaxed a bit, he rolled me a couple of times. The outcome of the match was different than I thought it should have been. I decided to pursue football instead of wrestling at that time.

I guess because I won nationals, everybody kind of knew who I was. They had a picture of me on a little jar that you put money in. Whoever, end up collecting the most money would get the award for "The Boy With the Best Smile," so I won the award.

I think a lot of my teammates came in and dropped a nickel or dime every now to get me the award. It was a great thing that the student body gave me that kind of recognition.

College Draft
I was drafted by Denver and was their first pick. The college scouts in the pros felt that I was a better student for offense. They just felt that I was too short to play D-line I guess mainly because of my stature, my size—my height.

I had an opportunity to participate in the College All-Star Game in Chicago. I was a little late getting into training camp in Denver.

Lou Saban was the Head Coach. Like the college scouts, he wanted me to participate on offense, and I did. I didn't like it, but I did it because that's what he wanted me to do. He gave me an opportunity to do both offense and defense. It just didn't work out there.

I had one game in the preseason and I thought I graded out. I did grade out better than everybody else on the D-line, but the following week, I was out of there. He traded me to Kansas City.

Hank Stram had come to Arizona State for an athletic event and he spoke to the athletes at the event. Afterward he told me if he ever had an opportunity to pick me up, he would. He didn't draft me, but he had an opportunity to pick me up from Denver when Lou Saban decided to let me go.

Chiefs training camp was structured a little differently. The organization was different in the sense that you had veteran ball players there, so things were done differently.

They had a weight-training program. Everybody lifted weights regardless of what position they played. When we moved over to Arrowhead in 1972, we had a big Jacuzzi for the players.

In that building, they had a racquetball court. Everybody was kind of fascinated by racquetball. I start playing racquetball for the first time. I truly enjoyed it because I think the quickness in playing the game allowed me to hone some of the things that might be productive on the football field.

Kansas City Chiefs Defense
It was a great bunch of men. You had Jerry Mays on one side and Aaron Brown on the other side as ends. Then you had Buck Buchanan and me in the middle. Willie Lanier, Bobby Bell, and Jim Lynch were the linebackers. Johnny Robinson and Emmitt Thomas were in the secondary. We had a great bunch of guys.

Jim Marsalis was the guy I roomed with a lot. I think we started rooming together the first year I was there. It was a great fit with the blend between young ballplayers and veteran ballplayers. It was one of those teams that you wanted to be on because it was a good chemistry and Hank Stram was such a great coach. He was an innovator on a lot of things he tried to do as well.

Tom Pratt was the defensive line coach. Most of the time, my interactions were with Tom Pratt. If there was a situation with the team that Tom Pratt thought Hank Stram should become involved with, he would do that.

Hank Stram held two roles. He was a head coach and he dealt with contracts. I thought that was kind of a conflict of interest, but he did that.

Move To Houston Oilers
I played with Kansas City for six and a half years, and six and a half years with Houston. I was in my sixth year of my contract with Kansas City that's when the World Football League started out. I was having some difficulty getting things ironed out with Hank Stram. I decided to move on and pursued playing in the World Football League by signing a contract with the California Suns.

During the 1974 NFL Season, I was basically playing out that year with all expectations of playing with the World Football League the following year. During the middle of the season, Hank Stram and me had a little disagreement of some sort, so Hank Stram decided to let me go.

The World Football Leagues first year was in 1974 and it just dissolved. I worked things out with Houston and stayed in Houston from the middle of 1974 to 1980. In 1981 I finished up in Detroit.

Bum Phillips
Bum Phillips was quite different than Hank Stram of course and even Tom Pratt. I think Bum was with Sid Gillman in San Diego.

Bum came over to Houston when Sid came in as head coach. Bum was a player's coach in a lot of respects. He was a great guy. He was really hands-on and let people do their own thing, so-to-speak.

Bum was the defensive line coach. The following year he became the head coach and Eddie Biles became the defensive coordinator.

I believe his son; Wade Phillips became the defensive line coach if I'm not mistaken.

3-4 Defense
In Kansas City, we had the "Triple Stack". We had two defenses primarily the "Triple Stack" and "Under". The "Triple Stack" was the one in which the defensive line would slide to disturb the formation. The "Under" defense, we would slide away from this vent.

In the Super Bowl, I don't know if I was assigned to the center all the time or if it just so happened. I think it was more situational than anything else.

In this matchup between the D-line against an offensive center the main responsibility of the center is to hide the ball. He has to hide the ball before he does anything else.

I'm engaging him probably at the same time he's hiking the ball. It's an advantage to the defensive line in those kinds of circumstances, although you could have a situation where you have the guards coming down on you too. It's interesting to say the least.

Transition To Oilers
In Kansas City, there were occasions I would get on the nose because it shifted the formation. Then when I go down to Houston, I'm stuck right there with the center. You don't have much movement, you're just right there kind of an apex of action. You can't relax. You're always involved in what's going on, on the football field.

Elvin Bethea

Elvin Bethea was a great one out there playing the right end position. We had Teddy Washington too. Robert Brazile came in 1976 and he helped out. The other guy inside was Gregg Bingham.

We had a good bunch of individuals, not the same talent that was in Kansas City, but we played well. We had good chemistry.

Defensive Touchdown Scored

Against the Chargers in San Diego I picked up the ball and I was just rumbling down the field. Elvin Bethea yelled, "You're going the wrong way." I turned around, and squabbled into the end zone. That was the first one and the last one I had in fourteen years in professional football, is quite neat to say the least. When you're down and you're eating all that grass and you pop-up, man, you just start running.

Toughest Offensive Linemen Faced

There were a lot of tough offensive linemen in the league during that era. I took pride in trying to keep myself physically fit to play the game. With Kansas City, we had the weight training.

Then when I shifted to Houston, James Young and me worked out extensively during the off-season trying to stay strong. We knew that was helpful when you're dealing with offensive linemen.

Favorite Coach

There were so many great coaches. Lou Saban was a good coach. We just didn't get along, but he was a great coach. Hank Stram was a super coach. Bum Phillips was a great coach. They were all good coaches. They just did things a little differently.

The greatest coach that I've been involved with was probably Hank Stram because of the fact that the team went to two Super Bowls, –the first and fourth Super Bowls. Even with Bum, we got to the championship game and played Pittsburgh two years in a row. They were both accomplished, so I guess, we're right there together.

Kansas City's Curley Culp pressures Dallas Craig Morton
Photograph courtesy Associated Press

Chapter 39

Ron Yary

College:
Southern California

Career History:
Minnesota Vikings (1968–1981)
Los Angeles Rams (1982)

2001 Inductee Pro Football Hall of Fame

Move To Offensive Line At USC

What happened was all of our offensive line members were
seniors my sophomore year. They lost everyone, so they moved
me to strong side offensive tackle. Then they flipped lines, the
left and right played both sides with the "I" formation. They told
me after my junior year, that my senior year that they were going
to play me both ways, which really got me excited but they never
did. We were having a really good year so they thought it wasn't
necessary. I was really disappointed they didn't call me to play
both sides of the ball.

Playing fullback in high school was enough for me. I realized
those guys get beat up. I was sorer after a game as a fullback
than I ever was as an offensive lineman. You've got nine guys
coming at you. I couldn't run away from guys and I wasn't that
nifty. It was either I run over them or through them, that's the
type of fullback I was. I was more of a blocking fullback. They
let me lead on plays to block the defense end, or block the
outside linebacker. They used me more as a blocking fullback
than a running back.

College Choice

Nobody recruited me except the coaches. No former players
came out or called me. I was, I think, maybe a borderline guy

who they wanted. I went to Cerritos College for a semester. I got good grades in high school. I took all college prep courses. For me, I needed to go to a junior college first. I was too immature with study habits, discipline, and areas that are required for you to succeed in college. I just wasn't ready for it.

USC offered me a scholarship; I didn't qualify to get in. I think USC shipped me off to a junior college with the expectation that I would turn out to be ok, but if I didn't they'd have an out. That's what happened.

O.J. Simpson
You never appreciated having O.J. Simpson until you played against him. To me, he was just another running back. He was a very nice guy in college. He was very personable and engaging with people. Everybody liked him. He never hung out with any of the players on the team. I don't know where he was. It was the same with Mike Garrett. You never knew where they were. They were probably in Hollywood or something, hanging out with all the celebrities. The guys that had to work stayed in the dorms.

John McKay Offense
John McKay liked to run at people. You run at them and if it works, it works. USC didn't have the quarterbacks that they have today. They didn't have the 6'3" or 6'5" quarterbacks to throw 50 yards. It was old time football.

You weren't any good unless you could run the ball. I was raised in a generation where that was your mental approach. If you were to throw the football, it was an insult to the offensive line. It was like, the reason we're throwing the ball is because we can't run the ball. The reason we can't run the ball is because we're not good enough. It was a big insult to you. That was the way that USC approached it back then. I'm sure that a lot of other colleges did as well. We were focused on run blocking and it turned out well.

Mike Holmgren
Mike Holmgren was a very smart guy. We had some smart players on the team, excluding me. Our two offensive guards became orthopedic surgeons. Another guard got his Master of Education.

One of our centers became a dentist. We had a lot of smart guys on those teams.

Mike was one of them. Mike was a throwing quarterback. They never gave him an opportunity to throw the ball. He had a heck of an arm. He could throw. He was a freshman or a sophomore my senior year.

He was a funny guy. Everybody loved Mike because he had a great sense of humor. He could take the worst situation and make it into something you could really laugh about and enjoy. You always need guys on teams like that, and Mike had that great quality. The quality came through when he was a coach. He was able to get players to play up to their abilities because of that. He was really a player's coach; I'm certain of that.

First Offensive Lineman To Be First Pick In The NFL Draft
I think if you're going to take a player and you're going to evaluate him to determine the outcome of his career, what kind a player he's going to be, it's easier to assess an offensive lineman more than any other position on the field. I think it's a safe investment to make when you pick an offensive lineman because of that.

Teams have had a lot of bad experiences drafting quarterbacks high in the draft. I know that they've had a lot of disappointments. I think there are maybe only one or two offensive linemen that they've been disappointed with in the draft.

You don't know how determined a guy is to play the game. A lot of guys don't have that hunger once they graduate from college, to make a career out of it. Chuck Arrobio, our left tackle, was a dentist as well. He was very smart. He went to the Vikings for a couple years and decided it was not worth it and became a dentist. He has had a great life as a dentist. Most of the other guys have done the same thing. They found alternatives or vocations that meant more than football.

Key To Minnesota Viking Success

What makes a great football team is how they handle adversity. We didn't like to lose. I knew that if we lost, the practices the following week would be worse than the game. Everybody would be angry with himself. Not angry at one another, but angry ourselves for losing the game. We were mad at ourselves for letting the game slip away. Once the team developed that quality, it was a tough thing to overcome for other teams. Once we lost that quality, the team began to lose.

We weren't replacing that type of a guy with the same type of a guy. You can't be happy losing.

Vikings Expectations Of Him

I didn't care about what the Vikings expectation were. I was going to do what I was going to do and that was it. I was going to live in my world, not theirs. I wasn't concerned with what their expectations were, or what they wanted me to do, I was going to do what I was going to do. I knew what I could do. I knew my limits. I knew how good I could be and I played the game.

The other thing is, I loved the game. I loved playing football. I would not have done anything other than football. It's the only thing in my life that I have done that I felt that way toward. Now, being a Dad is another. Up until this point, it was all me, everything. I loved going to work in the morning. I loved going to practice. I enjoyed hanging around that type of person. It was a simple life; it wasn't complex. You knew your outcome. You knew whether you'd succeed or fail immediately in your work assignment.

It's not like other occupations where you could go for six months and not know whether or not you're going to succeed. Your reward is known immediately. You can correct issues immediately as well. You can't find a better way to make a living in America than sports; it's ideal.

When you hear these guys talk about all the pressures involved, that's not true. To me I hear that and I don't understand it. You go to work every day, and you set your own goals. You reach your goals. You make a lot of money. You meet a lot of girls. If you're not

Married, you have a lot of opportunities to meet a lot of girls. What more can you ask for in life in your early twenties?

I've seen a lot of tragedies in marriages because of things that went on like that. I was married at 24, divorced at 26; perfect example of that. I was a bad husband; I was not a good husband. I had a great wife. I didn't get married again until I was 51, because I knew that failure ruined me for a long time. There may be reasons for that, but that's not what I'm here to talk about.

Bud Grant

Fran Tarkenton once said that if you can't play football for Bud Grant, you couldn't play for anyone. We all agreed on that. Bud had his ways that you may not have liked, but you could live with them. There wasn't anything he asked of you in terms of regimen or discipline that was something that you could not accept. He made it clear what he expected of you as a player. What was a good performance or what was a bad one. He never embarrassed you either. He never insulted you in front of your teammates.

He had the ability to stand up in front of the team and speak to you. He had that skill that all great orators have when they talk. It's like you're having a personal conversation with them. That was one of his great qualities. He left the coaching to the assistant coaches. He let our assistant coaches make decisions on the field. It made them feel like I they had a part in the success of the team. He was a great coach to play for.

The only thing that bothered me was that they sat me on the bench my first year. To this day, I can't accept it and I'm angry about it when I think back. I felt that I should have started from day one.

If that had been today, I would not have accepted that. I would have told him either get rid of me or put me on the field. I'm not going to sit on the sideline.

Bud Grant had the same offensive that Norm Van Brocklin had, except he changed the plays by moving the odd numbers to the right and the even numbers to the left. Under Van Brocklin's system, even was the right and odd was to the left. When I played in the College All-Star Game and Van Brocklin was the coach, every play that we learned was exactly the same as Bud had, except they were reversed.

When I joined the Vikings, I was backing up Doug Davis and Grady Alderman, a third tackle in training camp. When they'd run a play I would be thinking seven is to the right, but when you're tired it's hard to work through. I made a couple mistakes and I think it was because of that. I can't think of any other reason. Today I would probably quit the team and walk off. I would go somewhere where they needed a tackle, don't put me on the bench.

I really didn't like sitting on the bench. I'm still angry about my first year. You think about the past, that's one thing that always didn't sit well with me. That's my sole complaint in my life as a football player. That's pretty good.

Vikings Reacquiring Fran Tarkenton
Reacquiring Fran Tarkenton helped our team. It was a big benefit to our team because he could scramble. We were able to capitalize on his talent.

Being an offensive right tackle, I didn't like him scrambling because he liked to scramble to the right. He liked to drift to the right. If you look at the end zone films of Francis when he was playing, he would drift to the right and throw behind the right guard, even when he set up on a pass. I changed my style of play once I found that out. I think it was maybe two or three years after Francis came to the team they put an end zone camera in. I noticed he was drifting to the right when he set up.

I stopped using the normal drop back technique and started taking on guys who were on the line of scrimmage, sooner. I became a short pass blocker, rather than the regular drop back technique type guy. I had to be more aggressive with the defensive end. I couldn't let him get up field because he would be in the face of the quarterback because he was throwing behind the right guard.

That little nuance changed the way I played, which I didn't care. He always drifted right and I didn't have eyes in the back of my head. I couldn't see where he was moving. If I knew where he was, I wouldn't care. Then I could do something about it. When you begin to move and your quarterback is moving and that's not how you practice it or you're not aware of where he's going to be; it makes it more difficult. That's the problem with the scrambler. If there was some way you could determine where he's going to run that would be great.

Vikings Super Bowls
I thought our best one was against the Raiders. I thought that our first one with Kansas City was good as well. You go in thinking you can win them all. I thought we had the best opportunity to beat the Raiders. We never did very well in those games. The team that was better deserved to win. What more can you say? I'm happy for them.

Toughest Defensive Lineman Faced
In the beginning I didn't think anybody was any good. At the end of my career, everybody was great. You're tired of having to prove yourself every year. It's more the regimen that defeats you than the person telling you the truth. I'd have to say, if I picked out the lineman, Jack Youngblood, was good. Vern Den Herder played tough against me. I didn't know that he was from Minnesota when he was playing. I couldn't figure out why he came so hard against me.

Vikings Defensive Line Coaches
Buddy Ryan was our defensive line coach. Jack Patera built the defensive line. Jack left and went to Seattle where he was the head coach. Jack was the one that picked all those guys and he had a lot to do with developing them in the beginning. We were already into the peak of our careers when Buddy took over.

Chuck Foreman
Chuck Foreman made it a lot easier. He hit the hole so quick and he was so fast down the field that he made blocking a lot easier for everybody. That's what great running backs do. They turn

an average block into a pretty block. Chuck could hit a hole as fast as any guy I've ever seen.

I remember the first time he came in. The first play we ever ran with Chuck, he was through that hole so fast that he was five yards down the field. I was amazed. I said, "My God, he's going to help our team." He did, Chuck had great speed. Also, he had a great roll when he came to the Vikings. They'd hit him and he'd roll out of it, do a 360 roll and move down the field. He was very good.

Pro Football Hall Of Fame Induction
It's a very humbling experience that is a great culmination to your life and a career that you loved. If you love football and you go in the Hall of Fame, it's a big deal. If you really loved the game, wanted to play your whole life, and then you get recognized at what 50-some years old, it really is; it's like getting the Nobel Prize in Science to a football player.

Canton does such a great job. It's a great place to have the event. The whole town gets involved for that event. Nobody can give more than what the people in Canton, Ohio do. They make it worth the whole four days you're there. It's a big tribute and a great one.

When I'd go to a banquet, I'd sit out in the audience. Now, I sit at the head table and they introduce me. That's the difference when you make the Hall of Fame. They think that you have some insight about the game that nobody else has, which is not true. Actually, you have less insight probably than most people. That's how they are; you've become a big deal in life I guess.

Les Richter
I met Les Richter one time. He came to our market when I was 8 years old. I was overwhelmed with him. When I saw him, he made me want to play football.

The reason was he had cuts all over his hands and over his forehead. His eyes were all scarred over, he had nicks all over his arms and his face and I thought that was the greatest thing I'd ever seen. I said, "That's exactly what I want to be like. Just like him." I bet he left there and he never knew. I tried to meet him many years later, after I got into the Hall of Fame, to say hello to him. He got in the Hall of Fame in 2011. He's one that who overlooked.

He really loved kids. I could tell when he was there at the market that he really likes kids. He told me to go play football and made a big deal over me when I was a young boy. I couldn't talk to him because I was taken aback by his presence. I was tongue-tied. That was my introduction to football. It was more due to his appearance. He was in a suit, a coat and tie. I'll never forget it. I can see him as clearly today as I did as a young man. He influenced me.

Photograph copyright Associated Press

Chapter 40

Charlie Sanders

College:
Minnesota

Career History
Detroit Lions (1968-1977)

2007 Inductee Pro Football Hall of Fame

College Choice
I can't say so much a pipeline as much as it was a realization, that the black athletes down South really weren't afforded the opportunity to go to the major schools. They were confined to the smaller black schools.

If you want to give Minnesota and a lot of the other Big Ten schools some credit, it was their realization that the great athletes were left down South. If they [the athletes] were afforded an opportunity, they could not only benefit themselves, but more importantly, they would benefit the university and their football program.

The University of Minnesota was able to go down and recruit those black athletes. It really opened up the opportunity for the black athletes to not only participate at Big Ten schools, but also at the larger schools down South.

When I went to the University of Minnesota, there wasn't any snow on the ground. At least they were smart enough to know that if they were going to bring you up, they should show you the campus in the spring when it was beautiful. Then all of a sudden, you saw this snow falling and it kept falling for about four months, and you realize, "What have I gotten myself into?"

All in all, I wouldn't change a thing. It was a great experience for me, especially coming from the South, to not only get out of the South and the way of thinking that was going on at that time in my life, but to go North and see the difference in the way people thought and the way people were treated. So for me personally, being a black athlete, it was an experience that really opened my eyes as to what life is all about. It really gave me a different approach in terms of dealing with mankind.

Change In Blocking For Tight Ends
The defensive side of the ball has changed. Basically years before, you'd line up in your base 4-3 with your defensive end over your tackle. Now, they've gone to defenses where they put the defensive end over the tight end for that particular reason, and generally, the fact that most tight ends can't block a defensive end.

Schematically, from a defensive standpoint, they'd move people around to make it difficult for your running game as well as to aid the defense in the passing game. Most tight ends are not going to hold up against a good defensive end. That's a fact. If you can find a guy that can do both, then you've got yourself a jewel.

Memorable Game
I'm always going to be a little partial to the 1970 game against the Raiders when we made the playoffs. That was a team that started to develop late in the season. We had won our last five games, and four of those five games were against divisional leaders. We were able to do that and go on into the playoffs. Unfortunately, we lost to Dallas, but if you take some glory in it all, Dallas went on to win the Super Bowl. So we lost to the Super Bowl champs.

Dick Butkus
He was my favorite ball player. He was the one that every time I think about football and every time I take a step back, I know that he had something to do with it. He gouged the eyes. He did that.

Deacon Jones
I was a rookie and thought I could stand up to him, and luckily, the whistle blew before he got to my quarterback because I didn't lay a hand on him.

Best Player in NFL History

I had a chance to play against and see Walter Payton. I didn't have a chance to play with Jim Brown. I had a chance to see, coach, and be around Barry Sanders, and if he wasn't the best, he was a year away from that. So I'd have to say Barry was the best I've ever seen.

Coaching

I coached for 10 years, and I think I enjoyed coaching more than I did playing. As far as taking that next step from being an assistant to a head coach, I never aspired to do that. I was just wrapped up in what I was doing and in the glory of watching guys develop and perform out on the field.

Photograph copyright Associated Press

Chapter 41

Joe Greene

College:
North Texas

Career History:
Pittsburgh Steelers (1969–1981)

1987 Inductee Pro Football Hall of Fame

Adjustment To NFL

I had pretty good coaching there at North Texas. I was a big fan of Deacon Jones and I wore that number and I was a big fan of Bob Lilly of the Dallas Cowboys. I watched those guys play and I tried to emulate those guys. The defense we were playing at North Texas allowed me a little bit of latitude and I could do some of those things.

Fortunately for me when I came to Pittsburgh, we were doing some of the same things. It wasn't that big of a transition in terms of the things that I was doing, but obviously the people I played against were a great deal different.

Goal

My main goal was to win; it wasn't about sacks to tell you the truth. If the sacks were a part of winning then so be it. If I got a sack, the only way you would know I got a sack, is because you saw it. You definitely wouldn't see me dancing.

Steelers Key To Success

Why, over the years, have the Steelers been competitive, had a chance to get in the playoffs, and had a chance to go to the Super Bowl and win? It's because of the stability and the coaches who run the football operation. The bosses up on top, Dan Rooney, Art Rooney III, and before them obviously, Art Senior, understand the hierarchy. They understand the chain of command. They hire people to do a job and let them do it.

When someone has his own self-interest and his ego gets in the way, and that person wants to take control of the team's success, and when anything gets in the way of the team goal, then you have a problem. Again I say that's why the Steelers have had an opportunity each and every year to be competitive. They have seven or eight scouts and everybody has their own input. No one gets lambasted for having an opinion and everybody's opinion counts. They know that the final decision is going to come from the head coach and the ownership. I collect information and give it to them and they make the decisions and that's the way it should be. They've done a good job over the years. I'm just amazed. I'm really amazed that I've been able to be there and be in such a good situation after I have been in some pretty poor ones at times.

Rollie Dotsch
Rollie Dotsch was the offensive line coach back in the mid-70s. Rollie got the offensive line going. He was just a tremendous coach. He believed in technique, in developing those techniques, and hard work. A lot of times you see those big guys grazing as we call it. When Rollie was there, the offensive line guys didn't graze, they worked harder than the defensive line, I would say.

Now the first guy who was there did a great job for us. Then Rollie came in and just kept it going. We missed him when he left. He was one of the guys that incorporated the punch and the tight fitting jerseys. We had smaller offensive lineman who could move, pass protect, run, pull, get out and block on screens, and they could trap. That was the Pittsburgh Steelers way and Rollie was a big, big part of that.

Toughest Opponents
We faced Earl Campbell, the Juice (O.J. Simpson), Do It Pruitt (Greg Pruitt & Mike Pruitt) in Cleveland, and we faced Kenny Stabler. It was always those guys who could hurt you with the ball. There were some great offensive linemen, no doubt about it. Some gave you more difficult times than the others, but in my mind they were incidental. Now I got my butt kicked a lot, but they were

337

incidental because they couldn't score. My thought process was to stop the people who could score—running backs. In my day, teams ran a lot and the quarterbacks threw the football. If you get to the quarterback, usually the team is going to have a difficult time.

Larry Little was an offensive lineman for the Miami Dolphins in those days. He was an outstanding player and I did have some struggles with him. So there Larry I said it, okay.

Miami Dolphins In The '70s
During the '70s, especially the early and mid '70s, the Dolphins were a machine. They didn't make mistakes. They had a very, very good offense, with Bob Griese as the quarterback. By today's standards he didn't have the rifle arm, but he had great touch, great timing, and great leadership. He had just enough maneuverability in the pocket to make you miss and get the ball downfield. They had an outstanding offensive line. They had three running backs, Larry Csonka, Mercury Morris, and Jim Kiick along with Paul Warfield at wide receiver; not too shabby. They were a good football team.

NFL Offenses
Being on the defensive side of the ball my entire playing and coaching career, I just learned to hate those guys on offense. They would make us stay up late at night trying to figure out ways to stop them. As soon as we figured a way to stop them, they would go to the commissioner and have the rules changed on us. Then we had to start all over again. So, I hated those guys and still do.

Best Defensive Line Of All Time
I grew up watching the Fearsome Foursome; the group in New York, the Doomsday Defense, and the Purple People Eaters. Anybody can lay claim to a title, but you have to win to have it. My argument for my group is that we won four Super Bowls. When you start talking about defensive lines, you have to talk about the Steel Curtain, but you also have to talk about the Fearsome Foursome and the Purple People Eaters. That's my

take and because I played, I know how difficult it is. I know what we go through and I would never ever say that we were better than someone else if we didn't have an opportunity to play those guys. I'm not going to say that. Me saying it would be a disservice to them and I just haven't been that kind of guy.

Pittsburgh Steelers Players Off The Field Success
I coached on Chuck Noll's staff in the mid-80s and what Chuck and the scouting department wanted to have on their football team was first quality people. They started from there. They didn't always achieve that, but that was the goal. In my adult life in terms of someone who impacted my life, that guy is Chuck. In all of these years I've never met another guy who was as solid, as honest, as sincere, and as smart as Chuck Noll.

Favorite Season
Our first Super Bowl season was very, very rocky. We lost to the Oakland Raiders the second or third ball game of the year at Three Rivers Stadium, shutting us out 17 to nothing. We had a quarterback controversy with Joe Gilliam and Terry Bradshaw. We lost a division game to the Oilers in Pittsburgh, probably the 12th game of a 14 game schedule. It was very rocky. We got it together in the playoffs and we beat the Raiders for the AFC Championship. That would be maybe the best season, because of the ups and downs we had and how we came through it. There was a mystery in that first one though, for sure. That would probably be my favorite season.

In 1976, we lost four of the first five ball games. Then we went undefeated the next seven games, only giving up 28 points. That was a fantastic year also, although it wasn't a championship year. We fell short, but it was a great year for me. We had a lot of good years, but probably my favorite season was the 1974 season. When you talk about Super Bowls, I don't have a favorite, they were all good.

Pittsburgh Steeler Joe Greene in pursuit of Dallas Cowboy Walt
Garrison Photograph copyright Associated Press

Chapter 42

Larry Csonka

College:
Syracuse

Career History:
Miami Dolphins (1968–1974)
Memphis Southmen (WFL) (1975)
New York Giants (1976–1978)
Miami Dolphins (1979)

1987 Inductee Pro Football Hall of Fame

1972 Miami Dolphins Undefeated Season

If you look at our team during the undefeated season, if you went player by player and you staked us against the teams that were in the playoffs in those years, the Kansas City Chiefs who went to the Super Bowl, the Pittsburgh Steelers who would later go to Super Bowls the next couple of years, the Redskins, the Minnesota Vikings ... we probably wouldn't have won those match ups individual to individual. The intangible is what they call the will to win. That makes people like Howard Twilley, our wide receiver from Tulsa, Oklahoma, a kind of guy that got open even in the old bump and run. He would manage to get open somehow, someway. You can't measure that. That's what we had a team full of back in 1972.

Don Shula's Role in Perfect Season

Don Shula was the primary ingredient in the perfect season; make no bones about it. I don't care what anyone else on the undefeated team says, or the media for that matter. I know what the key factor was that season. I was there and it absolutely was Don Shula. He was, for lack of a better description, possessed after he came to us from losing that Super Bowl with

Baltimore. He came down to Miami and twisted, prodded, screamed, hollered, and insisted on tremendous attention to detail. I don't think he could coach that way in the NFL today. I don't think the players today would respond to him, but back then they did. We did and got into that first Super Bowl when we lost at the hands of Dallas in Super Bowl VI.

I think his finest moment in coaching was right after that loss because that's what lead to the undefeated season. He pulled us together through defeat, even stronger than we were prior to that happening.

Don Shula Becoming Coach Of Miami Dolphins
I thought he was pleasantly surprised by how much talent had been amassed by a fellow there named Joe Thomas. He was the Personnel Director who put the Minnesota team together prior to coming to Miami. After Miami, he put several other teams together including the 49ers, before he retired from the league. There was quite a litany for his success in the NFL. I think the Dolphins' nucleus of players was certainly there. I think he was somewhat surprised by how Joe Thomas put together a power running game and ball control game. Coach Shula had never had that in Baltimore. He suffered at the hands of Green Bay when he was a head coach at Baltimore, when Green Bay perfected that with Jim Taylor, Paul Hornung, and their great offensive line.

When Coach discovered he had that here, then we were set to go. He knew how to utilize it because he had suffered at the hands of it at Green Bay when he was with Baltimore.

Paul Warfield
Paul Warfield got open in the old bump and run. The strong safety and weak safety could come across and literary take your head off. He was tough enough to get open even when getting knocked, bumped, and jammed all the way down the field. Think about taking a time machine and putting Paul Warfield in today's game where you can only bump him in the first five yards, and the give him an equal opportunity to the ball downfield. How well do you think he would do today?

I think he qualified for the Olympics or came close to it in the low hurdles and he also ran the high hurdles. There's a guy who had to have a fluid motion. Anyone under Olympic consideration in the hurdles definitely has strong self-discipline and a smooth gait. He was perfect in that capacity and then moved it over to football. If you remember, he played for Woody Hayes. He was a halfback at Ohio State. Paul Brown saw the possibilities with Warfield and brought him to the Cleveland Browns.

College Choice
I attributed most of my success in the pros to Don Shula. I attribute my success in college to having the right coach in Ben Schwartzwalder, a fellow who believed in me enough to let me run the ball. It was questionable at the start. A lot of people, including Woody Hayes, had me pretty much set to be a middle linebacker. I wanted to run the ball. Ben Schwartzwalder was a guy who had a history of having a strong offensive line, not throwing the ball much, and the history of great large running backs. If I was going to have my shot at running the ball, it certainly would be with Ben. That's why I went to Syracuse.

Woody Hayes got us in a room and said we owed it to our state to go to Ohio State. I was about 16 years old and didn't figure I owed anybody anything, so I went to Syracuse.

Best Team Of All Time
When you say best team of all time, first you've got to set the parameters. You know you can't make a statement like that. I just alluded to the fact that Paul Warfield would be a wide receiver in today's game.

The rules today mostly enhance the offensive play a great deal and detract from the defensive play. You've got to look for a team that was a great championship team and had a great defense. You also have to look what rules they played under. There are a lot of prerequisites before you can make an assumption like the greatest team ever. In my era, I think the team that was the most powerful and came the closest to doing what we did was the Chicago Bears in 1985, under Ditka. They seemed so much more powerful than every other team they played in the NFL that year. Their greatness ran deep. They had great backups as we did in 1972, people who could step in and take over. That's what the Bears had that year.

Best Running Back Combinations On A Team
Again, you've got to look at the different decades. At the time, Jim Kick, Mercury Morris, and I were together, other teams had some great running backs too. The Steelers had Franco Harris with Rocky Bleier. The backfield is only as great as the offensive line can substantiate. When you talk about groups of running for different teams that's all predicated on the ability of the offensive linemen. It's maybe less important today than it was in past decades because the rules changed, but it still plays a major part.

You have to look at the quality of the offensive line. Also, whether they had a great blocking tight end and whether or not the wide receivers could block. Things like that made a tremendous difference in the running game.

Early Years With Miami Dolphins
My first couple of years with the Dolphins was also the first few years of their existence. The team logo and mascot was Flipper, not exactly the most macho thing. When you are out of college, you think a team with a macho mascot like the Cowboys, Bears, or Lions will draft you. The Dolphins drafted me. Our logo was Flipper. Our team colors were orange and aqua, for crying out loud. It was kind of a setback. We were absolutely the doormats of the league. The first two years of my career, things were tough.

Then Coach Don Shula came. He hired Monte Clark and the rest of the assistance coaches. Through trades and signings, the team put some people together. We got Jim Langer, Bob Kuechenberg, Larry Little, Wayne Moore, and Norm Evans. All of the sudden my headaches went away and we started to be a force to be reckoned with.

It was a great transitional period. You can really relate to winning if you've been losing for a while. I think that helps to make a stronger champion.

Hardest Hit Received

The hardest I've ever been hit in the NFL is by a guy named Roy Winston from Minnesota. He was backup linebacker for the Minnesota Vikings. It was a relief pass from a passing receiver on a play when we played Minnesota in 1972. I went out for a pass and was standing there. There was nowhere else to throw the ball. We had Mercury Morris, Jim Kiick, Paul Warfield, and Howard Twilley. Jim Kiick managed to throw the ball to me. I didn't have much chance of getting relief out of the pitch. That hit from Roy Winston on me just about retired me. I think of Roy every once in a while, on cold days when I get up. I think of several people when get out of bed on a cold morning in Alaska and I walk across the floor and my left ankle starts up. I think about Bill Bergey, and then I take another step and think of Joe Greene. I put my pants on and I think about Roy Winston. Then I think to myself, I wonder if any of them are thinking about me?

Miami Dolphin Larry Csonka drives between Minnesota Viking Jeff Siemon and Paul Krause Photograph copyright Associated Press

Chapter 43

Charlie Joiner

College:
Grambling State

Career History:
AFL Houston Oilers (1969)
NFL Houston Oilers (1970-1972)
NFL Cincinnati Bengals (1972-1975)
NFL San Diego Chargers (1976-1986)

1996 Inductee Pro Football Hall of Fame

College Choice
Eddie Robinson didn't recruit me. I was recruited by my high school coaches to play for Grambling, because both of them played for Eddie Robinson.

That's the way it was in Louisiana back then in those days. When he was going really good, he had been at Grambling for maybe 25-30 years. He was pretty well established within the city because almost everybody went to Grambling for college down in Louisiana. At the black high schools, Eddie Robinson would get most of the best athletes because the coach, the principal, or the athletic director went to Grambling as student athletes, or as students.

It was a joy to play for him. He was tough. He had very long practices, but I think he really taught you how to compete. He taught, don't let anybody get on top of you. You've got to be on top all the time. He was a great coach. His tactics may be a little outdated now, but back then I think he was good for the kind of people we had.

The only time I went to switch from one side of the ball to the other was when I was freshman. We had to have a loop team for the first team. I was a freshman so I was on a loop team. I was moved to the back on the loop team and I played offensive wide receiver for the defense, not offense. When I actually started playing, which was during my sophomore year, I only played one spot.

That was a tough transition for me because I was a small guy. I weighed about 185 pounds. Then I went to Grambling, which had some enormous, massive people. I'm saying to myself, "What am I doing here? I'm just too small. I won't survive." It was just the size of the guys that got me down because Grambling had big people. They had 300 pounders before the 300 pounders became popular.

We were a running offense. When we got James Harris, we started throwing the ball just a little more. Basically Grambling was a rushing offensive team. We ran the Wing-T. We didn't have a split out wide receiver.

1968 Grambling/Morgan State Game
That was a pretty good experience for us. We were a bunch of small college guys from Louisiana. The farthest state we'd been to was Tennessee, and we had to go there by bus. We got the chance to play this game in New York. They couldn't drive the bus that far, so we had to get on an airplane. That was a new experience for us. Plus, we were playing somebody we had never played before, which was another new experience for us. We enjoyed that and we relished the opportunity to be the first ones to do it. It was a big event for us.

Draft
Most of the professionals that used to train us and be with us at Grambling were in the AFL. Willie Brown, who played for the Denver Broncos and the Oakland Raiders, is a Grambling Knight. He would always come back and coach us during spring training. I think the only guy who went to the NFL who trained us was Henry Dyer. He went to the Rams.

Going to the AFL, was kind of a treat for me. I wasn't expecting to get picked high in the draft. I knew I was going to get picked, but being the second pick in the fourth round, surprised me. The reason why is a friend of mine had just become a scout for the Houston Oilers. Tom Williams of the Oilers drafted me that high. From this day on, God bless his heart and soul, I always thank him for drafting me that high. It was a miracle being drafted higher than I was expecting. It got me just a couple dollars more so I could help my parents out.

James Harris A Black Quarterback at Grambling

He just came along at the wrong time, that's all. Just born too soon. He was a drop back passer. He was not a runner though. He wasn't a moving around guy like the guys they have today, but he was a classic drop back passer with a great arm and great accuracy, a very good player.

Houston Oilers Offensive

Back then the coach of the Houston Oilers team was a basic run the ball first coach. He ran the ball to set up the pass. At the time I was with him, I was drafted as a defensive back too. I didn't play wide receiver fulltime until about my third year there.

Floyd Little & Tom Jackson

Floyd Little and Tom Jackson were the only two people that ever knocked me out of a game.

Both were damn good football players. One is in the Hall of Fame and the other one should be in the Hall of Fame, as good as he was. Floyd Little knocking me out got me to be a full-time wide receiver.

Paul Brown

He was very stern and ran that ship with an iron fist. The way he'd talk to you was very intimidating, but he's one of the most knowledgeable men I've been around. He knew how to pick talent. Paul Brown had some great coaches behind him. He was good for the league. He was good at discipline because he always scared the hell out of me.

He was our head coach, but I think Bill Walsh, Bill Johnson, and Jack Donaldson, his assistant coaches, did the most coaching. The defensive coach was Chuck Weber. I don't know what kind of coach he was. Bill Johnson was the offensive coordinator. Bill Walsh and Jack Donaldson did almost everything else on offense. Paul Brown was not an active coach. He was the head coach in name only.

Cincinnati Bengals
Isaac Curtis, Chip Myers, and I were the wide receivers. Bob Trumpy was the tight end. Bob Trumpy was one the fastest tight ends I have ever seen. He wasn't one of the bigger tight ends, but he was really fast and was more of a receiver than he was a blocker.

We had a really good passing game. Ken Anderson was an extremely accurate passer. He should be in that Hall of Fame also. I think the completion percentages were high every year I was there.

Bill Walsh
Bill Walsh was a kind of a jovial guy. He liked to laugh and joke with the players sometimes. He got real serious when the time for football came, but other than that he was a real joker. He wasn't the type who you would think was going to be one of the greatest coaches of all time. You just didn't think that with Cincinnati, but hey he had the mind and he put it to work. I bet his personality in San Francisco did not change from when he was in Cincinnati.

Trade To San Diego Chargers
San Diego had a wealth of former first and second round picks. They had Louie Kelcher, Gary "Big Hands" Johnson, and Woodrow Lowe. They had a bunch of talent there and all they needed was somebody to put it all together. Coach Tommy Protho was the coach there and from what I heard, he was a very, very smart man. What really sold me on going to San Diego was the fact that they hired Bill Walsh to be the offensive coordinator in San Diego the same year I got traded there. With Walsh going there, I knew that was the place I wanted to go too. Walsh came in for one year as coordinator, and then he left to be Head Coach at Stanford University. From Stanford he went on to the San Francisco 49ers.

Don Coryell

Coryell did an excellent job of getting some very skilled players. I think we had the best players in the league at the six skilled positions. I was out there catching balls. Whether I was an average player, a great player, or a very good player, I was just having fun going out there on the football field. Coryell excited people before a game. It was fun playing for him. It was really fun. It was more fun than anything else. It wasn't drudgery. It was like you wanted to go out there and participate. It was hard work, but it was fun and we loved looking at Coryell on the sideline every Sunday.

AFC Title Games

One of the AFC title games was against the Oakland Raiders. Oakland came in, and they just ran the football, keeping the ball away from our offense. The offense couldn't do anything because Oakland just came and ran the ball. Then we went to Cincinnati to play in the Cold Bowl. Unfortunately it never rains in San Diego, but it rained that Sunday. It shut down our passing game because it made us feel real slow.

The other AFC Championship Game we went to was in Cincinnati. The wind chill factor was 60 below zero. We just caught some bad weather. They really put a bite on us. It was unbelievable up there. I still say that game should not have been played. That game should have been moved to a central site somewhere. We could have had a better AFC Championship Game.

The football was like picking up a concrete brick. We had to try to throw it because we got behind pretty quick. We were trying to throw the football. There is just no way you can throw that ball, no way. They should have cancelled that game.

Don Coryell Not Being in Pro Football Hall of Fame

Don Coryell was probably the greatest offensive innovator around. I cannot understand why he's not in the Hall of Fame. It's strictly up to the writers and the voters. I think I'll just leave it at that because I think I've done as much as I possibly can. I've talked about it as much as I possibly can. I've written about it as much as I possibly can. It's just up to the writers and the voters now, but I just don't understand why he's not in the Hall of Fame.

Comparing San Diego Chargers Offense Of Late '70s & Early '80s With Buffalo Bills Teams Of '90s

The only difference between what we did when I was a receiver for the Chargers and receiver coach for the Buffalo Bills, is Jim Kelly actually called the plays. Dan Fouts did not call very many plays. He got the signals from the sideline and that's the way he liked it. He liked for the coordinator to have the pressure of calling the plays or having the luxury of calling the plays, and he would execute them on the field. If there was a play the coordinator called that Fouts didn't like, he would definitely change it, but he was more receptive to being told the play from the sideline. Kelly, in a huddle fashion, called every play. He and the coordinator did a great job of setting their game plans every week. Both offenses were very similar. They both had three wide receivers in the game most of the time, and they both had one great tight end that could catch and also block. They both had great quarterbacks. Basically that offense was almost the same, the teams just got to it in a different way.

Toughest Cornerbacks Faced

I always thought Willie Brown was the best bumper at cornerback I ever faced because he was a little bigger and a little stronger than me. I always thought Mel Blount of Pittsburgh was the best cover-two cornerback that ever played. Those two guys gave me fits because they were so big. They were a little bigger and a little stronger than receivers were back in those days.

I don't know if they could handle a receiver today. The wide receivers today are just a little bigger than we are, but they could handle the wide receivers back in my era. Those two guys gave me fits because they were bigger and it was just hard to get around them.

San Diego Charger Charlie Joiner makes a leaping catch between
Denver Bronco Steve Foley (43) and Bernard Jackson (29)
Photograph copyright Associated Press

Chapter 44

Roger Wehrli

College:
Missouri

Career History:
St. Louis Cardinals (1969-1982)

2007 Inductee Pro Football Hall of Fame

Missouri
I think Coach Clay Cooper, who was the defensive back coach at Missouri, and the Head Coach, looked at me from the start as a defensive back at Missouri. My sophomore year, they decided to use me on punts a few times. I played quarterback and some safety in college. All three years of my college career, I returned punts. Back then you didn't play as a freshman; you could only play on the freshman team. They didn't allow freshmen to play on the varsity back then. We only had three years of varsity in college.

Johnny Roland was a senior when I was a freshman. They gave me the same number that Johnny had my sophomore year. Obviously I was very thrilled with that because he'd had such a great career at Missouri. Then I was drafted by the Cardinals, and obviously would have like to have had 23, but Johnny was already on the Cardinals and he had 23. They gave me the next number down, which was 22.

Dan Devine
I think Dan Devine's degree was in psychology. He was very exacting. The two best coaches I ever had were Coach Devine in my college years, and Coach Don Coryell when I was with the Cardinals. They couldn't have been more different.

Coach Devine was more the type of coach that was up on a pedestal looking down over everything and letting individual coaches do most of the on field coaching, as far as technique and things like that. Coach Devine would take the team over on Friday and start getting us ready for the game. I always had a great mental frame of mind going into every game, no matter whom we played.

Coach Coryell with the Cardinals was just the opposite. He was a fiery type of coach. He would get right in your face or be your best friend. He was very much into the offensive side of the game. He didn't coach the defense much. He was an offensive innovator and had his hands on every little bit of the offense that we had in the mid '70s when he was our coach with the Cardinals.

Beating Alabama In The Gator Bowl
We always had great seasons at Missouri. The most games we ever lost in a season was three, but never won the conference championship. We would have had a shot at it, but Kansas beat us the last game of my senior year. Obviously getting an invitation to the Gator Bowl was a big deal at that point because we wanted to redeem ourselves after that loss. To go down there and beat Alabama in the Gator Bowl by a pretty good margin was a great way to end my college career and a great thrill for all the players.

Mel Gray
Mel Gray came in as a junior college transfer. The first time I didn't know who he was. I guess it was training camp before my senior year. We were just running patterns one on one against each other, the defensive backs against the receivers. I came up in line against him. He reached to the outside and got about a step on me. We went down the field about 40 yards and he still had a step on me. I went back to the hurdle and I said, "Who is that guy I can't even catch him?"

One of the other defensive backs told me who he was and how he was a junior college transfer who won the Junior College 50-yard Dash before he came to Missouri. After that, I remembered who he was. He was a great receiver. I played with him that one year at Missouri and then the Cardinals drafted him a couple years after me.

We had Johnny Roland, Mel, and me all on the Cardinals there for a while.

Jim Hart

I've never seen a better pinpoint passer who had an arm like Jim Hart. He could break open defenses. When Don Coryell came to the Cardinals in 1973, he had the offense that he needed. Hart threw pinpoint passes and quick passes to the backs out of the backfield. Basically, it was the west coast offense that Coryell brought which was kind of ahead of its time. Hart was the perfect quarterback for that. He had a great career with the Cardinals and is one of my better friends.

NFL Draft

It's amazing the way the draft is today. It's on television; they have tryouts and do timings on the players, strength testing with weights, the vertical jump, the long jump, and all of those things that they test the players so extensively on now. I hadn't really even talked to any of the Cardinals. I had letters from different teams … San Francisco, Dallas, and a lot of different teams, but none from the Cardinals.

As it turned out, apparently one of the Cardinals' scouts, I found out later, was in Hawaii at the Hula Bowl. He was the one who asked me to run the 40-yard dash for him at the Hula Bowl after practice, which I did. A few years later he told me that when I ran the 40 there, they decided to draft me because I was actually faster than they thought I was going to be. I guess they thought I could play cornerback. That was what resulted in me being drafted in the first round by the Cardinals.

Jimmy Marsalis and I played in a couple of all-star games together. He was drafted, I think, two picks later by the Kansas City Chiefs.

I think the fastest I ever ran was a 4.4 on Astroturf. Back then you didn't prepare for the draft like they do now. The first time I ever ran the 40 was when we were out in Hawaii. I ran that 4.5 on grass.

I just had a helmet, shoulder pads, and shorts on when I ran it, just like we worked out at the Hula Bowl.

Transition To NFL

It's always a tough transition. You're going up against the best players in the world. The best players on every team are the best players out of college. In college it's just not that way. I was really fortunate when I came to the Cardinals to have two guys playing safety there—Larry Wilson and Jerry Stovall. They were veterans and excellent ball players. When I first came in, they mentored me a little bit; Larry was calling the defenses and alerting us to team tendencies. That was something I really appreciated. It helped me a lot early in my career for sure.

It's a big transition no matter what and I got my jock handed to me a few times in my rookie season. You just have to go through that, learn from your mistakes, and work to get better. That's what I tried to do all during my rookie year with St. Louis.

Roger Staubach Called Roger Wehrli Best Cornerback He Played Against

Roger Staubach was such a great athlete. We played in the same division so we had to play against each other twice a year. The '70s was a big decade for him. Early in the '70s, he went to the Super Bowl a couple of times. In the mid '70s, we hit our stride and won the division a few times. During the mid '70s, it was always a challenge to beat Dallas because they had such a great team. They were an innovative team and had a lot of good receivers, Drew Pearson and those guys.

Obviously with Staubach at quarterback, as a defensive back it was a nightmare. You knew you had to cover the receiver not only the first four or five seconds of the play, but if nobody was open he had the ability to scramble. Then he was just looking for whoever was open, so we had to chase the guys all over the field. Playing his team was a struggle. To get those praises from him really meant a lot to me. I think it probably meant a lot to help me get into the Hall of Fame.

Beating Cowboys 38-0 On First Season Of Monday Night Football in 1970

It was wonderful. It was the first year of Monday Night Football. It was the first time that we had ever played on Monday Night Football, and I'm sure it was probably the first time for Dallas too. Don Meredith was in the booth with Howard Cosell. Don had just retired from Dallas and was obviously very partial to the Dallas Cowboys. We played in Dallas and had a great game. I had a couple of interceptions and a couple knockdowns on passes to Bob Hayes, deep down the field. We just pretty much dominating them.

Roger Staubach did not played in that game, and not played very much with the Cowboys at that point. He was just back from his service duties. I think that game spurred the coach to put him in more during upcoming games. They started alternating quarterbacks after that.

That was the last regular season game they lost that year. They ran the table, ended up beating us out for the division title by a game, and then went on to lose to Pittsburgh in the Super Bowl. I think the turning point for them was when Staubach started playing more and they started winning more after that game.

Toughest Receiver To Cover

That's tough to say. I think when I first came in, I look at Charley Taylor as a guy who was as tough as anybody to cover. Throughout our careers, we were in the same division so we had to play against each other twice a year. He came to the NFL as a running back. He was great receiver, had all the moves, he was tough, a great blocker, and a great pattern runner.

Bob Hayes with Dallas had speed, so he was a great receiver. Drew Pearson, on the other side down in Dallas, was a great pattern receiver.

Quarterback Who Had Most Interceptions Against

I had my most interceptions against Roger Staubach. Even though he was probably the best quarterback I played against, I had more opportunities against him. I think he was more stubborn than the rest of them and kept throwing the ball at me. I think I had six interceptions off of him. That's the most that I had off of any one quarterback.

I played against Billy Kilmer and Sonny Jurgensen; they didn't look very athletic back there at the quarterback position. I swear they could fling that ball in there. Many times I thought, "How did that guy get the ball to that player". They just were wily veterans and were able to get it done.

Jackie Smith

Jackie Smith was something else. Jackie was a competitor. Even in practice, he hated to get the ball knocked down from him if you were covering him or whatever. Once he caught the ball, he was something to see. I can still remember one of the greatest plays I've ever seen is when we were playing Dallas in St. Louis in the mid '70s. He took a ball across the middle about 10 yards, and broke five tackles from two linebackers, a corner, and a couple of safeties, and scored on the play. We were standing on the sidelines and just couldn't believe what we saw. I think it's one of those highlights that they always show when they're talking about Jackie Smith.

Favorite Moment In NFL

My favorite moment, other than the day that I got elected into the Hall of Fame, was early in my career, that Monday Night Football game in Dallas, when we beat them. That was such a great thrill.

Then in the mid '70s, when we won the division and had good teams. We were nicknamed The Cardiac Cardinals. We won the division a couple of times, and made it to the playoffs after falling short the first five or six years in my career. That was the most fun time to play with Don Coryell as our coach. He was such a great coach, a great offensive innovator, and a great coach to play for. The players just loved him. We had a lot of fun in the mid '70s, playing football in St. Louis. We had the town behind us. I think it was the most fun I ever had playing football.

Firing Of Don Coryell & Hiring Of Bud Wilkinson

We had such a great team and Coryell wanted to a draft a big defensive player. Instead we drafted a quarterback when we didn't need one because we had Jim Hart. Coryell basically blew up and went to the press. He ended up getting himself fired. That's when management hired Bud Wilkinson. It was tough for him because the players loved Coryell and we had winning seasons under him. Obviously the Cardinals hadn't really drafted the people that were needed. It was a tough situation for Bud for to come into. He was a great individual, a great man, and a great motivator. He was more the Devine type of coach. He left the nuts and bolts to the assistant coaches. He came in and was more of a motivator. Some of the stories that he told about his experiences kept you on the edge of your seat as a player. He was well respected in the sport as well as respected outside of football. It was kind of an odd time. It was a thrill to interact with him because he was kind of a legend at the time. Still, the football situation was not that good in St. Louis. He was only here a year and a half, and we didn't win that many games during that time. We weren't able to continue the good times that we had under Coryell. Bud came into a very tough situation because a very popular coach had been fired.

Pro Football Hall Of Fame Induction

Just basically a dream come true. I had been out of football for a good number of years. They put, I think, 100 people on the ballot, and then they vote it down to 50, then down to 25, and then down to that final 15 that they actually do the voting on. I had made those other lists numerous times and had been down to the final 15 one other time. I knew that it was a possibility that I could be voted in, but I think I had pretty much made up my mind that they'd probably pass me up. I probably wouldn't make the Hall of Fame unless I made it through the senior legends category.

Then I made the final 15 and was on edge again. When I got the call it was just an amazing time. I was so happy to be included with the players that I had played against and played with all those years. It's been a thrill to go back every year and be a part of that and be a part of everything that being in the Hall of Fame means.

Scoring Touchdown On Fake Field Goal
It was very satisfying because it was actually the last home game that I played. When I first came to the Cardinals, Jim Bakken was the place kicker and Larry Wilson was his holder. In my fourth year after Larry retired, I started holding on field goals for Bakken and then the other kickers that we had throughout my career.

I'd already announced that I was going to retire at the end of the season right before our last home game. We had a ceremony before the game. We were playing the New York Giants and needed to win the game to make the playoffs. That was the strike-shortened season. It was a very important touchdown that put us ahead. We had seen in the films during the week that there would be an opportunity for a fake field goal if they lined up in a certain way.

The coach put the play on and the alignment was right, so we tried it. I obviously got into the end zone, which is a big thrill any time, but especially during your last home game. It was really a special treat.

Photograph copyright Associated Press

Chapter 45

Jim Langer

College:
South Dakota State

Career History:
Miami Dolphins (1970–1979)
Minnesota Vikings (1980–1981)

1987 Inductee Pro Football Hall of Fame

College Choice
I played high school football in a town of 500 people. If you ran
an out pattern in the end zone, you ran into the Platte River. A lot
of the end zones I played in were partial cornfields. I don't think
I was ever recruited. My high school baseball coach had been a
quarterback at South Dakota State. I played baseball, football,
and basketball. Those were the three sports we had in high
school. I was actually a pretty good pitcher.

My high school coach said, "Jim why don't you come out to
South Dakota State with me? We'll go visit the campus. You can
play two sports out there." South Dakota State was Division II at
that time in the North Central Conference with North Dakota
State, North Dakota, and those schools. That's where I went to
school. I never heard from the Gophers.

When I went out to South Dakota State, I ended up playing on
the offensive line and I did play some linebacker. I didn't carry
the football at all. I played offensive tackle and some offensive
guard. I played a couple of years at linebacker.

Cleveland Browns
I actually went to Cleveland as a free agent. My baseball coach
knew a scout from the Cleveland Browns named Bob
Nussbaumer. He signed me as a free agent in 1970.

I was intimidated. I had been a commissioned second lieutenant. I was supposed to report for active duty in October 1970. I went to the summer training camp just for the experience. In fact, I talked to a good friend of mine, Gale Gillingham, a great guard for the Green Bay Packers at that time who was from Little Falls, a town near where I grew up. I was hoping he would help me talk myself out of going. He said, "There's going to be a strike this year. You aren't going to embarrass yourself. Go out there. The veterans aren't going to come to camp. You'll get a good look and if you can't play with the Browns, maybe somebody else will see you. Just take it a day at a time and do the best you can. What the hell do you got to lose?" It was the best advice I ever got.

I went over there and the Browns had drafted Mike Phipps, Craig Wycinski from Michigan State, who was my roommate, and Bill Yanchar from Purdue, a defensive tackle. These were all guys I had been watching on Saturday afternoons on TV. It was pretty humbling. Nobody knew who the hell I was. I really didn't have to prove anything to anybody. So I just took it a day at a time and went at it as hard as I could.

It got down to the last preseason game and I was still on the roster. Blanton Collier called me in and said, "We think you can play. We're going to put you on our taxi squad. We're going to pay you $500 a week." I went to Cleveland with $50 so I was pretty elated. I called my wife and told her what was going to happen. He said, "Now, we're going to put you on waivers tonight. For 24 hours any team can pick you up.

The next morning I get a call, go into his office again and find out the Dolphins had picked me up off of waivers. So I flew down to Miami. Quite honestly, I didn't even know Miami had a football team. I landed there and we played the Atlanta Falcons that night. The rest worked out pretty well.

Rookie Year With Miami Dolphins
The Dolphins were staying out at Doral, at the country club. That's where they stayed the night before the games. I got picked up at the

airport and went to my room at Doral. Wayne Moore, who they had just picked up from the 49ers and became our great left offensive tackle, was my roommate. We had no idea what the hell was going on. You just take it a day at a time. You go where you're supposed to be. At that time, I didn't know Don Shula from any other coach. We were practicing four times a day.

Coach Shula was the most intense man I had ever seen. We had 22 rookies on the team that year. I was on the taxi squad for about three weeks, and then I got moved onto the roster, and started playing center.

Monte Clark was my line coach. Monte became a great friend. He was the key that got to me to Miami. I didn't know that for quite a few years. He played for the Browns for 11 years and had just retired. He became a coach for Don Shula. It was his first year as offensive line coach. About two weeks before I got picked up off of waivers, he talked to a couple of his old buddies that were still playing for the Browns on the offensive line. He said, "You guys got anybody up there you think can play? I'm looking for a couple more linemen." They told him that I was a possible prospect that had some upside and that's how I got down there. It turned out just how old Gale Gillingham said it would.

It was quite a whirlwind. I remember the first game. My wife was going to drop me off at the stadium; that's when the Orange Bowl was still there. We stopped at a minor-league baseball park I thought was the Orange Bowl. It looked like there was a game going on. There was no GPS or cell phones or anything like that at that time. We stopped at a gas station and said, "Where the hell is the Orange Bowl?" It was quite a time and Miami was one step from being out of the league. After being with the team for several years, I started finding out the history of the team and how all this went together.

That team was literally one year from being insolvent. Joe Robbie picked up Shula and Paul Warfield, put this team together, and they started winning. By the time I got there, it was the last preseason game. There were 80,010 in the Orange Bowl and they were going nuts. They hadn't lost a game yet in the preseason.

It just all came together. It's one of those things. I don't know if you can duplicate that by some formula. Don is still, obviously a dear friend. That was one of the most incredible bunch of people who ever got put together. Whether it was just a stroke of genius, by accident, or whatever the hell happened, it was the damnest group of players I had ever been around in terms of how hard they worked and how they approached the game.

The coaches were incredibly dedicated people. It became a very cohesive well-oiled machine. We accomplished a lot in the world of football. We broke our team up even though we probably could have gone a couple more years. That was the way things were back then. It's an interesting period of time because my first contract I signed was $14,000. The year we went undefeated was the first year I started. I played every play that season, 17 games and my salary that year was $26,000. To win the Super Bowl was another $15,000; that was a big deal. Now these guys spend that much on dinner at night from what I've heard.

Pro Bowl
I went to six Pro Bowls. The winner's share was $2,500 and the loser's share was $1,500. That was a big deal to win that damn thing because another $2,500 that was a lot of money to me.

Bob Griese
As great as Bob Griese was and he truly was, he wasn't a physical player like Peyton Manning or Tom Brady. If you look at Bob in his playing days and saw him with his helmet on and glasses underneath, you'd swear he it was an accountant playing football. He was a student of the game. He was an analyst on the field. Of course, the rules were different. Out of 70 to 75 plays around 40 of them were running plays.

The offensive line was very methodical and very well schooled. The plays that we ran were executed with a lot of precision and consistency, much like Green Bay had done. You knew Green Bay was going to run the sweep, but you couldn't stop that damn thing.

The Dolphins were a very well oiled machine and weren't that fancy. The offense was very effective because it was executed; the perfection of the execution was the goal.

First Game Starting
My first game starting was the first game ever played in Arrowhead Stadium against Curley Culp, Buck Buchanan, Willie Lanier, and those guys. That's the year we beat the Redskins in that Super Bowl. The next year we went back and beat the Vikings in the Super Bowl.

I'll never forget my first game because it was 110 degrees on the field and was the first game of the season. Buck Buchanan was a pretty imposing figure. I'm probably 6'2" and he was 6'8". I got to know a lot of the Chiefs. Curley Culp and I became good friends. Curley Culp was the best damn nose guard that ever played the game. He was something, and he was an NCAA heavyweight wrestler.

Dick Butkus
I remember the first time I lined up against the Chicago Bears and Dick Butkus was out there. This is a guy I watched as a kid and as a college player. I had a hard time believing I was looking at this guy.

I always had a white towel tucked in my pants in the back. Bob Griese had a fear of lining up behind a guard. He was very attuned to looking down the field, looking at coverages, and looking at secondary. He wanted the towel so when he'd break the huddle, he would automatically have a visual as to whom the center was. As silly as that sounds, that was a very good thing to do.

Butkus pulled that towel out of my butt every play and laughed. He was a great player. There were some great players back then. They played every down. They didn't come out on nickel and dime packages. I was looking at Dick Butkus the whole game. I'm talking about Ray Nitschke and all those great players; it was quite the time.

Monte Clark

Next to Don Shula, Monte Clark was probably the most intense guy I've ever known. Monte was a master of attention to detail and the psychological part of the game. He taught us to visualize the game and to play the game over and over in your head before you actually played.

Other teams had cut our whole offensive line. Bob Kuechenberg was drafted by the Eagles then got cut. Then he played for the Chicago Owls, an amateur team, before joining the Dolphins.

Larry Little and Wayne Moore had been cut. Monte wanted us to make the right step, get in the right position, and get our head on the right point. Through our effort and execution, we became one line that could execute as well as any I've seen since. It was a great bunch of guys.

We started to play as a unit. We started to know each other as a unit. It became a really close bunch of guys. That whole team, those guys are like brothers to you. We paid our dues. It was a hard-working team. We put in a lot of time working on that field and working on execution. I look back and see it was quite a journey.

Don Shula's Concept

Don Shula's concept was if somebody got hurt, somebody came in. The year we went undefeated, about the fifth game of the season, Bob broke his ankle. Earl Morrall, at 35 years old, replaced Bob. Earl ran the 40-yard dash in about eight flat and couldn't throw the ball maybe 40 yards. Earl took us all the way to the AFC championship game in Pittsburgh. By the way, we were undefeated at the time. We got to go on the road and play Pittsburgh at their place, to win the AFC Championship; because that's the way the rules were then.

Earl takes us all the way. We didn't think anything of it other than Bob was hurt and Earl's our quarterback. Earl, of course, had the respect of everybody. He could run our offense. Everybody respected him and everybody picked up the pace. The defense played harder, probably subconsciously. The offensive line knew that we had to get an older guy behind us, not as mobile; we had to do better. Our running game, of course, was still there. We went undefeated with our backup quarterback.

Garo Yepremian

For the first few years, I didn't really think too much about the kicker because I was just worried about my job and worried about what I was supposed to do. Gary Yepremian talked funny, but he could kick the ball pretty well. I think the closest Garo came to death, was when we played the Chiefs in the Super Bowl out in Los Angeles. We were dominating the game, but were not ahead by much. I think the game ended up 14-7. He tried to kick the field goal, but the kick was blocked. He caught the ball and tried to throw a pass. The Redskins ran it back for a touchdown, which at the time put them back in the game. There was still some time left on the clock. It got a bit hairy. Even though we pretty much had our way with the Redskins that day, they were back in the ball game.

Garo's a great guy. I always felt kickers were an important part of our team. They certainly didn't take the abuse that the front line players took, but when the game's on the line, they're carrying a lot of the load on their shoulders. I always felt Garo was a good teammate. We were a very close bunch.

NFL Coaches

Don Shula is an amazing man. There have been great coaches in the past, and there will be great coaches in the future. All of these guys knew how to push players to a point they didn't think they could go. It's a hard thing to describe. Coach Shula worked as hard as we did. The coaching staff lived and slept the game just like we did. During the football season, I never got away from football. You didn't take off for the birth of your child. I had two sons born while I was playing football. One son was born the night we played Oakland in a playoff game. There was no thought of leaving while my wife was in labor. That might offend some people, but that thought didn't exist. The number one thing you did was take care of the team. You take care of the team; they'll take care of your family.

I think it was my second year of training camp and we were playing a scrimmage against the Saints. Coach Shula walked in before the game, called me in a little office and said, "Jim I'm going to tell you now. I just got a call and your father died. After the scrimmage, we'll get you on a plane and we'll fly you back home."

Comparing Bud Grant To Don Shula
It was a 180-degree difference; both were successful. Don Shula was very much hands-on, in your face, and dominated the meetings. He was in charge of the offensive meetings game film. Bud Grant sat in the back, ate granola bars, and Jerry Burns did the critiquing and film study. Bud would always say, "There's more important things than football." He was very philosophical about the game. Don was more we're going to win or I'll kill you.

Minnesota Vikings
When I got to Minnesota, I had a good time here. The Vikings were great to me. It's a great organization. It was just a different philosophy. I remember the first game. I wasn't starting then, I was playing a backup role. We got beat. We weren't a dominant team by any means in 1980 and 1981. I was struck by the fact that after a loss, the team went in the locker room, and the music was on. Everyone showered, cleaned up, and was ready to get back on the bus and fly back home.

I remember talking to Ron Yary one day. He's a Hall of Fame tackle, a great guy, and a good friend of mine. I said, "I can't believe this." He said, "What's the matter?" I said, "We just lost a football game." I wouldn't smile for three days after that. It would just eat the shit out of me. He said, "It's no big deal. It's just a game." I said, "I guess I'm from a culture that didn't look at it that way."

It was a different way of looking at the same occupation. It just wasn't something you carried with you outside the locker room in Minnesota. In Miami, I didn't turn that switch off until after the season.

Miami Dolphins Perfect Season
I have always said somebody will break it. I thought the 1985 Bears were a team capable of breaking it. The Patriots came within

an absolutely astonishing play of doing it. I think someday it will happen. People say the Patriots played two more games than you did. I say, "Yes, but you've got to remember, back in my day we played six preseason games the first four or five years of my career. I played every game in the preseason, which would be six games plus every game of the regular season, which would be 14. We didn't look at preseason games like they do today.

We didn't set out to go undefeated. I remember sitting in a hotel room with Bob Kuechenberg prior to playing the Giants, in the last game ever played at Yankee Stadium. Kuech says, "I don't know how to say this. I'm not so sure it's a good thing we win every game in the regular season." I said, "What are you talking about?" He said, "Well, it's an odd thing. Sooner or later it's going to bite us."

Yet once the game starts, you don't think about that. You go out and you execute the game plan. You play as hard as you can and you hope you win the game. You hope everything turns out. Your defense, your offense, special-teams, you hope everybody comes together and you end up winning the game. We had several games that year we could have lost quite easily. Minnesota should have beaten us. The Bills should have beaten us.

There's a record nobody talks about, by the way. I think the Dolphins beating the Bills for 20 consecutive games is still the longest winning streak against a team in the history of the NFL. I never lost to the Buffalo Bills.

I still give Joe DeLamielleure a hard time about that. They had a couple of games when O.J. Simpson was running wild. If they would have kept trying to build up his running yardage, they could have won a football game. I think we beat the Buffalo Bills 20 times in 10 years.

Preseason Games For Miami Dolphins
Preseason games were a big deal with Don Shula. There was none of this, we won't play the veterans for the first two weeks, and we sure as hell won't play them the last week. The first team

played every game, not necessarily four quarters. When the backup quarterback came in, I would usually play because they wanted to make sure the offensive line was intact to give that guy the best opportunity. I might sit out in the preseason after my fourth or fifth year of starting in the league. I might not play the fourth quarter, but I played three quarters for ten years.

Miami Dolphins & Minnesota Vikings Practices

I would like to say that the practice habits of the Dolphins were very hard. The guys worked hard. We didn't practice very long. I remember going to the Pro Bowl and I had John Madden as head coach two or three times. John would always come up to me and say, "You guys execute better than any team I've ever seen. How long do you practice?" I said, "An hour and 45 minutes." He'd say, "You're shitting me." I'd say, "No. You've got to understand that's preceded by an hour and 45 minutes of meetings."

Don Shula was very precise in practice. There was absolutely no standing around. In an hour and 45 minutes you never stopped moving. The plays he wanted to run were absolutely choreographed, scripted. He knew exactly what he wanted to run. He knew exactly what he wanted to get accomplished. If you didn't do it right, you still got it done in an hour and 45 minutes, you just had another practice that day. He could not get over that.

When I got to Minnesota, we'd practice for two hours, two and a half hours, or three hours. I would notice that when you got one of these marathon practices going, if the players didn't know exactly how long they were going to be on the field, they would save themselves. In Minnesota our practices went boom, boom, boom. You went from this drill to this drill to this drill, team drill, individual, team passing, team defense, and practice was over. I think that was a very critical part of our organization.

Pro Football Hall Of Fame Induction

I was totally overwhelmed to be amongst those great players. To be considered part of that—it's hard to describe. It's just an overwhelming feeling. They're tremendous people.

You listen to Hall Of Famers talk about their day and how they played for $3,500. It leaves you with a sense of what you are actually a part of.

I'm not so sure today in the high-tech world we live in, that we're not losing that. I think it's easy to lose that. I think those guys are incredible with what they went through. They formed the game. I go back and watch Monday night football every once in a while. We played St. Louis with Conrad Dobler and those guys, and it's like watching a home movie compared to today.

The graphics were ridiculous. There were no TV timeouts, one or two camera angles, and no slow-mos. It's pretty remarkable what it's like now. It's just hard to believe where this game has gone and what a big production it is.

I remember the first couple Super Bowls I played in, the halftime entertainment was a high school marching band. Now, God knows what you see at halftime now.

How Teams Deal With Injuries
I think every team had its own way of dealing with medical situations. We had a team physician around. You'd have a hip pointer so bad you couldn't squat down. If you wanted to get a shot, you could get a shot.

We played the Steelers one Monday night. We got done with a play in the first quarter and Bob Kuechenberg couldn't get up. He said, "I think I broke my ankle." They got him off the field. He came back in the second quarter and played the rest of the game. He had broken his ankle in six places; six bones were broke.

You couldn't say I can't go. That wasn't in the gene pool at that time. We didn't think if I go out there and play I might shorten my career. It never crossed my mind.

I broke my ankle when we were playing the Packers. I was blocking back on a trap play inside. Anyway, the opposing player falls on my right leg and I know something's broken. I went down. I hadn't been injured before other than torn cartilage and stuff. I'd always get surgery in the off-season.

I know something's broke. I get off the field. They do an x-ray which shows the top of my tibia was broke off. We had six games left until the playoffs. I said, "What do we have to do so I can get out there and play?" He said, "I don't know." Then he said, "I've got an idea here. I'll meet you at the hospital tomorrow. I think I can screw that piece back on there." I said, "Let's do it." After surgery I wait five weeks and take the cast off. I work out a little bit, go back out and practice for a week. Then I realize it wasn't going to work.

I go back in for x-rays, and find out the screws had come out. They popped out about an eighth of an inch. He says, "You're done. We've got two choices. We can go back in and tighten the screws up with a screwdriver, or I've never done this before, but I think I can fix it externally." I said, "What have you got in mind?" He said, "We'll take a piece of wood and we'll just pound them back in."

So I go to University Hospital down in Miami. I get on the operating table and he brings in the x-ray so he can see exactly where the screws are. There is a 2 x 2 piece of oak, about 6 inches long and with a ball-peen hammer he pounds the wood which puts the screws back in. He pounded them so hard that it broke the incision open from five weeks earlier. I still have that block of wood.

Then I said, "Here's the deal. I can't play anymore this season. Make sure you put the cast on so I can drive my pickup back to Minnesota in the off-season." He made the cast so when I sat on the seat, it was at the right angle for my accelerator. What we did would cause today's players to pass out. They'd freaking pass out.

Mercury Morris
Mercury Morris, in his heart, was a great player and was a great asset to us. He was a little difficult maybe, but never to the point of being a problem. That was with our whole team. We didn't have any emotional issues. The team would deal with that. If Mercury started getting a little too cocky, we would deal with that. The coaches didn't have to; Mercury and Larry Csonka knew their places. Larry

Csonka knew his place. We all knew our place. We were one part of the machine and one part wasn't bigger than the machine. I don't think any of us ever felt that, including Mercury.

Snapping For Punts & Kicks

I had never snapped in my life for punts and field goals. The first time I ever did it was at my first Pro Bowl. There was nobody on the roster that knew how to snap.

The first Pro Bowl I played in was in Kansas City. I think John Madden was my first Pro Bowl coach. He came to me and said, "You're going to have to snap." I said, "I've never done it." He said, "You're going to learn." Jan Stenerud comes over and he says, "Jim look, it's no big deal, you can do this. We'll work with it this week. You can do it."

I'm left-handed and I snapped to the quarterback right-handed. He said, "You snap the ball left-handed, don't use your right hand like you do to snap to center. He said, "Pretend you're throwing a pass. Bend over and you can do it. He said, "Don't think about it. Throw it back there. They'll catch it."

He kicked five field goals that game and I snapped for every one of them. I don't know how they got there. Some of them might have gone end over end I suppose. Anyway, I came back to training camp and Monte said, "You snapped for extra points and field goals." I said, "Yes." He said, "We're going to start working on that. I was never that good at it." I practiced. My wife would catch snaps in the backyard. I snapped to everybody.

Miami Dolphin Jim Langer blocks for Bob Griese
Photograph copyright Associated Press

three guys along with a guy by the name of Gary Hull played defensive line. So we had a front four that could really get after it. At that time, freshman could not play. Most of the time you were fodder for the varsity.

I found out that I was good enough to play, and in spring practice I became a first team linebacker on defense. We had the guys already mentioned, as well as Dennis Onkotz, Jim Kates, and Neal Smith. We had a big time defense coming back. It wasn't where there were nine or ten spots opening up because of graduation, this was a veteran team coming back. I played with that group for a couple of years.

Franco Harris and Lydell Mitchell ran the football for us. Everything was predicated on the running game on the offensive side. We had gifted running backs and a solid offensive line. We won a lot of games 17-7, 14-3, scores like that.

Our defense was about as good as you're going to get. That front four was a critical part for us on the defensive side of the ball. That was the way you played the game back then, solid defense, run the football offensively, don't make mistakes, don't turn the football over, and you had a chance to win a lot of football games.

Freshman Year At Penn State
I played outside linebacker my freshman year. We played a cover two defense back then with our linebacker coach, Dan Radakovich. The key was you're never going to let the tight end inside release and get up the field because it was always stretched to two safeties downfield. So the first play of the first practice a tight end goes in, gives me a move, goes inside, and gets up to field. The tight end was Ted Kwalick, who was not some shabby tight end. He ended up being a two time All-American and played for the 49ers. My linebacker coach took the clipboard and his whistle and threw it at me. That was my first indoctrination into how to play defense and be disciplined out there.

I learned so much about how to play. If I could play against him, I could do a pretty good job against anybody I played against on a Saturday afternoon.

Penn State & Pittsburgh Steelers Defensive Lines

I played with Mike Reid, Steve Smear, and John Ebersole up front on defense in college football. In pro football, I had LC Greenwood, Joe Greene, Ernie Holmes, and Dwight White up front. When you are a linebacker, you are as good as the people up front, and I was fortunate in my college and pro careers to have that kind of talent up front. Those defensive front fours set the tone for us.

NFL Draft

I'm normally not a very gullible guy. The day before the draft, the Giants and San Diego both called and told me they were going to draft me in the first round and I actually believed them. The next day, I didn't get drafted until the beginning of the second round. Pittsburgh took Frank Lewis, a really gifted wide receiver out of Grambling, and I was drafted by Pittsburgh in second round.

I grew up in Johnstown, Pennsylvania, and then I went to Penn State. I thought pro football would give me an opportunity to live and experience a different part of the country. It was not meant to be. I really wasn't all that happy about being drafted by Pittsburgh. Pittsburgh was not a very good football team. So it wasn't this euphoric day for me. I thought that I was going to go somewhere else and get drafted a round earlier so it was actually more disappointing, in a sense, for me. In retrospect, it could not have turned out any better for me in my career.

No one from Pittsburgh even called me prior to the draft to ask me any questions or conduct any kind of interview. So I never expected to get drafted by the Steelers.

There was a debate between Chuck Noll and other members of the Steelers. Coach Noll wanted to take me in the first round and others thought get Frank Lewis first and then you can get Ham in the second round. It turned out fine for me. I have no complaints about it at all. I was going forward.

Chicago Bears

I was late coming into my first training camp. I actually scrimmaged against the Chicago Bears when I was a member of the College All-Stars. We ended up beating the Bears in the scrimmage.

Our first regular season game was against Chicago. Back then, Chicago was not a very good football team. We were winning 15-3 in the fourth quarter. Butkus hit one of our running backs, who fumbles the ball, and Chicago runs it in for a touchdown. The next series, he does the same thing again to another running back and we lose the game 17-15. We lost to a bad Chicago Bear football team and I'm thinking, "Is this what it's going to be? My career is going to be just like this? Oh God, this is going to be a terrible, terrible situation here."

We kind of plotted along my rookie year, and then in 1972, we drafted Franco Harris in the first round. All of the sudden, things turned around. I think we were eleven and three that year. We went to the playoffs and Super Bowls from there.

Chuck Noll

I think we bought into Chuck Noll's style. He was a very business-like kind of a guy. We knew he was a real smart guy. He was more of a renaissance guy as a head coach. He was a wine connoisseur and flew his own plane. I think we all felt we have Chuck Noll, so we have a little bit of an advantage over everybody else because we have him on our side of the field. He was a stickler for detail and treated the first to the 50th player the same way. If you weren't good enough, you knew you weren't going to be on our football team.

The best thing he ever did was after we won our first Super Bowl. The first day in training camp the following year he told us, "You can put your Super Bowl rings up on the shelf because there's not a damn thing you did last year that's going to win you a job on the team this year." We bought into that. He said, "Each game you're going to play this year after winning that championship, every team is going to be gunning for you." We took that as a challenge and we bought into all of it. I'm proud that we were able to win back-to-back Super Bowls twice. I hold that in very high regard.

We had great players, but you don't win and have the chemistry needed unless you get it from the top. I don't think we would have won our four Super Bowls if we didn't have Chuck Noll.

Andy Russell 93-Yard Touchdown

Andy Russell was playing with a pulled groin muscle. I came to Pittsburgh and Andy had already been playing for about five or six years on the team. He was a smart guy, anticipated well, prepared, and knew how to watch tape. I was smart enough to realize I could learn a lot from this guy who was on the other side playing right linebacker. I was like a sponge with him. In meetings and out on the field, we would talk about different techniques. I learned a lot about playing the game from Andy Russell. I don't know what his 40-yard dash time was, but he was All-Pro for seven or eight years. If we didn't win all those Super Bowls, I think he would probably be in the Hall of Fame right now. He has the credentials to be there. All of us get in and Andy Russell is the one guy who hasn't. I learned more from him on how to play and how to be professional than from anybody else in my career. It was great to be able to learn from him on the job.

Super Bowls

We won our Super Bowl against Minnesota. Two weeks before that, we beat the Raiders out in Oakland, to go to the Super Bowl. The games against the Raiders were the most fun. I don't know if I made one or two tackles in the Super Bowl against Minnesota. Minnesota tried to run the football right at Joe Greene and Ernie Holmes. To this day, I don't know why you would try to do that. That was the strength of our defense. After that game, not that I wasn't thrilled that we won the game, but when we played the Raiders, those were epic games for us.

My favorite Super Bowl was probably the first one because it finally gave Art Rooney an opportunity to win a championship and get him the Lombardi Trophy. I think to any man in that locker room, that was probably the most important thing for us.

Franco Harris Immaculate Reception

All I knew was that the crowd was going crazy, but at that time, I had to make sure they weren't going to call the play back. I didn't really see the play, but it was amazing. I think that stadium held about 50,000 people. I probably met about a hundred thousand people who said they were there that day for the game. I think the stories get embellished as they go along. I did not have a good view of that play. The Franco Harris run was just an amazing thing. It is one of the most exciting plays in NFL history.

Terry Bradshaw

A lot of people don't realize Terry Bradshaw called his own plays out there. Back then, that's what quarterbacks did. The thing I admire most about Terry is the fact that in our first two Super Bowls, we ran the football and played great defense. Normally, quarterbacks want to throw the football 35 times a game and throw touchdown passes. He was very content handing off to Franco Harris and winning low-scoring games. When we needed him to throw the ball, we probably weren't as good defensively in the last two Super Bowls. He was never a quarterback who complained and bitched about not being able to throw the football enough. All he cared about was winning football games. The team's personnel evolved where we had to throw the football. Obviously he had that talent. He was able to put together incredible years passing. That's what I admired about him. All he cared about was winning, and whatever way that was, he was happy with that.

Toughest Running Back

I think for me, it was Earl Campbell because I had a misfortune of playing against him twice a year since we were in Earl's division. Then we would play against him again in the playoffs. O.J. Simpson was illusive, but Earl Campbell had such power, you could not get underneath him. He was about 5' 10" and 240 pounds. If the Oilers had an average offensive line, he would've racked up some numbers that would've just been incredible. He was, by far, the toughest running back that I had ever had to fill up against. I wish he was not in my division.

We played in the AFC Championship Game in Pittsburgh. It was cold and rainy. It almost turned to snow in the second half. This was kind of the worst weather in the world for the Oilers. We're winning the game 34-5, with two minutes left in the game, and we know we're going to the Super Bowl. You want to make sure you don't get hurt in the last two minutes of the game. The next play Earl Campbell is running away from me. I'm thinking "Okay, I'll just kind of jog along here so I don't have to make the tackle over there on that side of the field." Then he bent the play all the way back toward me, and we have a collision. He shattered the facemask right off my helmet. I could have lost an eye. I'd never had that happen before. The facemask was in pieces and I was on the ground. I said, "Earl, it's 34-5." He said, "You know Jack, I'm going to go a hundred miles an hour on every play. I don't care what part of the game it is or whatever."

That's the kind of running back he was. Fortunately, I got to play with him in a couple of Pro Bowls and finally got him on my side. What a class guy and a great, great competitor. That's the way he played on every play.

Defensive Philosophy
Well, you know, as a linebacker even in college, I always enjoyed the passing game. I always felt that if you're a linebacker and you can't cover, or you can't react in zone defenses, then you have become a live dummy. That's why they take a lot of these guys out on third-down situations now. I was always very good at ball reacting and zone coverage. I took a lot of pride in man-to-man coverage out in the backfield, or on tight ends or whatever. I wasn't rushing off the edge a lot and bluffing. I was more in coverage. It gives you time. You know the quarterback doesn't have the luxury of pump faking because we've got a darn good front four just going to collapse the pocket, and we anticipated that in that secondary. So it gives you a chance to anticipate jump routes and react on your own coverage.

Joe Greene
Joe Greene got into the Hall of Fame the year before I did. He was the cornerstone of our football team and the true team leader out there. I knew how intense he was when we'd lose a football

game. We lost that Chicago Bear game my rookie year and he threw his helmet against the doorpost and shattered it. He was so mad after that game. I know people talk about not wanting to lose, but he took it to a whole new level there at that game and I knew how intensive a player he was going to be.

I think that Coke commercial he was in goes down as one of the best commercials of all time. He did a fabulous job. It was a great, great commercial.

Pro Football Hall Of Fame Induction
When the Hall of Fame committee called me I was ecstatic. Joe Greene got in the year before me. When I got in, it said so much about our football team and about all the guys that are in the Hall of Fame now from the Steelers. We had a great collection of guys. When you get into the Hall of Fame, I think it reflects more on your football team. I think because we won championships, people look at that football team in a different light and that's why we ended up getting so many guys in.

Two Defensive Touchdowns
The one I just fell on the ball. I forgot what team it was but they were on the one-yard line and the quarterback fumbled the snap from center. I fell on it for a touchdown. How much credit can I take for that? It probably was the most embarrassing touchdown, to tell you the truth.

At that time, Jim Plunkett was playing with New England. He threw an interception that I couldn't, even if I had the worst hands in the world, I could not have missed that one. I don't know what he was thinking on that play, but I ran some 30 yards for a touchdown.

Chapter 46

Jack Ham

College:
Penn State

Career History:
Pittsburgh Steelers (1971–1982)

1988 Inductee Pro Football Hall of Fame

College Choice
I was not a five-star recruit coming out of high school. One of
my teammates, a guy by the name of Steve Smear, was already at
Penn State. He recommended me to Joe Paterno and the Penn
State coaching staff. At that time, I was in a military school in
Virginia. I was going to go to Virginia Military Institute but the
more I got involved in a military life, the less I enjoyed it. I
ended up getting a scholarship from Penn State. I was very
fortunate that they gave me an opportunity. I only had a
scholarship offer from Penn State.

Penn State
Penn State was very strict; there was no question about that.
Education was always paramount. Joe Paterno felt that only a
few people would get the opportunity to play pro football and
even if you play pro football, your chance of getting hurt is
pretty high. So education was very, very important to him. Plus it
was during the Vietnam War era, and if you didn't stay in school,
you ended up being drafted. You'd be surprised how hard guys
worked in school when there was that kind of incentive to
continue with your college deferment time.

John Ebersole and Mike Reid went to Altoona High School and
continued to Penn State together, joining Steve Smear and me.
John Ebersole played for the New York Jets for a number of
years as a linebacker, but he played defensive line for us. Those

Photograph copyright Associated Press

www.ingramcontent.com/pod-product-compliance
Lightning Source LLC
Chambersburg PA
CBHW070641150426
42811CB00050B/491